PALGRAVE MOD

PALGRAVE MODERN DRAMATISTS

SAM SHEPARD: A 'POETIC RODEO'

Carol Rosen

First published 2004 by
PALGRAVE MACMILLAN
Houndmills, Basingstoke, Hampshire RG21 6XS and
175 Fifth Avenue, New York, N.Y. 10010
Companies and representatives throughout the world

PALGRAVE MACMILLAN is the global academic imprint of the Palgrave Macmillan division of St. Martin's Press, LLC and of Palgrave Macmillan Ltd. Macmillan® is a registered trademark in the United States, United Kingdom and other countries. Palgrave is a registered trademark in the European Union and other countries.

ISBN 0–333–38002–9 hardback
ISBN 0–333–38003–7 Paperback

This book is printed on paper suitable for recycling and made from fully managed and sustained forest sources.

A catalogue record for this book is available from the British Library.

Library of Congress Cataloging-in-Publication Data
Rosen, Carol, 1950–
    Sam Shepard: a poetic rodeo/Carol Rosen.
        p. cm.—(Palgrave modern dramatists)
        ISBN 0-333-38002-9 (cloth) – ISBN 0-333-38003-7 (pbk.)
            1. Shepard, Sam, 1943—Criticism and interpretation. 2.
    Dramatists, American—20th century—Interviews. 3. Shepard,
    Sam, 1943—Interviews. 4. Playwriting. I. Title. II. Series.
    PS3569.H394Z855 2004
    812´.54—dc22   2004042102

10   9   8   7   6   5   4   3   2   1
13   12   11   10   09   08   07   06   05   04

Printed and bound in China

In memory of my father, Hyman Rosen, and for Sarah, Rebecca, and Ben

How could I settle for this poetic rodeo all the time
knowing that my true art lies in transformation?

(Sam Shepard, *Man Fly*)

Contents

vii

Contents

List of Illustrations

Acknowledgements

Thanks go to Sam Shepard for his body of work and for his gracious and open discussion about it.

Thanks also go to Anna Sandeman and Sonya Barker at Palgrave for their patience over the long haul. Overdue thanks go to the wise Bruce King and John Russell Brown. The English Department at Stony Brook University, especially Peter Manning, its Chair, has been most supportive of this work in its final stages. Clare Logan and Janet Cea helped enormously with production of the last drafts. Jason Beardsley provided expert assistance in the home stretch.

More thanks go, also, to the late John Lions for advice and access; to Ed Harris, Gary Sinise, and James Houghton for their insights into the plays as performance; and to Johan Callens for his perseverance and overview. Some excerpts from this work have appeared in various forms in *The Village Voice*, *TheatreWeek*, *Modern Drama*, and *Contemporary Theatre Review*; I am grateful to the editors of those publications for their responses to the work. Judy Boals of Berman, Boals & Flynn was also very helpful.

Finally, I am grateful beyond words to my enthusiastic drama students, and to John Harris, Jonathan Levy, and the

Acknowledgements

much missed Ross Wetzsteon, exemplary in their advice and encouragement, as well as to Joseph Chaikin, whose life and work cut short will continue to inspire all of us who love theatre.

The author and publishers wish to thank the following for the use of copyright material in the book:

Sam Shepard, for material from interviews and published and unpublished works; Martha Swope, for photographs 1, 7 and 8. Copyright © Martha Swope; Sylvia Plachy, for photograph 4. Copyright © Sylvia Plachy; Carol Rosegg, for photograph 5. Copyright © Carol Rosegg; Anne Militello, for photograph 9. Copyright © Anne Militello; Bancroft Library, for photographs 2, 3 and 6, taken by Ron Blanchette; reproduced courtesy of the Bancroft Library, University of California, Berkeley. Cover photo from *Simpatico* copyright © Michal Daniel.

Special Rider Music, for the lyrics from 'Brownsville Girl' by Bob Dylan and Sam Shepard. Copyright © 1986 by Special Rider Music. All rights reserved. International Copyright secured. Reprinted by permission of Special Rider Music.

Every effort has been made to trace the copyright holders, but if any have been inadvertently overlooked the publisher will be pleased to make the necessary arrangement at the first opportunity.

Editors' Preface

The *Palgrave Modern Dramatists* is an international series of introductions to major and significant nineteenth- and twentieth-century dramatists, movements and new forms of drama in Europe, Great Britain, America and new nations such as Nigeria and Trinidad. Besides new studies of great and influential dramatists of the past, the series includes volumes on contemporary authors, recent trends in the theatre and on many dramatists, such as writers of farce, who have created theatre 'classics' while being neglected by literary criticism. The volumes in the series devoted to individual dramatists include a biography, a survey of the plays, and detailed analysis of the most significant plays, along with discussion, where relevant, of the political, social, historical and theatrical context. The authors of the volumes, who are involved with theatre as playwrights, directors, actors, teachers and critics, are concerned with the plays as theatre and discuss such matters as performance, character interpretation and staging, along with themes and context.

BRUCE KING
ADELE KING

Introduction

Sam Shepard crashed onto the New York theatre scene during the 1960s with an intensity and passion unmatched by any American playwright since Eugene O'Neill. He immediately established himself as an original on the New York stage, composing what one critic of his early work admiringly called plays with time-stopping declamations rather than dialogue, spoken in the voices that Shepard would later identify as the 'demons and angels'[1] at war in a single consciousness. Play after play poured forth in an unstoppable flow of pleasure and daring and rock-and-roll rhythms.

After a while, the Shepard who wrote all those early free-wheeling plays – plays such as *Red Cross* and *LaTurista* that evoke what he has called 'visions in the eye of the audience'[2] – burned out. A second Shepard emerged during the playwright's three-year stay in England from 1971 to 1974. There, Shepard began to harness his verbal and visual gifts to a desire to see into the self. In suddenly classic dramas, most notably in *The Tooth of Crime*, this playwright who had peopled his early plays with cowboys, film stars, and other mythic American adventurers now grappled boldly

1

with what it means to be a hero, with what it means to be an artist burdened and consumed by the voices and visions of myth.

When Shepard set up residency at San Francisco's Magic Theatre in 1975, his previous concern with self-destruction and the voice of the hero gave way to yet a third kind of playwriting. He began to build his dramas around the nexus of the family. In plays such as *Curse of the Starving Class*, *Buried Child* and *True West*, and then, devastatingly, in *Fool for Love*, with the wreckage of a home stuffed into a battered suitcase and sprawled across a motel bed, Shepard began to extend the boundaries of conventional psychological drama, making palpable the ways in which identity is an inescapable legacy, the ways in which the bonds of flesh and blood are potentially tragic. With *A Lie of the Mind* in 1985, Shepard once again broke new ground, escaping from received ideas about character and conflict to create a world of devastation on stage, a world bereaved of myths, energized by basic emotions and atavistic impulses.

In the years since the sprawling *A Lie of the Mind* premiered, Shepard has taken a new turn, sporadically returning to the theatre with plays that mine familiar ground, but always reveal some new properties of the Shepard domain. Tourists, wanderers, and heirs continue to unpack and dust off souvenirs, nurse still open wounds, restake old claims, and vanish, but with a previously unseen interiority and resignation. Shepard has meanwhile also been complementing his work for the theatre with film projects and prose works.

His work for the stage seems to have tapered off since 1986. In addition to a short nostalgic piece characterized by transformations, *When the World Was Green*, coauthored with his mentor, Joseph Chaikin, in 1996, only four full-length plays have been produced since *A Lie of the Mind*.

States of Shock (1991), occasioned by the first Gulf War, is a *tour de force* food fight set in a roadside diner. *Sympatico* (1994) examines new ways to pay old debts and settle old scores as a race-track scandal from the past reverberates in a shaky motel room. *Eyes for Consuela* (1998), adapted from 'The Blue Bouquet' by Octavio Paz, tracks the disintegration of a tourist on the run. And *The Late Henry Moss* (2000) uses flashbacks to revisit the troubles sons can never resolve, troubles caused by a damaged, dangerous, careless father who will always be for Shepard a 'dead man living in a dead house' in the desert.

Shepard's plays have steadily gained critical acceptance and ever widening audiences on both sides of the Atlantic. His plays have won more than a dozen Obies (annual awards given by the *Village Voice* for off-Broadway productions), including a special Obie in 1980 for sustained achievement. And in 1979 *Buried Child* was awarded the Pulitzer Prize for drama.

While a playwright, Shepard has also been developing as a prose and screen writer and as a public persona, a popular identity. First, in addition to seeing more than forty of his plays produced since he began drumming out plays for many off-off Broadway theatres in the 1960s, then, later, ever since he found himself comfortable at home at San Francisco's Magic Theatre in the late 1970s, tending to direct them himself, he has also produced a body of prose works and screenplays. The awestruck chronicler of Bob Dylan's Rolling Thunder Revue in the collection of short sketches composed on the road with that tour has matured into a short story writer in the Hemingway tradition. 'Tales' compiled in *Cruising Paradise* (1996) and the anthology of 'stories' published in *Great Dream of Heaven* (2002) present haunting snapshots of loners driving rattletraps or marvelling at

3

their moments of respite as they 'dodge the black hole', the 'panic of aloneness'.

Ironically, it has been Shepard's movie career – not his daredevil plays that interrogate the chasms beneath reunions and reconciliations, nor his stories that offer short takes on hostility and disconnectedness – that has made him famous, and forced such a clearly fun-loving hedonist into the life of a recluse.

His career in film, of course, differs from his career in movies. As a writer with an imagination the size of a drive-in screen from the start, Shepard started writing screenplays early on, most significantly for *Paris, Texas*, the Wim Wenders film tracking broken hearts along an American highway that won the Best Picture award at the 1984 Cannes Film Festival. Shepard has thus far auteured two films of his own, *Silent Tongue*, a neo-Native-American western with shamanistic aspirations, and *Far North*, a farcical depiction of 'the female side of things' in Minnesota. A documentary, *This so-called Disaster: Sam Shepard Directs 'The Late Henry Moss'*, was filmed by Michael Almereyda in 2000, and premiered in 2004. Another collaboration with director Wim Wenders, *Don't Come Knocking*, written by and starring Shepard as an over-the-hill movie cowboy who rides off the set in the middle of production, was set to start filming in Arizona in 2003.

But the famous Shepard is the one who has also worked as a rock musician and who has acted in many major films. Today this playwright who once said, 'I don't want to be a playwright, I want to be a rock and roll star,'[3] this playwright who made his screen acting debut in Bob Dylan's movie *Renaldo and Clara* (1977), now finds himself a known commodity as an established character actor in films. Shepard first attracted public attention in movies such as *Days of Heaven, Frances, Country, Fool for Love* (based on his own screenplay of his stage play), and was nominated for a 1983 Academy Award nomination for his portrayal of Chuck Yeager in *The Right Stuff*.

Shepard has sometimes scoffed at his own film-acting career, crediting his success in this business more to his cheekbones than to his limited acting abilities, and more about financing than about art. Nevertheless, ever since he was deeply impressed by the real artistry in Ellen Burstyn's Actor's Studio technique, which he observed at close range in one of his first films, *Resurrection* (1980), Shepard has maintained respect – even awe – at the work of other film actors. Now, he crosses with ease back and forth between commercial Hollywood projects and independent films. In the last couple of years alone, his roles on TV and in movies have ranged from Dashiell Hammett to the Ghost of Hamlet's father in Michael Almereyda's postmodern film version featuring Ethan Hawke. In 2001, for example, he appeared both in the blockbuster, *Black Hawk Down*, as well as in Sean Penn's moody character study, *The Pledge*.

From childhood, both Shepard's life and the route taken by his drama have reflected the nomadic and chameleon-like impulses that are particularly American. After leaving his home in Duarte, California, where he was raised on ranching, movies, drive-ins, brawls and a teen car culture, he settled for several years in New York City, then in London, and then, as a family man in the Mill Valley outside San Francisco. Publicly linked since the mid-1980s with actress Jessica Lange, Shepard uprooted himself once again, and home for them has since then been Santa Fe, New Mexico, then, with their children in the Virginia horse country, and then, through their children's high school years in icy Minnesota, which Lange's extended family calls home, and then, in 2004, back to New York with plans for Shepard to appear on-stage in the East Village in a NY Theatre Workshop production of Caryl Churchill's *A Number*.

Wherever he has lived is reflected in the writing he has done there. 'For me,' says Shepard, 'language comes from the earth. If a man is raised on a mountain, he's going to talk according to that place. If a man is raised along a river, he's influenced by that river. And you can feel it in different areas of the country. The language grows like a crop from the place where it sprouted.'[4]

It is most productive to apply an 'auteur theory' to Shepard's dramatic works, for in his plays, as in the body of works by a singular film director, we can identify what has been termed a continuing artistic personality, one whose major ideas and images, one whose through-lines of action and attitudes towards plot and character, are as individual as a signature.

The chronological division of Shepard's work is not just a convenience here, nor is it an instance of the fallacy of artistic evolution and maturation (that is, the notion that an artist's body of work is analogous to a tree, with the later work perceived as an expansion of, or as an improvement on, or as an outgrowth from earlier work). But in Shepard's case a chronological division is useful; with so many revivals of his plays of different periods, even of early plays he jokingly dubbed 'disposable', audience members are sometimes puzzled. You can hear them asking during the intermission of, say, *Cowboy Mouth*: how could the author of *Buried Child* have now written this jumble of baroque language and rock and roll? Is this a new play or another old one? Add to this the fact that Shepard has been feeding this befuddlement himself. As an artist who, above all, will not be pinned down, with his *The Late Henry Moss*, produced in

2000, he harks back to the shenanigans of plays like *Seduced* and *La Turista*, while he echoes the dirges from plays like *True West* and *Fool for Love* for 'family stuff' and for 'the land of the living' by characters who have 'disappeared' with 'no destination'.

Nevertheless, the division of his work into phases makes natural sense. Shepard quite consciously does this himself. He has this 'thing' he says, about 'burning bridges and entering new territory'.[5]

From a variety of points of reference, we can consider Shepard's *oeuvre* in five distinct phases so far:

1. the early plays, celebrating myths, enchanted with the West, from *Cowboys* through to *Operation Sidewinder*;
2. the hero plays, analysing and questioning creativity and the artist's role in a society which seeks to possess, exploit and mythologise its heroes, starting with *The Tooth of Crime*, and *Angel City*;
3. the family plays that turn genealogy into excavations, including *Curse of the Starving Class, Buried Child, True West* and *Fool for Love*;
4. the play of cataclysm, *A Lie of the Mind*, which is a requiem for all that has befallen America, a dirge for the third phase – the family plays – especially; and
5. the plays of bold and broad strokes, including *States of Shock, Simpatico, Eyes for Consuela*, and *The Late Henry Moss*, that are sometimes rewarding fishing expeditions, harking back to a tried and true spot, where love pacts and legacies are quicksand. Yet these plays are slapstick tragedies, displaying the gusto and outrageousness and, yes, also the spontaneous devil-may-care looseness of the youthful plays whose wild narratives they also recall, like *Tooth of Crime, Geography of a Horse Dreamer*, and *The Holy Ghostly*.

Among the points of reference that underscore the shifting dramatic structure and style in Shepard's major phases are:

Spine or vector of action

In early plays, characters simply want to fly, to soar through language.

In the hero plays, characters want to escape. They attempt to connect themselves with an image of an artist.

In the family plays, characters want to unearth the past, to go beyond psychology and imagery to penetrate to a basic connection with blood ties.

In *A Lie of the Mind*, images dissolve, and we are left with natural phenomena in the moon, the earth, the snow, a fire.

Once again, in plays like *States of Shock* and *The Late Henry Moss*, wild, desperate characters have no sense of direction, landing at diners, motels, and dives on the way to somewhere off the map. They yearn to let it all go.

Characters

In early plays, they are actors, playing and shifting into trances.

In the hero plays, they are artists, figures from folklore, earnest transformers of self.

In the family plays, they are 'hopers' longing to connect with and to control the double-sidedness of their nature.

In *A Lie of the Mind*, they are hopeless, broken, with amnesia, no destination, no pretences.

In the bold plays of conflict and claustrophobia, such as *Simpatico* and *The Late Henry Moss*, they are often brazen and belligerent shoot-from-the-hip guys (still mostly guys, unless they bring some symbolic super-female saving force on board), nursing old wounds, settling old scores, revisiting the scene of some vague, half-forgotten crime.

Language

In early plays, language tends to be hipster slang, decorative, baroque.

In the hero plays, language is more self-conscious and self-referential in that these tend to be discussion plays about artistic creativity.

In the family plays, language grows progressively barer, more violent; Shepard pares down his metaphysical language to the anecdotes and the idiom of rural America.

In *A Lie of the Mind*, language is organic, unadorned. 'I love you more than the earth', says Jake.

In the bold plays of conflict and trying, as characters do in *The Late Henry Moss*, to reconcile themselves to the fact that they will never 'get to the bottom of things', language is fluid, characterized as earlier by anecdotes and bravura. Arias of betrayal abound.

Music

In the early plays, action mimics and invokes the energy of rock and roll.

In the hero plays, jazz is integral to the action, which itself strives to become 'visual music'.

In the family plays, country music is used incidentally, as a gloss on the narrative action.

In *A Lie of the Mind*, the music used to underscore action and as a bridge between scenes is blue-grass music, elementary music, straightforward in its expression of basic sentiments of love and forlornness.

In the plays characterized by bold stokes of conflict (although away from theatres, early in the twenty-first century he tries out some rock lyrics with Bob Dylan), onstage Shepard is aiming mainly for word-music. When used, like the guitar in *Eyes for Consuela*, or like the rumba in *The Late Henry Moss*, music is an organic part of the action.

Destination of the journey

In early plays, celebrating myths, there is no destination, just aimless cruising.

In the hero plays, where myths are contemplated and agonized over, the destination is westward, onward, inward on the frontiers.

In the family plays, which are archaeological in their approach to myths, the destination is the past, as far back as possible.

In *A Lie of the Mind*, a play which deconstructs myths, the destination is an atavistic world, a world without myths.

In plays like *The Late Henry Moss* Shepard just shrugs off endings. They are a false contrivance of modern drama. Like Joyce in *The Dead*, like Yeats in the Cuchulain plays or in *Purgatory*, Shepard is not just playing the Ghost father to Ethan Hawke's screen Hamlet, he is also foregrounding the conundrum of living ghosts in his plays.

Shepard has said, 'I've always had a problem with ending. I never know when to end a play. I'd just as soon not end anything. But you have to stop at some point, just to let people out of the theatre. A resolution isn't an ending: it's strangulation.' Some critics have argued that, 'if plays consisted of beginnings and middles only, this gifted playwright would rank even higher than he does'.[6] Nevertheless, in every phase, this original, innovative playwright fulfils an audience's desire to experience drama in a vital way, in what Shepard has called,

The language of the body, intellect and emotions. It is this 'body language' of actual experience which is theatrical. This perspective is not anti-intellectual, but the problem

10

is how to express ideas and emotions through 'direct contact'. In the theatre, language is in the air, not on the page, and that makes it physical.[7]

Shepard's work may resist endings, but it actively seeks out change. Quite conscious of the tensions in his dramaturgy and of the personal transformations they may signal, Shepard wrote in 1980:

I saw a man submit to a tempo
I saw a man taken over
I saw this man resisting the tempo
I saw the moment he gave in
I saw the man fighting to reach the rhythm
I saw him slashing the air
I saw the man finding a passage
I saw him scared to the bone
I saw the man facing the faceless
I saw his face lose its shape
I saw the man maintaining his struggle
I saw the moment he stepped into himself
I saw this same man become another man
A man inside the same man
I saw this man turned inside out
I saw this man released.[8]

1
'Ain't the Highway Fine'

Listen to the song that the V-8 sings
Watch the rhythm of the line
Isn't it some magic that the nighttime brings
Ain't the highway fine
(Becky's Song in *The Tooth of Crime*, Act I)

Until the late 1970s, even as he settled first in cities and then on a ranch, Shepard could thrive as an artist on the freedom offered by a highway society. If Shepard's plays can be seen as quintessentially American in their syntax, their imagery, and their characters' yearnings to hold fast to a dream slipping by, so can his life be understood in terms of the sounds, images and yearnings that are most profoundly American. Like the Young Man of his *Operation Sidewinder* (1970), Shepard was 'made in America. Born, bred and raised [with] American scars on [his] brain. Red, white and blue. [He must] dream American dreams' (Act I, scene viii).

Shepard's youth was spent covering the American continent as thoroughly as his plays journey through a highly

12

personal yet recognizable American territory. He was born Sam Shepard Rogers, VII, on 5 November 1943 in Fort Sheridan, Illinois, and was called Steve, going along with an idiosyncratic family tradition of nicknaming. As Shepard explains it in a *Motel Chronicles* entry dated 1980:

> My name came down through seven generations of men with the same name each naming the first son the same name as the father then the mothers nicknaming the sons so as not to confuse them with the fathers when hearing their names called in the open air while working side by side in the waist-high wheat . . . The sons came to believe their names were the nicknames they heard floating across these fields and answered to these names building ideas of who they were around the sound never dreaming their real legal name was lying in wait for them written on some paper in Chicago and that name would be the name they'd prefix with 'Mr.' and that name would be the name they'd die with.[1]

Following his father, a career officer in the Army Air Corps, who suffered after war service in Italy, the family moved from base to base: Illinois, South Dakota, Utah, Florida and Guam all within the first six years of Sam's life. These early years, marked by his parents' private turmoil and his family's upheaval, continue to haunt Shepard's writings. He writes in *Motel Chronicles* in 1981:

> My Mom carried a .45 for a while
> me on one hip
> the pistol on the other
> I lived in a community of women
> pilots' wives
> quonset huts
> it rained all the time.[2]

After his father left the service, when Shepard was about 12, the family finally settled on an avocado ranch in Duarte, California, a town located about ten miles east of Pasadena. Sense memories from these years surface most vividly in Shepard's *Curse of the Starving Class* (1978), a play in which everything – 'the house, the land, the orchard, the tractor, the stock, the whole thing the whole fandango! the air! the night sky!' – is threatened both by the lure of the desert and by the bulldozing land developers. In *Motel Chronicles* Shepard recalls the family house: 'the red awning. The garage door. The strip of lawn down the center of the driveway. The Pyracantha berries. The robins that ate them.' He can see 'close-ups of the Robin's beak guzzling red berries' and he can remember pretending to sleepwalk down the hallway, 'past the snarling tiger painted on silk, brought back by my Dad from the Philippines; past the portrait of a train conductor painted by my Grandfather; past the pink Hibiscus flowers glowing in the light from the bath-room.'[3]

Shepard's adolescence was a time for toughness and high-way adventure. The futuristic picture of scoring set to music, drugs and high rolling in *The Tooth of Crime* (1972) captures the spirit of those days when Shepard passed through high school, cruising, taking speed, drinking and fighting. He has said he was celebrating 'events of the body and feelings'. As he describes it, 'Fighting was a kind of badge. I never enjoyed it, but I never backed down. There would be these incredible slug-outs in the park. I remember some guys fought like wild men.'

There were battles at home as well. Shepard has described his relationship with his father during that period with compassion. 'My father had a real short fuse', Shepard has said. 'He had a really rough life. Had to support his mother and brothers at a very young age when his dad's farm collapsed. You could see his suffering, his terrible suffering, living a life that was disappointing and looking for another one. It was past frustration; it was anger. My father was full of terrifying anger.' As Shepard has explained it further, 'He was an alcoholic with a lot of problems that are still a mystery to me – connected with the war I guess. He never settled down and though he tried his best at all kinds of things, he never could make it. I had a real dropping out with him . . . I had to get out.'[4]

In that unfathomable way that the felt life of the artist often seems somehow fated to find expression in his work, an image of an unmoored, disappearing, disturbed and philosophizing father haunts and shapes Shepard's plays of every period. This is an image probably coloured by Shepard's complicated ties to his own father, who was killed in 1984 after wandering out into a road near Shepard's home in Santa Fe, where he had also settled. 'My Dad lives alone on the desert. . . . He says he doesn't fit with people', wrote Shepard in *Motel Chronicles* in 1979.[5] This image surfaces in early plays such as *The Rock Garden* (1964) and *The Holy Ghostly* (1969); it hovers about the shadow of the broken father played by Shepard in silence in the film *Raggedy Man* (1981) and played by Harry Dean Stanton in near silence in Shepard's screenplay for *Paris, Texas* (1984); it even offers hope in the voice of the father in *The Tooth of Crime*, who advises Hoss that 'The road's what counts . . . just look at the road . . . don't worry about where it's goin'; and it absolutely dominates the bold plays of confrontation such as *States of Shock* (1991) and *The Late Henry Moss* (2000). Shepard has said that some of the family stories recounted in *True West* (1980), *Fool for Love* (1983) and *A Lie of the Mind* (1985) are close to autobiographical. The father is revivified as the spectre who hovers outside the action of *Fool for Love*; as the broken-down Dodge, confined to his couch, cursing his kin in *Buried Child* (1978); and as the violent, derelict father reborn in the desert in *Curse of the Starving Class* and then lost to the desert in *True West* and *A Lie of the Mind*. All are related, as is the tenacious, cantankerous resurrected ghost of *The Late Henry Moss*, in that inexplicable way most art is wed to a biography of the artist, to Shepard's memories of his father and their troubles.

His father also led the young Shepard towards some of the pleasures that would later fuel his art. His father was an amateur drummer who played with a local Dixieland band. 'He had a great record collection, all old swing music, Dixieland, that kind of thing. I hated it all at the time', Shepard recalls, 'but now I know I was getting an education in American music without even knowing it.'[6] Shepard himself took up the drums, eventually even playing them 'loud and mean', both in isolation, while working on early plays in the basement of New York's experimental theatre club, Café La Mama, and professionally with the Holy Modal Rounders, a not-very-commercial but highly regarded rock and electric fiddle band in the early 1960s, whose founders, Peter Stampfel and Steve Weber, characterized their music as 'progressive old-timey' and 'rockabilly'.[7] He jammed with Ike and Tina Turner, Lou Reed's Velvet Underground, and Patti Smith. He toured with Bob Dylan's Bicentennial Rolling Thunder Revue as an unofficial chronicler, hired by Dylan to work on a projected film of the tour; his job was to provide 'dialogue on the spot for all the heavies'.[8] Later he played percussion for *Tongues* and *Savage/Love* (1978), two performance pieces he conceived in collaboration with Joseph Chaikin at the Magic Theatre.

Along with his sense of dangerous pleasures, family pain and jazz music, two other interests Shepard developed in

16

Duarte would later influence his playwriting. One was an interest in the potential freedom language could offer, a debt he owes indirectly to local members of the 'beat generation'. In a favourite anecdote of his, Shepard describes how a friend mentioned to him that

> there were these guys called the beatniks. One of these local guys was a painter. He wore sandals and had a beard – you know, all that stuff. One time I went over to his place, and he had all these books, and he threw this play at me. It was *Waiting for Godot*. I never had seen anything like it. I didn't understand it. I didn't know what the hell was going on, I didn't know what it *was*. I couldn't place it as a play, a poem, a novel, or anything else. It just seemed like a unique piece of writing. It didn't stick with me as a model or anything. But it just struck me suddenly that with words you could do anything.[9]

The other enduring interest of Shepard's that now took shape was an appreciation of the cowboy, both as a movie icon of individualism and as a real way of life on the land. Recalling the hypnotic effect movies had on him in those days, Shepard says:

> There was this powerful impression when I was a kid going to those films and absolutely believing that this was a way to *be*. It wasn't just an actor acting; this was a *life form*. One you could suddenly assume and step into. There were times – and this isn't special with me, it happens to other people – where you'd go into a film and come out feeling like John Wayne. That whole swagger, or whatever it was, you'd walk out of the theatre with it. Even now, after seeing a great film, I feel that little twinge of assuming the character. I come out of the theatre walking with it.[10]

Shepard's first produced play was *Cowboys* (1964); a short piece he composed in collaboration with rock-poet Patti Smith was *Cowboy Mouth* (1971); both the *High Noon* style showdown and Crow's ability to 'assume and step into' a 'life form' in *The Tooth of Crime* and the role Rabbit hopes to play when he rides into town in *Angel City* (1976) can all be counted among Shepard's many stage moments rooted in movie dreams of cowboy power and the assumption of voices and gestures that enlarge upon life. In *Fool for Love*, Shepard mocks American dreams of cowboy power as he focuses on the lost love of a stuntman, a stand-in for a fake cowboy, lassoing only bedposts.

Away from drive-ins, the real life of the cowboy also appealed to Shepard. An accomplished horseman, he has always been drawn to the range (as well as to rodeos, the track, and polo). His bond with the open country comes across in his film performances, especially as the farm owner suffering from others' sins in *Days of Heaven* (1978) and suffering from economic hardships in *Country* (1983), as well as in his plays, where it brings a special grace to the on-stage celebration of the heartland's potential fertility in *Buried Child* and to the rodeo-style wrangling that offers some measure of hope in *Fool for Love*. About those early experiences as a hand, Shepard has said he 'really liked being in contact with animals and the whole agricultural thing', he 'even had the grand champion yearling ram at the Los Angeles Fair one year'.[11] Shepard's work on a horse ranch and three semesters at Mount San Antonio agricultural college led to the possibility of a career in the country.

Shepard turned down a chance to run a sheep ranch in Chino, choosing instead to hit the road. On a whim he auditioned for the Bishop's Company, a touring repertory group that performed in churches across America. The next day he was on a bus to Pennsylvania. And over the next six months of 1962 he had a crash course in theatre crafts. He says:

It was a great time. I really learned what it is to make theatre. We'd go into churches, mostly in New England, set up lights, do make-up, do the play, tear it all down and leave to go down the road the next day. It really gave you a sense of the makeshift quality of theatre and the possibilities of doing it anywhere. That's what turned me on most of all. I realized suddenly that anybody can make theatre. You don't need to be affiliated with anybody. You just make it with a bunch of people. That's still what I like about it.[12]

When the Bishop's Company landed in New York, Shepard stayed. He gave himself a new name, anticipating the longing of many of his characters to reinvent themselves. 'I always thought Rogers was a corny name', he says, 'because of Roy Rogers and all the associations with that. But Samuel Shepard Rogers was kind of a long handle. So I just dropped the Rogers part of it . . . Now in a way I kind of regret it. But it was, you know, one of those reactions to your background. Years later, I found out that Steve Rogers was the original name of Captain America in the comics.'[13]

In New York in 1963, then, Shepard dropped his family name and became a playwright, eventually the author of play after play in which the hero dons a mask and loses himself. As Crow, the usurper of selves and the bearer of masks in *The Tooth of Crime*, sings it, near the start of Act II:

But I believe in my mask – the man I made up is me
And I believe in my dance and my destiny.

2
'Just Like Rock and Roll'

I'm listening to ole Bobby Dylan and trying to write something about me that might be of interest to folks out there. Maybe a few of my favorite words would do it. Here's a few of my favorite words: Slipstream, Tahachapi, Wichita, Choctaw, Apache, Switchblade, Bootleg, Fox, Vixen, Feather, Coyote, Crow, Riptide, Flash, Flood, Appaloosa, Pachooko, Cajun, Creole, Gris Gris, Mojo, Shadow, Cheyenne, Eucalyptus, Sycamore, Birch Bark, Creasote, Asphalt, Ghost, Saint, Aztec, Quaxaca, Messiah, Tootsie Roll, Abazaba, Cantalope, Antelope, Python, Yucca, Sapling, Waxing, Waning, Moxie, Hooch, Wolf, Pine, Pistol, Abalone, Cowboy, Stranger.

. . . Writing is neat because you do it on a very physical level. Just like rock and roll.

> (Shepard, 'Autobiography' for *News of the American Place Theatre*, Apr 1971)

In New York at the age of 19, Shepard 'really just liked that whole idea of being independent, of being able to do

something on your own'. He briefly tried acting, but, finding self-promotion demoralizing, he 'soon dropped out of
that'. He was living on the Lower East Side, and, although
he was also involved in music, he found that:

> the world I was living in was the most interesting thing to
> me, and I thought the best thing I could do maybe would
> be to write about it, so I started writing plays. I always
> liked the idea that plays happened in three dimensions,
> that here was something that came to life in space rather
> than in a book . . . I didn't really have any references for
> the theatre, except for the few plays that I'd acted in. But
> in a way I think that was better for me, because I didn't
> have any idea about how to shape an action into what is
> seen – so the so-called originality of the early work just
> comes from ignorance.[1]

His first production, a double bill of two one-acts,
Cowboys and *The Rock Garden*, was mounted by Theatre
Genesis at St Mark's Church in the Bowery in October
1964. *Cowboys #2* (the first script was lost) brought Shepard
a lot of critical attention, most of it unpleasant. But Michael
Smith of the *Village Voice* was engaged by the life captured
in this quick play that moves through Cowboy-and-Indian
games, through tall tales of coyotes, and through reveries
about breakfast foods, while two pals wait for rain. Smith's
appreciative write-up brought in audiences eager for new-
wave theatre. *The Rock Garden* (which later supplied
Shepard with a small regular income – about $70 a week –
through some rough years, thanks to its third scene being
featured in Kenneth Tynan's *Oh! Calcutta!*) also breezes
through Americana vignettes and makes some stops for
monologues about food, fences and sex. Homemaking,
homesteading and orgasm, themes to which Shepard plays

21

often return, are first sounded here, in one of Shepard's first plays. Later Shepard would say, '*Rock Garden* is about leaving my mom and dad'.

After this initial cult success, Shepard began churning out short plays; and all of them were quickly produced. As Shepard told *Theatre Quarterly* in 1974:

> I was very lucky to have arrived in New York at that time . . . because the whole off-off-Broadway theatre was just starting – like Ellen Stewart with her little café (Café La Mama), and Joe Cino, and the Judson Poets Theatre and all these places. It was just a lucky accident really that I arrived at the same time as that was all starting.

Today, Shepard can barely remember some of the early instant plays he wrote as fast as images came to him. Plays such as *Cowboys* or *Fourteen Hundred Thousand* or *Dog* or *Rocking Chair* faded fast; they were self-indulgent outpourings by a playwright who would rather be a rock star. Still, at their best, these early plays can burst forth with unself-conscious language to break through everyday discourse, unleashing in its place a stream of rhythmic energy. They put us suddenly in touch with physical reality, with the way bodies fill and respond to their natural environment.

The best of these early plays are collected in *Five Plays*, reprinted as *Chicago and Other Plays*. These are colourful excursions that start out in the mundane world and then take flight through dream-like torrents of language and images. In 1966, three of these short plays of altered selves and location, *Chicago*, *Icarus's Mother* and *Red Cross*, were performed at Cafe La Mama, toured abroad, and were presented off-Broadway at the Martinique Theatre. These three plays combined to win him his first Obie Award for Distinguished Playwrighting in 1966.

All three of these plays begin in ordinary situations and erupt with ferocious energy into compelling monologues about being caught, and about evolving to survive natural forces. And all three revolve, not about plot or action, but about physical sensations, especially felt between water and air.

Chicago, for example, moves from Stu splashing in his bath which becomes a boat, into the kitchen where friends eat biscuits and create images of a fishing expedition and a train ride, to a vision of doomed life on a beach. Stu's final speeches evoke sensations of emerging from the depths of the sea, back into the air, and learning how to breathe again. The play ends with all the actors breathing in unison as they follow Stu's lead to 'taste' the air, 'all this neat air gathered before us . . . The place is teeming with air'.

Red Cross begins with Jim in an unmade bed in a motel cabin where lice make him 'weaker and weaker'; and without a change of scene, while the maid makes the bed, the play moves through language into an exhausting swimming lesson. The last speech and stage image of *Red Cross* shows Jim and his girlfriend consumed by lice, bloodied and enervated, tearing apart motel beds. This is an image which Shepard would more fully tap in *Fool for Love* two decades later. Here, though, as in other early plays that black out on an image of ordinary waste – at a table, on a porch, in an unmade bed or at a beach – the last image is used as a snapshot, presented hot on the heels of a speech depicting out-of-body states or evolution, delivered by a character in a trance. Here, the final snapshot of the motel mess reinforces in colloquial shorthand the feeling of drowning, which the maid has just described. The maid's last speech, presented, according to the stage directions, *'very still'*, reverses the movement at the end of *Chicago*. It takes us from dry land to the bottom of a lake, where drowning leads to a reverse evolution. 'Once it's over it isn't bad at all', says the maid. 'Once you get over the shock of having water all around and dragonflies and water lilies floating by and little silver fish flashing around you. Once that's past and you get all used to your flippers and your fins and your new skin, then it all comes very easy.'

Icarus's Mother, directed by Michael Smith, the first critic who championed Shepard's work, begins with a Fourth of July picnic. Full and lazy after a meal, the characters belch and stare at a plane circling above them. They wonder whether the pilot is skywriting or signalling. In the time it takes the characters to 'rest and settle [their] stomach[s] and empty [their] bladder[s] and loosen their leg[s]', the play moves into drifting rhapsodies about firework displays and the beach. Gradually, while some of the picnickers go off for a walk, the play moves into a less familiar world: Howard and Bill, left alone, suddenly and in silence both get up at once and use the barbecue and table-cloth to send up smoke signals. When the two girls return from their walk, we learn through conversation that the pilot engaged them in a kind of long-distance flirtation. The girls recount how, while they urinated and danced at the ocean's edge, the plane dipped, buzzed low, did flips and slides, climbed high into the sky, and left a vapour trail that read '*E* equals *MC* squared'. By the time the play is over, the plane has crashed; Frank, another one of the guys at the picnic, saw the jet explode and go down in the middle of the ocean. Frank delivers the final series of trance-state monologues that characteristically close this early Shepard play. According to the stage directions, he remains '*oblivious to everything but what he's saying*' as he describes a pleasurable apocalypse while the audience is bombarded by resounding booms, flashes of light and colour, and the noise of a growing crowd, which finally becomes '*deafening*'.

In *Icarus's Mother*, then, the 'weather and atmospheric conditions' take on, as is usual in a play by the young Shepard, a kinetic force. Here, a beach party turns into a watch, and flashes of light display a negative charge. First, in fun, characters search the sky for a plane and try to connect their landlocked bodies with the sky by means of various gestures and signals, both natural (smoke signals) and technological (sparklers). But the plane, like the air itself in the final sequence, explodes over the water like a firecracker: 'watch it change colours . . . one beautiful flashing thing across the whole sky'.

In his director's notes to *Icarus's Mother*, included in *Chicago and Other Plays*, Michael Smith writes, 'It's always hard to tell what, if anything, Sam's plays are "about" – although they are unmistakably alive.' Asked about the impulse behind *Icarus's Mother*, for example, Shepard said:

> One of the weird things about being in America now . . . is that you don't have any connection with the past, with what history means: so you can be there celebrating the Fourth of July, but all you know is that things are exploding in the sky. And then you've got this emotional thing that goes a long way back, which creates a certain kind of chaos, a kind of terror . . . When you talk about images, an image can be seen without looking at anything – you can see something in your head, or you can see something on stage, or you can see things that don't appear onstage, you know. The fantastic thing about theatre is that it can make something be seen that's invisible, and that's where my interest in theatre is – that you can be watching this thing happening with actors and costumes and light and set and language, and even plot, and something emerges from

beyond that, and that's the image part that I'm looking for, that's the sort of added dimension.[2]

What happens on stage and in the audience during an early Shepard play goes beyond a vision of American youth in the sixties. It is true that all of these plays have about them a casual air of social commentary: *Up to Thursday* (1965) features a young man sleeping in an American flag; *Chicago* opens with a policeman clubbing the curtain, and an off-stage voice reciting the Gettysburg address; *Fourteen Hundred Thousand* (1966) ends with Mom and Pop reading aloud an essay on the urban 'linear city' while the rest of the characters hum 'White Christmas'; and, after all, *Icarus's Mother* does close with an apocalypse on the Fourth of July.

But the effect of these plays in performance is much more profoundly wed to body rhythms and life cycles – breathing in *Chicago*, drowning and evolving in *Red Cross*, and soaring in a flash over the sea in *Icarus's Mother* – than to sixties protests. In his director's notes, which accompany the published version of *Red Cross*, for example, Jacques Levy compares the effect of these early plays to the way 'changing a room's temperature does something to the people in it'. In a 1977 essay called 'Visualization, Language and the Inner Library', Shepard himself writes that:

The power of words for me isn't so much in the delineation of a character's social circumstances as it is in the capacity to evoke visions in the eye of the audience. American Indian poetry (in its simplest translation) is a prime example. The roots of this poetry stem from a religious belief in the word itself. Like 'crow'. Like 'hawk'. Words as living incantations and not as symbols. Taken in this way, the organization of living, breathing words as they hit the air between the actor and the audience actually possesses the power to change our chemistry.[3]

With their mind/body journeys into the elements of air, sea and earth, these loose and somewhat gawky early plays burst into monologues of memory and intense physical sensations: they explode (and sometimes fizzle) like firecrackers in a summer sky.

With *La Turista* (1967), Shepard hit on a form that could control and direct the energies of the 'living, breathing words' enlivening all those plays he would habitually 'sit down and whip off'. For a long time he had resisted structure because, in his mind:

> The structure of any art form immediately implies limitation . . . Language, then, seems to be the only ingredient in this plan that retains the potential of making leaps into the unknown. There's only so much I can do with appearances. Change the costume, add a new character, change the light, bring in objects, shift the set, but language is always hovering right in there, ready to move faster and pulling out a .38 when someone faces you with a knife.[4]

La Turista is a play that literally leaps beyond those 'manic monologues' that Ruby Cohn has identified as the young Shepard's trademark.[5] It penetrates physically as well as verbally to what Shepard has called 'a world behind the form'.[6] In Act I of *La Turista*, written while Shepard was using amphetamines and sick with dysentery, witchdoctors perform voodoo rituals over Kent and his sidekick Salem, American tourists (named by Shepard after American cigarette brands) whose Mexican vacation has been wrecked by an intestinal disease. In Act II, connected to Act I by a kind of hallucinogenic logic, a parallel disease still plagues Kent, who is now back at home in the States, where his witchdoctors reappear as country doctors, garbed in the clothes of the Civil War period, and sacrifice two live chickens.

Typically, for a play written by Shepard in the sixties, the engine of *La Turista* is the urge to escape, to get out of one's skin (sunburned here, just as it was blistered and lice-bitten in *Red Cross*), to be out there with the elements instead of inside a body. 'Relaxation is the thing you seek', says Kent, 'to just disappear for a while.' Finally, after a delirious monologue about a battle between 'the Doctor and the beast' – that is, between old Doc and the monster Kent has become – Kent does escape; he gets out. As Cohn points out in her book *New American Dramatists*, *La Turista* ends with a striking silhouette. The central character swings Tarzan-like over the audience and onto the stage. Then, according to the stage directions, '*He runs straight toward the upstage wall of the set and leaps right through it, leaving a cut-out silhouette of his body in the wall.*' This final gesture of the play – the actor literally and forcefully breaking free – creates a physical equivalent for what Shepard had previously counted on as the capacity of words 'to evoke visions in the eye of the audience' when in 'lightning-like eruptions words are not thought, they're felt. They cut through space.'[7]

Written in 1967, when he was just 23, *La Turista* was Shepard's first long play, and as he recalls, thanks to the encouragement of the director, Jacques Levy, and artistic director of the American Place Theatre, Wynn Handman, it was also the first play Shepard ever revised. Two weeks into rehearsals, Shepard walked in with a new second act. According to Shepard, 'That was the first taste I got of theatre as an ongoing process. I could feel the whole evolution of that play from a tiny sweltering hotel in the Yucatan . . . to a full-blown production in New York City.'[8]

When it was presented at the American Place Theatre, *La Turista* won Shepard his second Obie, and his first real critical praise in the form of Elizabeth Hardwick's review, reprinted with the published version of the text. Hardwick offered special praise for the play's particular American brand of 'despair and humour'. She wrote, 'His play ends with sweating, breathless actors in a state of exhaustion. The characters put on a shawl and begin to declaim like an auctioneer at a slave mart, or a cowboy suit and fall into Texas harangues. They stop in the midst of jokes, for set pieces, some fixed action from childhood.'

After five years in New York City, this stranger had become the most prolific and well-known playwright in the underground theatre. By the close of 1969, when 26-year-old Shepard married O-Lan Johnson, an actress, musician and writer who appeared in his plays, the *New York Times* covered their wedding. Appropriately enough, the ceremony was held at St Mark's Church in the Bowery, the home of Theatre Genesis, where so many of Shepard's early plays – including *Cowboy*s, his first produced piece – had been premiered.

From the age of 19, throughout the hell-bent early sixties in the East Village, in plays he wrote quickly, with urgency, and saw realized in every major off-off-Broadway house – from Theatre Genesis to Café La Mama to the Judson Poets' Theatre to the off-Broadway American Place Theatre – Shepard had readily conjured verbal and physical images of shifting selves. Now he discovered a way of yoking what Hardwick had dubbed his American 'despair and humour' to his longing to let his characters leap out of themselves. In *La Turista*, he jokingly called his characters Kent and Salem. Now, he systematically began to anchor his plays in pop-culture plots, myths, American legends and tall tales.

3
'In this Desert'

I'm interested in exploring the writing of plays through attitudes derived from other forms such as music, painting, sculpture, film, etc., all the time keeping in mind that I'm writing for the theatre. I consider theatre and writing to be a home where I bring the adventures of my life and sort them out, making sense or non-sense out of mysterious impressions. I like to start with as little information about where I'm going as possible. A nearly empty space which is the stage where a picture, a sound, a colour sneaks in and tells me a certain kind of story. I feel that language is a veil hiding demons and angels which the characters are always out of touch with. Their quest in the play is the same as ours in life – to find those forces, to meet them face-to-face and end the mystery. I'm pulled toward images that shine in the middle of junk. Like cracked headlights shining on a deer's eyes. I've been influenced by Jackson Pollock, Little Richard, Cajun fiddles and the Southwest.

(Shepard, quoted by Ruby Cohn in
Contemporary Dramatists, 1983, p. 722)

30

I am! I am! I am! I am! Tonight. In this desert. In this space. I am.

> (The Young Man in *Operation Sidewinder*,
> Act I, scene viii)

After *La Turista*, Shepard wrote several other ambitious long plays in the late sixties, and in all of them, as in that final crash through the wallpaper in *La Turista*, Shepard strove to find organic stage images to express the desire to break out of a fixed identity, to enter into another name, another time, another atmosphere, to penetrate into another world, into 'a world behind the form', as he phrases it in 'Visualization, Language and the Inner Library'. In all of these plays, as in the Civil War setting and voodoo action of *La Turista*'s second act, Shepard found two sources to tap for such organic stage images: he tapped into his American legacy of names and tales, *and* he tapped into his interest in other cultures' experiments in mind expansion and self-transcendence.

Some plays just mock the idea of a potential hero on that quest 'to find those forces, to meet them face-to-face and end the mystery'. Pulled toward 'images that shine in the middle of junk', these plays parody pop-entertainments such as mystery movies, comic books, or Westerns. In *Melodrama Play*, directed by Tom O'Horgan at the Café La Mama in 1967, Shepard follows the formula for a B-movie detective story in his treatment of Duke Durgens, a pop star who cannot come up with a new hit song. In *Forensic and the Navigators*, originally staged by Theatre Genesis in 1967, and later produced at the Astor Place Theatre in 1970 – and which along with *Melodrama Play* won Shepard his third Obie – revolutionaries may have Cherokee powers as well as sci-fi ray guns, but, when they face their enemies, the Exterminators, in a comic-book confrontation, nobody wins. The play goes up in smoke. In *The Holy Ghostly* (1969), another piece directed by Tom O'Horgan for La Mama in a very broad, physical manner, Pop, the image of the old time Western hero, is exposed and destroyed. On a camping trip in the desert with his son, Ice, Pop sees the Chindi, and, as the sound of an Indian drum steadily beating is heard off-stage, Pop wards off the haunting with a bazooka and a drum lesson, but a corpse that represents him is brought on by the white witch. Shot dead by his son in a showdown, Pop tosses his own corpse into the campfire.

In more ambitious plays written in the late sixties, Shepard went beyond parodying a *single* form of pop culture. In some plays, he packs myth upon myth, popular genre upon popular genre, achieving a dizzying effect. Sometimes, such plays are in danger of becoming unintentionally ridiculous. What salvages them is Shepard's impulse towards a single organic scenic image. Shepard's best plays of this period have protean characters, zap-pop-pow action, comic-book verbs, *and* a stage set that locates all the action in a very American physical realm. Never before had an American playwright achieved the equivalent effect on stage. For comparable evocations of American dreams and discarded hopes, we must look to F. Scott Fitzgerald's *The Great Gatsby*, a novel whose central image – a faded roadside billboard painting of an eye, promising an ophthalmologist's cure to drivers passing an ash-heap – reflects the careless destruction of the age it depicts; or we must look to Nathanael West's *The Day of the Locusts*, a novel set at the edge of America, where sham Hollywood images eat up everything natural, from grocery markets to homesites.

The Unseen Hand, a one-act play first performed at La Mama at the end of 1969, is a play in which an outer-space freak from the planet Nogoland needs to awaken the Wild

West's legendary dead Morphan brothers to help free his people from the Silent Ones, sorcerers who use 'the Unseen Hand, a muscle contracting syndrome hooked up to [their] will'. Whenever the thoughts of the captives 'transcend those of the magicians the Hand squeezes down and forces [their] minds to contract into non-preoccupation'. According to Willie, the space-freak who pleads for the aid of old Blue, Cisco and Sycamore Morphan, this feels like 'Living death. Sometimes when one of us tries to fight the Hand or escape its control, like me, we are punished by excruciating muscle spasms and nightmare visions. Blood pours past my eyes and smoke fills up my brain.'

This play draws its language from technological jargon, hometown teenage slang, and old Westerns. Willie speaks both in a kind of computer lingo and, when he goes into the by-now-obligatory Shepard-play trance, in a strange ancient language. Willie's appeal for aid is delivered outside Azusa, California, another kind of alien world, about which a hometown kid rhapsodizes. While the old C, A, F, G rock-and-roll chords are played in the background, the Kid yells out:

Don't make fun of my home. I was born and raised here and I'll die here! I love it! That's something you can't understand! I love Azusa! I love the foothills and the drive-in movies and the bowling alleys and the football games and the drag races and the girls and the donut shop and the High School and the Junior College and the outdoor track meets and the parades and the Junior Chamber of Commerce and the Key Club and the Letterman's Club and the Kiwanis and the Safeway Shopping Center and the freeway and the pool hall and the Bank of America and the Post Office and the Presbyterian church and the Laundromat and the liquor

> store and the miniature golf course and Lookout Point
> and the YMCA and the Glee Club and the basketball
> games and the sock hop ... (*The Unseen Hand*, near
> the end of the single Act)

And the old Morphan brothers, relics from a time of blazing
six-guns and trains to rob, speak in chew-and-spit drawls
about being 'long gone by mornin' if they could just appease
that old 'hankerin' to take stock a' things'.

This hybrid play has as its setting a landscape where all
three worlds can intersect: an automobile graveyard by a
highway just outside Azusa, California. 'A man's gotta be
still long enough to figure out his next move', says
Sycamore as he climbs into the back seat of a rusted '51
Chevy convertible. 'That's the great thing about this country, ya' know. The fact that you can make yer own moves in
yer own time without some guy behind the scenes pullin' the
switches on ya'. May be a far cry from bein' free, but it sure
comes closer than most anything I've seen.'

In 'Visualization, Language and the Inner Library'
Shepard defined a myth as something that:

> speaks to everything at once, especially the emotions. By
> myth I mean a sense of mystery and not necessarily a
> traditional formula. A character for me is a composite of
> different mysteries. He's an unknown quantity ... I see
> an old man by a broken car in the middle of nowhere and
> those simple elements right away set up associations and
> yearnings to pursue what he's doing there. (*Drama
> Review*, XXI [1977] 53–8)

With its image of human and mechanical wreckage at the
edge of town in the moonlight – quite literally an image that
shines in the middle of junk – sustained throughout the

1. Barbara Eda-Young as 'Honey, a Blonde', Roberts Blossom as a 'Prospector', and a huge snake take over the stage in the premiere of *Operation Sidewinder* at the Vivian Beaumont Theatre at Lincoln Centre in New York in 1970. Photo: Martha Swope.

action, *The Unseen Hand* at once uses both set and characters to present 'a composite of different mysteries', at once making a physical three of Shepard's concerns: his star-wars futuristic imagination, his highway point of view about Norman Rockwell Americana, and his mourning for the dead West.

Operation Sidewinder, Shepard's second lengthy play after *La Turista*, released myths of Hopi snake dancers, paratroopers, computers, extraterrestrials, carhops, revolutionaries, drug dealers and tourists before astonished 1970 audiences in the Lincoln Centre's Beaumont Theatre. This play's strength is also bound to its organic scenic image, again presented as 'a composite of different mysteries': the American desert. The Alien Song of *Operation Sidewinder*, for example, is about the feeling of being lost that faces a traveller in search of a familiar America. The landmarks keep changing here, even as they will for *Buried Child*'s Vince, who, coming home in a less schematic play, will take a while to learn of his alien status:

> It wasn't so long that I wandered
> It wasn't so long I was gone
> But now I come back and there's no wooden shack
> And the turnips I grew are all gone
>
> I couldn't go back where I came from
> 'Cause that would just bring me back here
> And this is the place I was born, bred and raised
> And it doesn't seem like I was ever here.
> (Act I, scene viii, leading to Intermission)

Even when he gets most despondent over everything 'considered in the light of the political situation – The soldiers are dying, the blacks are dying, the children are dying' – the Young Man of *Operation Sidewinder* can find joy in an open space. He delivers a speech that, like Shepard's *Zabriskie Point* screenplay, captures the mood swings of the late sixties, when Woodstock elation and angry Bob Dylan lyrics rocked back and forth, giving the body and mind what Shepard, writing 'Connecticut Blues' in his *Rolling Thunder Logbook*, called 'the shattered feeling'. The Young Man says:

> Let's wait till four years from now when we can take over the Democratic Party. Teddy Kennedy is still alive. Let's not do anything at all. It can only get worse. Let's give up. And then I walked through the crowd of smiling people. They were loving and happy, alive and free. You

can't win all the time. You can't always have everything
your own way. You'll be arrested. You'll be arrested,
accosted, molested, tested and re-tested. You'll be beaten,
you'll be jailed, you'll be thrown out of school. You'll be
spanked, you'll be whipped and chained. But I am
whipped. I am chained. I am prisoner to all your oppres-
sion. I am depressed, deranged, decapitated, dehuman-
ized, defoliated, demented and damned! I can't get out.
You can get out. You can smile and laugh and kiss and
cry. I am! I am! I am! I am! I am! I am! I am! I am! I am!
I am! I am! Tonight. In this desert. In this space. I am.

(Act I, scene viii)

The Mad Dog Blues, another play with music, first
performed by Theatre Genesis in 1971, has a campy quality
in its loosely jointed parade of famous faces, but it also has
an interesting way of locating those faces on an uncluttered
stage, which scenically represents 'a composite of mysteries' in the very relaxed mind of Kosmo, a rock-and-roll star.
Accompanied by Yahoodi, his sidekick and drug supplier,
Kosmo starts this play by saying, 'I've had a vision . . . It
came to me in music. It's like old rhythm-and blues and
gospel, a cappella, sort of like The Persuasions but with this
bitchin' lead line. Like a Hendrix lead line. Like a living
Hendrix lead line right through the middle of it.' Then
Yahoodi asks him, 'What about the visuals. Did ya see any
pictures?' Thus, the sidewinding action of the play is
launched. A hodge-podged American who's – who is
paraded across this landscape of the musician's mind as he
takes a trip past everybody from Marlene Dietrich to Mae
West, from Paul Bunyan to Jesse James, from Captain Kid
to an old time Westerner who thinks he is Jimmie Rodgers.

These plays of the late sixties, in which Shepard experimented with rock music and trips – trying to get beyond that

veil of language 'hiding demons and angels' from out-of-touch characters – are uncontrolled. The plays flash, zoom and screech across the stage. Primary colours ooze like neon; jazz and rock shoot through the sound system; and armed and dangerous characters, frazzled and scared, hurl words like weapons, wounding each other with Shepard's heightened and hip version of American English, a language culled from rock and drug slang, action comics, jargon, punk talk, dime novels, and B-movies. Shepard floods the stage now with such language. On a jag of hostility, raw nerves and all-American dreams of fame and fun, Shepard rolls up and codifies a language of energy, sounding through space.

He peoples his stage with characters in quest of the lone heroes of American myths, all of his characters painfully aware of how disconnected they are from the mystical powers they associate either with where a hero might live, with music, or with 'ending the mystery' by means of self-transcendence learned from other cultures. Gangsters, government agents, subversive forces, rock stars, cowboys, Wild West desperadoes, sci-fi creatures and dead movie actors bump into each other, all in a fog, looking for a quick fix, annihilation or personal obliteration. Hits, showdowns, rub-outs and blast-offs are so common in these plays, they seem to collide with each other as smoke and explosions repeatedly abruptly end the action.

Shepard's increasing fame in his off-off-Broadway world took a heavy toll on him now, bringing him offers to script movies for Hollywood moguls, and bringing him that offer to have his *Operation Sidewinder* mounted in the Vivian Beaumont Theatre at Lincoln Centre – that is, in a major theatre, in the equivalent of a Broadway house. By all accounts, both kinds of offers backfired, with disastrous personal results for Shepard.

His early work as a screenwriter soured him for years about writing for Hollywood films. Although his first screenplay, *Me and My Brother*, co-written with Robert Frank in 1967, was a non-commercial film about Peter Orlovsky, his next assignment, working on Antonioni's *Zabriskie Point* in 1968, placed him in quite a different situation, one in which high-powered wheeling and dealing stifled artistic collaboration. In 1975, Shepard looked back with disdain at screenwriting. 'I hate it,' he said:

> because it's never just . . . working on a film. It has to do with studios, with pleasing certain people, cutting things down, and rewriting. It's not a writer's medium, it's a director's medium – the writer is just superfluous. It's an old hangover fom Hollywood days, you know – 'we need a screen writer' – but as far as I'm concerned it's an obsolete profession.[1]

Asked if this was why he had only worked on the first version of the *Zabriskie Point* script, Shepard said:

> No, I didn't know how to continue with what Antonioni wanted. He wanted political repartee and I just didn't know how. Plus I was 24 and just wasted by the experience. It was like a nightmare. I was surrounded by MGM and all that stuff. I like Michelangelo [Antonioni] a lot – he is incredible – but to submerge yourself in that world of limousines and hotels and rehashing and pleasing Carlo Ponti [the film's producer] is just . . . forget it.[2]

Shepard spent almost two years, off and on, involved in the film business, working especially on three other interesting projects, all of which fell through: a screenplay called *Maxagasm* for the Rolling Stones; *Ringaleerio*, with playwright Murray Mednick; and *The Bodyguard*, an adaptation of Middleton and Rowley's Jacobean tragedy, *The Changeling*, to have been directed by Tony Richardson. Only *Zabriskie Point* made it to the screen. Seeing it today is like entering a time machine. Suddenly it is 1968: earnest, naïvely idealistic students passionately debate revolutionary tactics; youth and age seem to be fighting a war on campus; middle-aged America seems crass and complacent; the landscape is blistered by violence and dirtied by commercialism. But off the beaten track, away from radio static and bullhorns and cops and clocks and calendars, the land itself – even the deepest spot in the desert – seems potentially fertile, charged with the energy of young men and women, open to their pleasurable sensations and their claims on its natural resources.

Antonioni had sought Shepard to write the screenplay for this film because, as Shepard later recalled with more than a trace of irony, 'I had a play called *Icarus's Mother* which had an airplane in it; he figured that since he had an airplane in his movie we had something in common.'[3] The film follows the journey of a campus revolutionary on the run, as he rides down America's highways and over its skies in a hijacked plane on his way to the Mojave desert. There, he makes love with a beautiful girl who is on a spiritual quest, which she finances by occasionally working for an American corporation that parcels out condominiums in the desert, the 'Sunny Dunes Estates'.

This film has trance-like silent sequences that are analogous in form to the verbal reveries into which Shepard's characters launch themselves on stage. Scenes of mass lovemaking in the desert, played by actors from Joseph Chaikin's Open Theatre Company, and the film's final scene – a joyful apocalypse either willed or imagined by the film's young heroine, with Coke bottles and breakfast cereal and sofas and all sorts of plastics cascading in slow motion through space in a blow-up – especially communicate in a purely visual language what Shepard's late sixties characters talk about so much on stage: a sincere belief in sympathetic magic and in youth as powerful, capable of winning out over any and all of the demons and angels.

Like Shepard's run-in with Hollywood in the late sixties, which he would later turn into a vision of all movies as disaster movies in *Angel City*, his Lincoln Centre production of *Operation Sidewinder* was also a fiasco: it alienated critics, subscription audiences and the playwright himself. Asked why he has always made a point of avoiding Broadway productions, Shepard has said:

> The closest I ever came to that territory was when *Operation Sidewinder* was produced at Lincoln Centre, and that was a total disaster. The thing was mass-produced. There was all this money involved in costumes and sets, and that took precedence over the work between actors. It also had too big an audience. I don't think theatre can be received in a huge space with thousands of people. It becomes a spectacle.[4]

From this experience he learned, 'It's important to take into consideration the general environment the play's going to hit. It's more important to have a five-character play or less that can be done in a close, non-financial situation than it is to have a circus.'[5]

By 1970, the prolific rock-playwright was burning out. He had already written, according to some accounts, 'more than 100 plays, some in less than a week'. And, even in the grip of the whirlwind, Shepard was aware that his art was in a rut: he was taking short cuts to express the frenzy and the visions that were most easily available to his imagination. 'You get a certain spontaneous freaky thing if you write real fast. You don't get anything heavy unless you spend real time', he told the *New York Times* late in 1969. About those scores of 'fast' plays, he went on to say, 'They're kind of facile.' For example, critic Elizabeth Hardwick had managed to see *La Turista*, and she had proclaimed it 'a work of superlative interest', even though Shepard had banned critics from the audience. Despite Hardwick's assessment, Shepard now dismissed *La Turista* (giving further credence to his reputation as a quick writer who never revised, just moved on) with the words: 'I didn't think it was a finished thing.' Alluding to plays such as *Melodrama Play*, *Forensic and the Navigators*, *The Holy Ghostly*, *The Unseen Hand* and *Mad Dog Blues*, and revving up to his work on *Operation Sidewinder*, which he characterized as 'a movie for the stage', he said that now, 'I'm dealing more with mythic characters, a combination of science-fiction, Westerns, and television'.[6]

Shepard has talked quite frankly about this period. 'People will say the Sixties was the greatest thing that ever hit America, that it was peace and love. Maybe in San Francisco, but in New York it got very scary', he has said.

My plays were influenced by everything happening to me. A lot of them came out of fear and anger, because that's what was going on. There was an extreme kind of street paranoia in those days – the Kennedy trip, Malcolm X and the Panthers ... everybody had the sense that there was a flood coming ... I was using a lot of drugs then – amphetamines, smack. Drugs were a big part of the whole experience of that time. It was part of a feeling that you wanted to experience different aspects of reality. I didn't use drugs to write. I only used drugs to live. But I was using heavy stuff, and I saw a lot of people go under from drugs, which was one of the main reasons I left the streets, because street life went hand in hand with that.[7]

Along with *Melodrama Play*, *Forensic and the Navigators* and *The Holy Ghostly*, other low-ebb plays are of interest now mainly for the naked way in which they lope along or moodily crash out the qualities that haunt Shepard's best plays. *Shaved Splits*, done at La Mama in 1970, *Cowboy Mouth*, co-authored with Patti Smith in 1971, and *Back Bog Beast Bait*, presented at the American Place Theatre in 1971, are little more than physical expressions of paranoia, presented full-force in a now somewhat dated American slang of cowboys, hired guns, revolutionaries and the potential 'rock and roll saviour' doing battle with the beast within.

In *Shaved Splits*, for example, a revolutionary wrecks the pleasure palace of a sex-crazed woman; he describes deer hunting; and, finally, his disembodied voice imagines the magical transformation of a revolutionary into a rock star. *Shaved Splits* seems almost entirely silly now, completely self-contained in a time-capsule of late-sixties stoned fantasies and self-mockery, epitomized by the glazed looks, giddy inflections, distracted manner and exaggerated performance style of Madeline Leroux, an actress who was that era's specialist in campy parodies by playwright Tom Eyen presented at Café La Mama, and who originally played Miss Cherry, this play's voluptuous, voracious consumer of chocolates and pornography.

Only the final speech of *Shaved Splits*, a voice-over delivered while Geez stands with his back to the audience and with his rifle slung over his shoulder, saves the play. It lifts it towards the yearning that drives Shepard's later true heroes to Faustian pacts with private devils; this is a yearning for something in life – some art or some action, some adventure or human connection – to have the life-force, the luminous vitality of music:

> Somewhere in his mind a band was playing . . . All the sounds of the fifties and sixties combined in one band and all making sense . . . Then it seemed it came from the street itself. From out of the smoke and rubble. From out of the gutted tenements and ramshackle shacks. He followed the music like a dog scenting deer . . . until he came to a bar with the windows blown out . . . He walked inside, kicking aside a hubcap from a '49 Pontiac. There in the dingy back room, high up on the bandstand the band was playing 'Satisfaction' . . . Suddenly his eyes caught sight of a bright orange guitar all plugged in and ready to go . . . He set down his rifle carefully in a corner and walked over to the guitar. He picked it up and something happened to his hands. Gold light shot out from his hands and they began to move over the guitar in patterns and rhythms he'd never seen before. He was playing! . . . The music filled him up and poured out over the dusty tables and chairs. He was alive again. The war was over and he was alive!

Even in the most incoherent and personal plays written during this spell, then, a volatile and palpable Shepard signature is felt in certain recurring scenic images, vocal patterns, physical movements, and yearnings towards explosion, self-discovery *and* isolation. Such plays are frequently revived now, especially on college campuses, and in such revivals all those free associations and send-ups, all those relaxed, easy-riding revolutionaries full of fun and faith and hope – all those 'hopers' as Dodge will put it in *Buried Child*

– can, in sudden, lucid undated moments move or engage us still.

These plays are by no means whole, fully imagined dramas. They are uneven, jumpy, unmeasured and littered with images that do not often 'shine in the middle of junk'. But they sketch out with the abandon of an artist flailing, holding nothing back, many of Shepard's private 'demons and angels': images of the hunt and the devouring hunger, rhythms of rock drumming, characters facing a family heritage, settings in American open country, and action that leads to the end of one world and the start of a new one, alone in the desert.

Wasteland settings hold some of these plays together. The desert both in *Operation Sidewinder* and in *The Holy Ghostly*, as well as the highway en route to suburbia in *The Unseen Hand*, count among Shepard's most vivid inventions of a personal, resonant geography on stage. But in plays such as *Seduced, Curse of the Starving Class* and *True West*, the action of the play *itself* will make us feel as though we are riding down a highway that can turn off either to a land development *or* to a desert. With *A Lie of the Mind*, and with the even bleaker, circular road map of memory in *The Late Henry Moss*, Shepard succeeds at confounding geography with destiny.

Endings that go up in smoke start to seem predictable, even arbitrary, in Shepard's plays. He sometimes seems to fall back on this sure way out simply for want of any other strategy to resolve all battles. When *Forensic and the Navigators*, *The Holy Ghostly*, *Operation Sidewinder*, *Cowboy Mouth* or *Back Bog Beast Bait* have nowhere to go, they go to the light- and sound-effects of an apocalypse or to an actor's physical transformation, suggesting that some other form of life might better inhabit a desert, some other beast might better animate a man's dispirited body.

When Shepard later gains control over his dramatic structure, and when he discovers where a hero lives, then, when the worlds of *Curse of the Starving Class*, *Buried Child*, *Fool for Love* or *A Lie of the Mind* must of necessity collapse, the walls cave in, and nature itself responds.

4
'Where Does a Hero Live?'

Through bragging, a lot of early-day American heroes
sprang up. Paul Bunyan, Pecos Bill, all those mythic guys
emerged from fantastic 'tall tales', mostly based on
macho bravado and superhuman strength . . . Then there
were the real live ones like Jesse James, Billy the Kid,
Mickey Free, Buffalo Bill . . . Even now, when communi-
cations are almost down to teleportation of brain signals,
there's still an emotional space in us that needs filling . . .
Even with the advent of 'demystification', we get stoned
out of the gyrations of a few individuals. Somebody 'out
there' is actually doing what cries out in us to be done.
Something somehow that we know is in us, but it's
dormant. It's lying around and undeveloped. So we're all
applauding ourselves is what it comes down to. 'There it
is! Up there!' 'The whole of mankind in one single act!'
                    (Shepard, *Rolling Thunder Logbook*, p.76)

In this piece called 'Where Does a Hero Live?' written in the
year when Bob Dylan's bicentennial Rolling Thunder Revue

47

toured America, Shepard puts forth his theory about heroes. For Shepard, heroes are born of a craving for transformation, a desire to be animated by a spirit or music beyond our ken. Until 1971, his plays presented this craving for transformation from the point of view of characters who heard of, dreamt of, watched and applauded heroes, feeling heroic action dormant in themselves. Their longing was to escape their own identity, to get out of themselves, and to get in touch with an idea of a hero.

Shepard's drama has always dared to presume that identity is prismatic, that actors serve to refract the light of selves, and that the colours and aspects of self are always shifting. In later plays such as *A Lie of the Mind* or in the screenplay for *Paris, Texas* Shepard will experiment with altering the form, movement and memories of character, too, but throughout his career, he experiments with altering voices. A previously defined character will suddenly evaporate, his physical shell invaded by a new otherly self – or by an otherly facet of the same self, or by an atavistic version of his present self – with an other voice to animate the temporarily dormant shell of character.

Shepard's method of what could be called otherly animation draws on notions of 'possession' by a dybbuk, 'speaking in tongues' and trance utterances by a medium at a séance. Conventional action and dialogue are temporarily placed on hold, and in a moment in parenthesis, the actor becomes both ventriloquist and dummy, usually delivering in a voice not his own a long speech filled with vivid memories and desires of escape, even transcendence. Such speeches, filling a stage moment in parentheses, are directed *not* towards other characters on-stage, but, like Beckett's silences, such speeches are directed towards a universalizing place of heroic yearning within all of us.

In Shepard's early plays, transformation as a means of

escape was hoped for or described by voices not wholly their own, in long speeches that floated away from the rest of the action, which still remained grounded on stage. Starting with *La Turista*, Shepard sought physical expressions for these sudden moments of otherly animation: we get a crash through a wall in *La Turista*, travel through time and outer space in *The Unseen Hand*, a human body changing into an animal form in *Back Bog Beast Bait*, or an animal slouching into the shape of a saviour in *Cowboy Mouth*; and then there are all those brawls, bullets, and bombs tossed by Shepard's 'macho bravado' forces toughing out an apocalypse – made physical on the grandest scale in *Operation Sidewinder* – to warn us that such moments of otherly animation are due.

'Escape' is the final word of *Cowboy Mouth*, Shepard's last short-circuit play of casual desperation. After this piece, which Shepard and Patti Smith knocked off in two nights by shoving a typewriter back and forth, and then acted themselves in a special performance at the American Place Theatre, the artist stopped pressing his luck. Shepard credits Patti Smith with having shown him 'what it's like to construct a line of language in a different way, putting ideas and images together . . . you learn it through the skin, you don't learn it through the head. She writes an animal poetry.' But performing in *Cowboy Mouth* drained him. 'The thing was too emotionally packed,' he has recalled. 'I suddenly realized I didn't want to exhibit myself like that, playing my life onstage. It was like being in an aquarium.'[1]

In Spring 1971, Shepard broke through a wall as surely as Kent had at the end of *La Turista*. With his wife and infant son in tow, he tore free of his New York connections, escaping from the world that he imagined in *Cowboy Mouth* to be holding him captive, trying to turn him into a 'saint but with a cowboy mouth'. Shepard moved to Shepherds Bush in

London, and he stayed there for about three years, supported mainly by small royalties in Hampstead, racing two grey-hounds at the tracks in Walthamstow and Birmingham, and, in summer, raising alfalfa and wheat on a 50-acre farm in Nova Scotia.

The trip to England was engineered as an escape, a moulting for a playwright who otherwise could not stop spinning his wheels, could not connect with any world outside the one in his head. He felt his identity as a play-wright closing in on him. As he put it at the time:

> When I first got to New York it was wide open, you were like a kid in a fun park, but then as it developed, as more and more elements came into it, things got more and more insane – you know, the difference between living in New York and working in New York became wider and wider, so that you were doing this thing called *theatre* in these little places and you were bringing your so-called experience to it, and then going back and living in this kind of tight, insular, protective way, where you were defending yourself. And also, I was into a lot of drugs then – it became very difficult you know, everything seemed to be sort of shattering. I didn't feel like going back to California, so I thought I'd come here – really to get into music, you know. I was in a band in New York [The Holy Modal Rounders, the electric-fiddle group with which Shepard played drums] and I'd heard that this [London] was the rock'n'roll centre of the world – so I came here with that kind of idea.[2]

Once in England, Shepard let go of the rock fantasy. Instead of joining a band, he went beyond all those lucky voices, images, and action that smacked of what the Doctor in *Geography of a Horse Dreamer* (1974) diagnoses as 'the dreamer's magic'. Shepard now moved to track down the luck itself. He wrote three plays-of-ideas about art, luck and escape: *The Tooth of Crime* (1972), directed by Walter Donohue and Charles Marowitz at the Open Space Theatre; *Geography of a Horse Dreamer* (1974), which is the first play of his that he directed himself, at the Theatre Upstairs at the Royal Court; and *Action* (1974), directed by Nancy Meckler at the Theatre Upstairs. Shepard also wrote some lesser pieces, including *Man Fly*, an unproduced adaptation of Christopher Marlowe's *Dr. Faustus*; *Blue Bitch* (1973), a short play for the BBC about Dixie and Cody, expatriates from Wyoming, hoping to sell their greyhound; and *Little Ocean* (1974), an unpublished sketchy play about three women's conflicting feelings and fantasies about pregnancy, produced at the Hampstead Theatre Club.

Shepard's split from the American landscape, from 1971 to 1974, yielded him a way of seeing that gave theatrical shape and symbolic meaning to the voices, images, and trajectory of action into rhythm that had long obsessed his art. This was lucky, because, as the sixties came to a close, these voices, images and self-propelled, incremental actions had all been in danger of self-destructing, the way a frequently replayed track on a vinyl record can wear itself out. After 1971, Shepard's plays take on a much larger task. That is, transformation is *not* presented as the desire of one who wants a hero's voice to animate him, a hero's shape to fill that 'emotional space' inside him, a hero 'doing what cries out to be done'. The craving for transformation is presented more frequently from the *hero's* own perspective. And, so, it is not a desire to escape out of the self, but a desire to see more clearly into the self. This is presented on stage as 'one single act', wilful and dangerous.

What Shepard would now seek to present on stage was nothing less than 'the whole of mankind in one single act'.

He would begin to recognize the tangible power that the true artist holds, the power to take an audience past entertainment to experience; he would seek to show how one single act can transform all those who witness it. This uncanny power is the 'dreamer's magic', which is luck. 'Luck is no accident', says the Doctor in *Geography of a Horse Dreamer*, searching through his black bag for a scalpel with which to remove from the back of Cody's neck the magical 'dreamer's bone' potent with 'valuable substances'. According to the Doctor, luck is 'a phenomenon. Luck is a living thing. The problem, of course, is tracking it down.'

In a series of dazzling plays, most notably including *The Tooth of Crime*, Shepard imagines a world of heroes, usually artists, whose dreams have been usurped, kidnapped or bought out by slimy profiteers, promoters, wheeler-dealers, gamblers or the other hangers-on who seem to be part and parcel of sudden success, called up by great good luck to bring down the hero. In these plays, the creative artist feels himself and his imagination – what Shepard calls the 'gyrations . . . the whole of mankind in one single act', and what Cody in *Geography of a Horse Dreamer* calls 'the magic space inside where the dream comes' – slip away. It is a terrifying loss of power; it hurls the hero towards oblivion, towards a loss of self, towards what Shepard calls 'demystification' with terrific velocity. The hero hardly knows what hit him. It usually turns out to be someone without a face, without a name, someone who is one of us, one of the anonymous audience 'applauding ourselves', 'feeling the same act in us but it's dormant'.

The Tooth of Crime is Shepard's breakthrough play: for the first time nostalgic voices and American roadside images are not random or whimsical, not hit-or-miss scenic side trips or wrong turns taken by the script. In plays from *Red Cross* to *Operation Sidewinder*, notably in *La Turista*,

The Unseen Hand and *Shaved Splits*, Shepard would time and again present sudden, extended moments when a character would find himself filled with words and images, possessed by a boundless burst of vocal athleticism. As Shepard saw the problem at this time, 'One of the things I've found is that it's too much to expect an actor to do a vocal aria, standing there in the middle of the stage and have the thing work in space, without actually having him physically involved in what he's talking about . . . The characters are physically marooned by their speaking.'[3] In early plays, Shepard often relies on such moments of otherly animation as a way out, at least vocally, even if the characters stay 'physically marooned'; such 'arias' are escapes both for his characters trapped in their skins, and for his plays, locked in a holding pattern, wanting to take flight, looking about for a climax.

In *The Tooth of Crime*, these 'arias', to use Shepard's term, finally belong to the character, Hoss, who is now a whole, rather than a fragmented creation; the solos are the character's, not the playwright's. The drugged rhythms of Hoss's singing, talking and slipping-away are all fully psychologized. And so are Hoss's monologues, especially the two wrenching memories of American roadside adventures at the close of Act I. Instead of addressing us in a new voice and taking us away from the present action, as Shepard's earlier solos are wont to do, these extended disclosures bring us directly in touch with the character we see right now on-stage.

Anxious about his ability to face his challenger, Crow, the Gypsy Killer, Hoss delivers two such speeches of personal intensity at the close of Act I. In the first, he describes and re-enacts a memory of the triumph he and two other buddies, also outsiders, felt when they beat some toughs in a high-school 'class war' in the parking lot of a Pasadena burger palace. In the second such speech, Hoss is taken over by his father's spirit, who reminds Hoss of their fishing expeditions and the pleasures of the way. 'The road's what counts. Just look at the road. Don't worry about where it's goin', says Hoss in his father's voice. Both of these speeches reassure Hoss; they are alternative ways of thinking about the open highway. They are fixes of hope, self-administered from Hoss's still vital imagination. Both of these passages yoke language to a physical reality on stage, riveting our attention to the inner life of the hero.

The Tooth of Crime may be considered as Shepard's first structured play, his first play that does not depend on a final crescendo of words to contain and present a whole glossary of transcendent selves, iconic images and hypnotic rhythms. The plot is basically a simple and archetypal one, as simple as Shepard's earlier shoot-out scenarios, as archetypal as the triumph of the new over tradition. Hoss and Crow are hero and villain, straight out of melodrama. But they also come across as King and victorious Challenger, for Hoss's first-act monologues are organically related to the action of *Tooth* in a more seamless, calculated, necessary way than ever before in Shepard's plays.

With the *Tooth of Crime*, then, Shepard's signature skills – his ability to create vivid theatrical moments using spirits of heroism; his ability to create a language of American images, slang, and totems; and his ability to harness action to raw musical rhythms – take us *into* the play, not out of it. In *Tooth* those solos bring otherly animation to a character already shaped; they bring senses and memory to bear on images, slang, and totems already defined: and they bring intensity to a beat and vocal range already established in language and movement on stage.

Indeed, Act I of *Tooth* continues beyond those soaring speeches, finding a way to make actual an image of Crow, a name that Shepard has called up time and again, but, until now, never projected full force, never given physical substance. Act I of *The Tooth of Crime* ends with a shadow and an echo of what is to come. We see a huge shadow of Crow cast behind Hoss's throne, and we hear Crow's voice over the public-address system. Crow's first song celebrates the new age, the age after heroes, when a creature like Crow nurtures evil, strangles the angel in himself and ejaculates poison.

In *The Tooth of Crime*, then, which is still considered by many to be Shepard's most exciting, original fully realized play to date, Shepard's three earlier escape routes – the mystique of heroes, the belief in a palpable language, and the release through music – are all confronted directly and simultaneously.

This play grapples most directly with heroic energy, its sources, its creative and destructive manifestations, and its styles. Hoss, the hero of *The Tooth of Crime*, was in the past a true artist, but he now performs only when he must, preferring to inhabit a drug-induced stupor in moneyed isolation rather than to make music for a world of fallen sensibilities. Computer-driven 'keepers' make a 'clean killer' such as Hoss long for the days 'when we were warriors'.

The Tooth of Crime plays for what Shepard dubs 'high stakes'. At the time it premiered, Shepard said:

It's been called an American play, right, but it was written in the middle of Shepherds Bush, and for about a month before that I was struggling to write this other play called *The Tooth of Crime*, which was a three-act epic number in a jail . . . and at the end it was a complete piece of shit, so I put it in the sink and burnt it, and then an hour later I started to write this one that's been performed . . .

It started with language – it started with hearing a certain sound which is coming from the voice of this character, Hoss. And also this sort of black figure appearing on stage with this throne, and the whole kind of world that he was involved in, came from this voice – I don't mean it was any weird psychological voice in the air thing, but that it was a very real kind of sound that I heard, and I just started to write the play from there. It just accumulated force as I wrote it.[4]

When the play opens, we see that throne which Shepard first imagined as the kernel of the play, and then Hoss appears onstage. In front of his 'Egyptian Pharaoh's throne', looking like a wild, mean, young Rip Torn, decked out in black leather and silver-studded rocker's gear, and backed by a band that should sound like the Velvet Underground, he sings 'The Way things Are', a song that sets the mood and situation for us:

> Everybody's doin' time for everybody else's crime
> and
> I can't swim for the waves in the ocean
> All the heroes is dyin' like flies they say it's a sign a'
> the times
> And everybody's walkin' asleep eyes open – eyes open
>
> So here's another sleep-walkin' dream
> A livin' talkin' show of the way things seem.

In this opening song, Hoss laments the hero's crisis, his doubts, and his diminishing powers. As he tells his sidekick, Cheyenne, 'It's gettin' lonely as an ocean in here.'

In his time, Hoss was himself a 'mad dog', a 'cold . . . sideways killer, a complete beast of nature'. Deep down he knows that making it in the game does not really count. 'That stuff is for schoolies', he says, after consulting and dismissing his stargazer, who advises him to sit tight and wait out the imminent wars over territory. Another member of his entourage who thinks Hoss 'can afford to take it easy' is Becky Lou, his tall, blonde, weapon-toting groupie. Becky Lou cautions Hoss to cool out, to 'hold down the pressure circuits . . . put it in fourth for a while . . . cruise it'. But Hoss remembers how it used to be. He can still hear the true music – the music of 'genius killers' – in his head. 'I'm too old fashioned', he says:

> Gotta kick out the scruples. Go against the code. That's what they used to do. The big ones. Dylan, Jagger, Townsend. All of them cats broke codes. Time can't change that . . . The next genius is gonna be a Gypsy Killer. I can feel it . . . We don't have the whole picture . . . We're insulated from what's really happening by our own fame. (*The Tooth of Crime*, early in Act I)

Everything Hoss does – even rhythm and blues – goes down in doubt. Vulnerable now, Hoss has been 'marked' by a gypsy killer, and 'Gypsies don't play by the rules'. To stay on top, in the lingo of the play, to stay number one with a bullet, to keep controlling borders, to stay on the charts and in the game, he needs more than one more 'global glow' or 'interplanetary flash', more than one more 'clean kill'. He has been 'marked', and so he must fight however he can with honour.

What Hoss has got to hold onto goes deeper than the code. It has to do with the felt life of the artist, the hero's magic. He must find something to believe in, some 'little light . . . in the darkest night' to 'keep [him] rockin', that is, to keep him breathing, to keep him alive. But Hoss's first strategy, which he rehearses by stabbing a dummy in Act I, sticks to the code. Hoss begins to worry, and he anticipates his doom. 'What if the neutral field state failed one time . . . what if an emotional field came through stronger . . . something subtle like the sound of his voice or a gesture or his timing.'

Hoss feels 'stuck in [his] image . . . stuck in a mansion . . . waiting for a kid who's probably just like [him]', contemplating suicide because, as he says towards the end of Act I:

> The whole thing's a joke . . . He's my brother and I gotta kill him. He's gotta kill me. Jimmy Dean was right. Drive the fuckin' Spider till it stings ya' to death. Crack up your soul! Jackson Pollock! Duane Allman! Break it open! Pull the trigger! . . . Drive it off the cliff! It's all an open highway. Long and clean and deadly beautiful. Deadly and lonesome as a jukebox.

The play's central image of the dissipated, lost hero gains strength from the language that dislocates us as well, launching us into a rock-future where we exist only as a half-remembered frame of reference, where Hoss, a hero for our time, finds himself out of time. We hear that Hoss was 'good on the streets', a 'true hustler', way back when. He was so formidable, he could even manage to score, he could even make it big, in the tough heart of the East Village, on New York's Second Avenue. But that was then, when the old geography held true. Now, Hoss 'wouldn't stand a snowball's chance in hell of makin' it outside the game'. So long cushioned by success, so long quieted by easy money, sex, guns and drugs, Hoss has lost touch with the special music that marked him as a hero. In the code language of *Tooth*, he has lost touch with his genius killer's lust.

Hoss has also lost touch with the way things are in the world outside his enclave. 'What Second Avenue? There ain't no Second Avenue', he is reminded by Becky in the middle of Act I:

> They're all zoned out . . . the streets are controlled by the packs. They got it locked up. The packs are controlled by the gangs. The gangs and the Low Riders. They're controlled by cross syndicates. The next step is the Keepers.

Then Hoss poses a question that pitches us forward into a no man's land where familiar landmarks would have vanished and where contemporary American road maps would be obsolete. 'What about the country?' he asks. 'Ain't there any farmers left, ranches, cowboys, open space? Nobody just livin' their life?' The answer is no, delivered with a flippancy that chills us. 'You ain't playin' with a full deck, Hoss', is the answer. 'All that's gone. That's old time boogie. The only way to be an individual is in the game. You're it. You're on top. You're free.'

The time-warp language gives *Tooth* its terrifying edge. These words, so familiar to us, are co-opted to haunt *Tooth's* new country, a zoned-out, marked-off appropriated landscape, just as the play's very familiar rhythm-and-blues and rock music, and its hero's classical act of self-assertion are consistently played off against a hard-edged futuristic controlling organization devoid of values, empty at the core. Through language, then, *The Tooth of Crime* conjures up a future wasteland where the thrill of the hero's clean kill and personal voice is gone, where nothing counts but the scavenger game itself. Shepard uses language here to ground both the play's music and its hero in a very specifically imagined future vacuum, a world vacated of meaning and emptied of true music, a country without cowboys, where a true hero such as Hoss is an anachronism.

Hoss's electronically guarded compound, and then his inner sanctum, is invaded by Crow, a 'gypsy killer' who doesn't follow the rules for clean kills. Crow is a Shepard demon-force: a hollow man who fights for power, usurps territory, stakes a claim, and challenges the artist to question and to give up his luck. Crow's verbal footwork as he tracks down the luck is dazzling: he fights, usurps, steals, stakes, and challenges Hoss's very essence in Shepard's most consistent hybrid language culled from picture shows and codes of cool behaviour.

The language itself finally wins. It takes on a mysterious energy, a dangerous significance that goes beyond psychology towards a more universal sound. It is a rocker vocabulary, a code garishly coloured by an insider's slang for cool attitudes: for the right cars, drugs, music, fifties American Westerns, and black-leather-jacket teenage-rebel movies. As in Anthony Burgess's novel *Clockwork Orange*, we can track the language back to our own; and we also learn to understand the language on its own ground, that is, to hear it as a future-dialect, invented to conjure a world rooted in and sometimes nostalgic for our own, but a world far gone, long past our own.

Act II of *Tooth* revolves around Crow, whose very presence is kinetic and volatile, whose physical bearing – whose attitude of connection to unheard music – should suggest, according to the stage directions, Keith Richard, the eeriest, most spectral member of the indestructible Rolling Stones. Crow's language goes a step beyond the argot shared by Hoss and members of his inner circle: Becky, Cheyenne and Galactic Jack. Crow speaks in clipped cadences, in a machine rhythm that wastes no breath as this very shrewd and sharp – in his language, 'very razor' gypsy killer – susses the scene and computes his odds, sizing up Hoss. 'Very razor to cop z's sussin' me to be on the far end of the spectrum', he compliments Hoss at their first meeting.

Then, left alone for a minute, Crow instantly starts to fill his own body with Hoss's style. 'Cut at the gait. Heel-toe action rhymes of New Orleans . . . Mashing patterns. Easy mistake here. Suss the bounce,' he instructs himself. In these gestures, we see that Crow is immediately attuned to Hoss's attitude, and that he has done his research. He can call up in his mind the Cream's recording of the old Skip James tune 'I'm So Glad', to identify the 'ancient . . . inborn' pattern he wants to cop. What Hoss was drawn to as an artist, the music that engulfed him and gave him vital energy, is what Crow has scientifically studied. Hoss, who knows nothing of pretence, is drowning in this music and in the painful memories of all its long-gone sources; Crow, an image of performance as ever-shifting, daemonic and consuming, has got it all under control.

To kill Hoss, to beat the hero, Crow must go past mimesis to the music inside Hoss, to his pulse. Crow must connect on a visceral level with a mode of being, in solitude and in essence. From the moment he enters at the start of Act II, we sense that Crow can and will do this. According to the stage directions, '*CROW tries to copy Hoss's walk. He goes back and forth across the stage practising different styles until he gets the exact one. It's important that he gets inside the feeling of Hoss's walk and not just the outer form.*' On Shepard's terms, music is the most potent force with which to create or destroy life. In *Tooth*, we discover that Hoss is hooked on his music, while Crow, a breathing radio, is the scourge personified. He assaults and incarnates the hero with a Mephosophelean relentlessness that gives Act II of *Tooth* an inevitability and inner logic unprecedented in Shepard's earlier plays.

If *Tooth* is Shepard gaining distance, breaking free of contemporary packages, lingo and jingles; indeed, if the play seems suspended, hovering above the seventies junkyard, making us see it in the context of the dramatic tradition of heroic tragedy, then this reaching-out to a larger context is even more clear in *Man Fly*, the adaptation of Marlowe's *Dr. Faustus* which Shepard wrote at this time, but has chosen never to publish or to see produced. The unpublished type-script of the second draft of this play is now in the University of California at Berkeley's collection in the Bancroft Library. (A shorter first draft of this play is in the Boston University collection at the Mugar Memorial Library.)

In *Man Fly*, Shepard adapts Marlowe's play to his own subject: the hero as successful artist, seduced by worldly deals just as he feels himself losing touch with what is called in *Geography of a Horse Dreamer* the otherworldly 'space inside where the dream comes'. *Man Fly* is about Skeetz, a writer trying to write. The play is transparently Shepard's most personal work, but it is also somewhat tongue-in-cheek, an ironic treatment of all those elements Shepard's heroes elsewhere hold holy. Words as incantatory, art as the shaman's gift, the American West as a goldmine of images – all these are blasphemed and travestied by Shepard's Skeetz, who sells out.

The action of *Man Fly* requires the ultimate Shepard setting. It is envisioned as a '*vast, empty space surrounding this very cluttered and crammed room*'. Like other of Shepard's characters – the artists and heroes as well as the unfulfilled dreamers of artists and heroes in the early plays and the misfits and hermits of later plays – Skeetz never takes out the garbage, so his life, like that of the others who want to fly, is bordered by Styrofoam coffee cups and cigarette butts, beer cans and papers and unmade beds.

The room itself objectifies the paradox felt by Shepard's

heroes: for them, the personal clutter of hangovers and rough times is always set against a backdrop of natural resources, timeless and vast spaces, sources of untapped power. In *Man Fly* this tension between spaces, this contrast between breathing the stale air inside and the air between the sky and open land, is presented with special self-deprecating whimsy. For until he writes *True West*, which shares much of *Man Fly's* ease of self-mockery and ironic distance, this is Shepard's only play directly placing a writer in the hero's predicament.

Man Fly is still, in fact, the only play Shepard has set in the writer's study. And what a study it is! Shepard mocks his own occupation and his notorious preoccupations in a room decorated with gleeful abandon. Skeetz's room is '*a primitive structure of four poles, split shingle roof with antelope skins hanging underneath forming the ceiling . . . The poles should be notched with a primitive design, not highly painted, having a feeling of age and weather. Eagle and hawk feathers tied to the poles in small bunches . . . In the centre of this space is a large, very old, black Remington typewriter set on a Formica-top table . . . The seat for the person typing is an old Western saddle set on a horse tree, facing the typewriter and table. These objects rest on a large Navajo rug.*' The outer side of the structure in which Skeetz works should give the feeling of '*a Plains Indian burial site where the corpse is elevated on a crude platform and left to the sun.*' And Shepard does not stop there. The photographic backdrop is '*the Rocky Mountains with snowy caps*'.

In Skeetz's opening soliloquy, Shepard is his own sharpest and most wicked critic. Skeetz berates himself for the limits of his art:

Squashed from the effort to raise myself. The very urge to soar, to climb the heights of words and dazzle all

America with my shimmering tongue. Hypnotized with
my collection of inside goods . . . Pieces of Americana
flashing on the page. Broken Antelope horns, drum
heads, Indian skin. Literature crammed into a ball of cow
flop. Whitman, Kerouac, Faulkner. Heroic death and
dying still. Nothing to study. Never was. No body of
information. No whole body . . . The whole escapes me.
Always will. Still, behind it, dancing, the pull from those
who know . . . How could I settle for this poetic rodeo all
the time knowing that my true art lies in transformation
. . . The power to change my shape to empty space. But
that was how it started anyway. Those were the stakes.
Way back in the days when volumes reeled off me like a
ticker tape. The pure impulse to be re-born through
words. Through shaping structures line by line until
tornadoes ripped across my desk. A pure alchemical
transformation from the demon-dog to the angel-cowboy.

The writer who wants inspiration and to play for high stakes
now calls upon Lucifer, who rips a page from Skeetz's typewriter and sneers at it. 'Look at this! Simpering romanticism', says the Devil. 'What's he know of God and country.
That's what comes from riding the middle rail too long . . .
this stuff is full of puss (*rips paper into shreds*). Kid dreams.
Movie fantasies, while all the time the syndicate fattens, the
world bleeds, the laws of heaven and earth are played out all
around his typing machine but never find their way to the
page.' The Devil dismisses Skeetz and his worldly praise,
praise that has even led to an honorary doctorate of letters
degree. 'America's starving from the spirit out', explains
Lucifer. 'Any rancid piece of bacon can easily pass for the
whole pig.'

What Skeetz, the Shepard hero *redux*, wants is to fly.
When he gives up his soul, the words 'MAN FLY' appear in

blood on his arm. Lucifer convinces him that 'Anyone can be a poet. But a devil!' The real power he offers Skeetz is to 'open up this country . . . change [things] at . . . will . . . Roll Mt. Rushmore to Boot Hill . . . Re-create the Civil War . . . Tear apart the Great Divide and have the Rockies sink and hide.' By the close of the play, however, when Skeetz longs in vain to repent, he discovers what those words really mean. As he realizes his soul is disappearing, and only his arm remains, appearing almost alive in front of him, Skeetz cries out to his arm:

> Speak to me! I was a part of you once! Not cut off! NOT CUT OFF! Speak! No. I'm only crazy. Nothing heroic in it. Just blind insanity. It wrote it plain before. 'Man Fly'! Now I know the meaning of it. Now it strikes me plain as day! I had the chance to soar and now it's gone! Oh God! All I wanted was to love America! But I turned it on myself! LOVE MYSELF SKEETZ! LOVE MYSELF!

Man Fly shows Shepard is both quite aware of and able to poke fun at his own insistent romanticism and catechism of Americana, which, as he acknowledges through Skeetz's distress, have sometimes enabled him to construct plays on automatic pilot. In *Man Fly* Shepard looks long and hard, and with a wry wit, at his own writings. He sees how easy it has become to turn a true impulse into a formula, how facile he can be at calling up his sure-fire short-hand popcorn movie indicators of Americana, and how his technique has sometimes supplanted his style.

Skeetz' crime is that he has lost his touch with the quick of the plays he writes. In Shepard's ontology, this quick is a constant value; it is an atavistic rhythm of being that is expressible only in animal howls or jazz wails: it is the unmoored, expressible yearning – the desire to soar past history, geography, and language – that obsesses and identifies the hero.

From play to play, Shepard recapitulates this 'feeling [which is] like a curse . . . but even so it's what adventure's made from'. Even his heroes who come home feel this need to fly, the need that belongs to the hero whose romantic inner world is at odds with present-time reality. The hero feels himself marooned in a world which refuses to recognize his claim to the hallowed land that rooted him; and he feels himself outlawed in a world which disregards his reverence for the discarded modern vehicles – the abandoned heaps of rust and dust that used to be the cars, planes, music, drink, drugs, films, and poetry – that beckoned him to adventure. This archetypal feeling finds its most apt voice in *The Tooth of Crime*, where Hoss's original deep-down rasp should rival the sound of the broken string in *The Cherry Orchard* or the sound of Katrin's drum in *Mother Courage* in its ability to put us in touch with a nexus of response to pain beyond words. This feeling will also find its visual expression in *Seduced* (1976), when Shepard, dramatizing the end awaiting a Howard Hughes-like hero, makes literal the desire to fly. This feeling will even erupt in the backyard that awaits Vince, the heir who comes home in *Buried Child* (1978) to save his lineage from the curse of those half-remembered giants in the earth, Vince's forebears who still haunt the family, making their presence felt in the hall portraits, in the wallpaper, in the windshield, and in the rich replenishing Midwestern soil.

In *Man Fly*, this feeling finds its most general, and hence, its least specific mode. When Billy Lee, in his baseball cap, tries one last time to urge Skeetz back to the Shepard paradise, to the hallowed roadside attractions, he implores him, 'Turn back to poetry Skeetz. We'll hit the streets. Hitchhike like we used to. Poetry is prayer. You knew that once. Pray now Skeetz.' But Skeetz cannot. In a speech that baldly puts forth *an idea* of the heroic feeling, Skeetz realizes that his pact with Lucifer has made rescue impossible, that his animal nature is cruel, for it keeps him earthbound even as it heightens his instinct for flight, and even as it intensifies his senses, especially his hunger:

> Now, this is it. At the lowest point. Where a man feels his animal crawl along the ground. Here on the earth. Nowhere else. Not in mind or dreams . . . Right here. Crawling. Like a snake. Even a snake is free to crawl without this constant nagging. It's knowing that I'm stuck! Marooned. Pinned by gravity. No matter how many bouncing Southern boys there are in outer space, it's me that hurts. Me that hungers for my wings. But even with them I wouldn't know where to fly. Now this feeling's like a curse. But even so it's what adventure's made from. It's what moves explorers. But everything's been discovered except the source of this great need. So still I'm stuck and always will be. No matter where I flew there'd always be a 'somewhere else'.

Man Fly, then, is a most curious play for three reasons: it presents Shepard's on-the-money parody of his own other works – their verbal styles, their sets, their props, and their angels and demons; it places Shepard's heroes squarely in a dramatic tradition, most often in a maudlin but nevertheless unequivocal way, relocating the pact made by Marlowe's Faustus to a world of front porches, holy rollers, and dirt roads; and its hero's soliloquies and its devil's explanations of the way things are supply a blatant gloss on Shepard's more subtle plays, belying Shepard's usual public pose as a taciturn, unreflective playwright. Mustafo sums it all up on Shepard's terms when he finally gloats over Skeetz' 'last attempt at honor' in the face of 'a sneak preview of things to come' in hell.'Remember,' says Mustafo, 'it's from hunting pleasure that you fall.'

Shepard's rehearsal in *Man Fly* and in *The Tooth of Crime* of the hero's fall from grace is, of course, rooted not only in the playwright's own personal adventures as an American artist pursued as a potential hot property before he left for England. It has been Shepard's subject from the start, ever since *Cowboys*. But until *Tooth*, we have never seen a fully imagined depiction of Shepard's subject, which, as *Man Fly* makes transparent, is rooted in the archetypal self-destructive energy of the new Faustian hero as artist, conjurer, and lost soul. Until *Tooth*, we have never seen fully imagined a necessity for Shepard's action, the engine of which is the delicate transference of heroism from one age to the next. And most important, until *Tooth's* inherent musicality, Shepard has never controlled the form of theatrical expression to so fully underscore the intensity and high seriousness of this subject of heroism.

The Tooth of Crime is driven by what the playwright would later term 'visual music', then, as well as by kinetic language characterized by sudden leaps from jargon to incantation, from pop lyrics to lamentations. We are dazzled by the quickening rhythm of the language in this play described by Shepard as 'built like *High Noon*, like a machine Western'.[5] 'Can't you back the language up, man?', Hoss asks his killer in the manic 'gestalt match', the rhythm'n'blues fight between these two futuristic rockers battling it out for the number one spot on the charts. 'I'm too old to follow the flash', he says.

Although he had used music in earlier plays (notably the pop hit parody in *Melodrama Play*, the easy tunes in *Mad Dog Blues*, the rockabilly protests in *Operation Sidewinder*, and the drum solo in *Cowboy Mouth*), this is the first play in which Shepard fully integrates music and action on stage; where, in fact, making music can itself be a heroic act. In a letter to Richard Schechner, who in 1972, without the play-wright's collaboration, mounted an environmental, ironic production of *The Tooth of Crime* at the Performing Garage in New York, Shepard describes how integral the music is to the action in *Tooth*, how the creativity and survival of his characters are now bound to the vital force of the simple, passionate rock progressions his score provides:

> about the music. Most of it is very simple: rock progres-
> sions from Velvet Underground to The Who. It's gotta be
> electric! No other way for it to work. The songs were all
> built for electric guitar, keyboard, bass, and drums. All the
> music is written down and fits each section of the play
> according to the emotional line that's going down. It's
> gotta be played by rock musicians who've got their chops.
> Actors who aren't musicians just couldn't handle it.[6]

In *Tooth*, rock celebrates and becomes a mode of action, an assertion of self, a way of being.

At the heart of Act II is the 'style match', a 'gestalt match' in three unfairly refereed rounds. Singing and music never interrupt the action. They *are* the action. Shepard's stage directions are crucial here, for they point to the vocal athleticism required in performance to realize this script, cut clean and lean, with no false moves, faked rhythms, or dialogue just there for the flash. As Shepard envisions and hears it, Act II is a 'sort of talking opera', enhanced by a band with a '*lurking evil sound*', complete with drums, guitars, bass, piano and microphones for Hoss and Crow. During the match, '*Their voices build so that sometimes they sing the words or shout. The words remain as intelligible as possible, like a sort of talking opera.*'

Shepard's instructions take us to his purist attitude towards music and, by extension, towards acting, that energizes this play, and that will now start to characterize his work both as a playwright and, starting with *Geography of a Horse Dreamer*, as a director. Although major productions of *Tooth* have focused more on surface moves and outward rhythms, Shepard insists here on what is akin to a classical style of acting for his play: let the rhythms develop out of the language; let the actors approach the script as they would an opera, where emotions can penetrate to one's very breathing, where no emotion is beyond the possibility of complete vocal expression.

Music now identifies the hero. Hoss, who at bottom is a conventional, traditional hero, is always himself, and no one but himself. The voices that fill Hoss are not otherly animations; they may link him to other transcendent, sympathetic spirits, but they are filtered through his own. Because this is how it must be with heroes, when the referee calls Round Three as a technical knock-out, we in the audience must side with Hoss, who knows better, and who kills the referee rather than accept the decision, which is based on Crow's false logic, a logic that equates all new music with stolen energy, a logic of the future that has no room in it for the original gifts that are handed down to shape a tradition of 'visioners'.

Hoss never did steal his image or his voice from *his* predecessors. The heroic age to which Round Three harks back is the age of 'the origins', the age Hoss knows in his bones:

Little Brother Montgomery with the keyboard on his back. The turpentine circuit. Piano ringin' through the woods . . . Back when the boogie wasn't named and every cat house had a professor . . . Diplomats and sailors

gettin' laid side by side to the blues . . . so bad the U.S.
Navy have to close down Storyville. That's how the
move began. King Oliver got Chicago talkin' New
Orleans. Ma Rainey, Blind Lemon Jefferson. They all
come and got the gangsters hoppin'. (Act II)

So Hoss, who feels himself to be the last survivor in the line
he traces with reverence, does not lose to Crow. As Hoss
tells Crow in Round Three, 'Yo' music's in yo' head. You a
blind minstrel with a phony shuffle. You got a wound gapin'
'tween the chords and the pickin'. Chuck Berry can't even
mend you up. You doin' a pantomime in the eye of a hurri-
cane.' Crow is the weapon, not the actual killer. Crow's
assault, leading to what he finally calls ' a snake dance to
heaven' of future challengers, makes Hoss see that the
throne he will relinquish is a relic. When Hoss commits
suicide, he takes with him his music, his heroic gift. Hoss
takes with him what Crow, who never really understands the
art, disparages as 'all that power goin' backwards'.

In every play Shepard has written since *The Tooth of Crime*,
especially in *Suicide in B Flat* and in *Angel City*, the two
plays he wrote upon his return to America, his two jazz
meditations on melodrama that grapple directly with (and
then let rip) rhythmic structure and cadences of emotion,
Shepard has relentlessly applied a musician's attitude and
criterion of authenticity to ideas of acting and directing his
plays.

Even before he wrote *The Tooth of Crime*, Shepard had a
reputation for being uncompromising, and a difficult writer
to please because, as Kenneth Chubb, a British director of
several of his works, observed, 'he has seen in his author's
eye a potential production . . . if Sam is around you are
aware of the one in his imagination'.[7] But his experience

with directors putting their mark on *The Tooth of Crime* cinched it for Shepard. The music that pulses through this play, and that determines the outcome of the second-act duel, poses a special challenge for the director: how to let loose for an audience at a *representational*, scripted performance the vibrancy and danger that would be experienced by witnesses present at an *actual* event like a rock concert, or a title boxing match, or a courtroom trial.

The job of the director of *The Tooth of Crime* is to make sure the music really has the killer force behind it that the play says it has. Charles Marowitz, co-director of the Open Space production of *The Tooth of Crime*, said, 'Shepard has a fierce dislike of "flash", which tends to turn away from bold, "outside" theatrical effects. I, on the other hand, have a fondness for artifice which, when properly conjugated, seems to me to get closer to inner truths than brow-beating interior probes.'[8] Shepard himself went straight to the point. He saw his play thrown into chaos by Marowitz's direction, and he also focused his concern on the performance possibilities not tackled. Kenneth Chubb writes, 'Sam suggested that Lou Reed, the ex-lead singer of the Velvet Underground, would have been right in *The Tooth of Crime* [for the role of Crow]. Perhaps the only way to find the right style is to utilize the performance skills that certain rock musicians and singers have derived from spending all their energies on finding their own personal style.'[9]

Discussing the 'powerful emotional influence . . . in the nature of music', Shepard referred to Brecht's plays. 'Plays like *Mahagonny*. He's my favourite playwright, Brecht', said Shepard in 1974, and then he acknowledged the obvious but nonetheless subtle influence of *Jungle of Cities* on *The Tooth of Crime*, where music has an emotional, metaphysical significance, not a literal interrupt-the-action-with-a-number effect. 'If you look at *Jungle of Cities*', said

Shepard, it's 'a bout, between these two characters, taken in a completely open-ended way, the bout is never defined as being anything but metaphysical.'[10]

About Richard Schechner's environmental production of this play, Shepard again found disheartening the misplaced theatricality and the insufficiency of the musical expression. 'Well, I think he's lost', said Shepard kindly about Schechner's adaptation of *The Tooth of Crime* to a playing area composed of various wooden structures through, on, and around which audience members scurried as scenes shifted location. This was a poor theatre version of the play, and the music was intimate, accompanied on a very small scale, mainly with homemade instruments. No attempt was made to make music into action. When it was all over, Shepard clarified his position, saying:

> When you write a play it sets up certain assumptions about the context in which it's to be performed, and in that play they had nothing to do with what Schechner set up in the theatre. You can take that or leave it. It can be okay – the playwright isn't a holy man, you know. Except I'd rather that the experimentation took place with something that left itself open to that – a play that from the start defines its context as undefinable, so that you can fuck around with it if you want to.[11]

Shepard wrote a letter to Schechner to make his position plain. Shepard put forth a rather traditional assertion of authorial rights, privileging the published text over a director's new concept (Shepard has held steadfast to this position in the years since, repeatedly refusing permission to directors with notions of producing female versions of *True West*, for example, his later play about wrangling brothers):

I've laid myself open to every kind of production for my plays in the hope of finding a situation where they'll come to life in the way I vision them. Out of all these hundreds of productions, I've seen maybe five that worked . . . It seems to me that the reason someone wants to put that play together in a production is because they are pulled to its vision. If that's true then it seems they should respect the form the vision takes place in and not merely extrapolate the language and invent another form which isn't the play.[12]

This letter reinforces the point Shepard stressed in his letter consenting to the environmental production. 'The main reluctance I have', he wrote, 'is that the play will become over-physicalized and the language will fall into the background.'[13]

Now Shepard began to try his own hand at directing. Indeed, after the Marowitz and Schechner productions of *Tooth*, what did he have to lose? After years of sometimes-heated debates with directors who had encumbered his plays with surface flash, Shepard now decided to try his own luck at serving his visions in a clean, ungimmicky, actor-centred way. Even a great playwright like Beckett found it difficult to protect the integrity of his texts from well-meaning directors eager to deconstruct and reconceptualize his plays. Furthermore, Shepard himself was most closely in touch with the essence of what his plays had to say through action and sound, and there was the possibility that he would also be most conscious of how to make that felt meaning relentlessly present without falsifying it with an over-theatrical style.

As a director, Shepard has always been influenced by Joseph Chaikin's Open Theatre techniques of heightened vocal and physical expression as well as by the Open

Theatre's emphasis on ensemble work and on the importance of the actor's personal authenticity. In 1969, he wrote monologues called 'Voices from the Dead' for *Terminal*, and in 1972 Shepard joined Jean Claude Van Itallie and Megan Terry, two other playwrights, to collaborate with the Open Theatre company on monologues for *Nightwalk*, a performance piece that delved into dreams.

In one sense, this method of directing is precisely outlined in *The Tooth of Crime*, with its emphasis on Hoss 'riding a state of grace' because he possesses 'True courage in every move . . . True to his voice. Everything's whole and unshakable . . . Lives by a code. His own code. Knows something timeless. . . . Can't do anything false.' Hoss compromises this mode of being when he tries to make a survival deal with Crow, to learn his moves, to reprogramme the tapes, to put on his gestures to remodel himself after Crow, a 'master adapter'.

This kind of attitudinizing proves fatal for the hero. When Hoss commits suicide by shooting himself in the mouth, *Tooth* finally holds up for our admiration a clean, cool kill. Hoss has been cheated out of the match; he is the loser; and now he shows his stuff. 'I can take it in death. I'm a born Marker, Crow Bait. That's more than you'll ever be', he says. 'Now stand back and watch some true style. The mark of a lifetime. A true gesture that won't never cheat on itself 'cause it's the last of its kind. It can't be taught or copied or stolen or sold. It's mine. An original. It's my life and my death in one clean shot.' The stage directions that follow specify that the same criterion is applied to actors as to heroes. Shepard cautions his actor that, when Hoss falls in a heap, '*This gesture should not be in slow motion or use any jive theatrical gimmicks other than the actor's own courage on stage.*'

Shepard began to take charge of realizing his own scripts

on stage, always keeping in mind each actor's relentless task of finding the 'true gesture that won't . . . cheat on itself'. He directed his next two-act play, *Geography of a Horse Dreamer*, at the Royal Court. Since one critic suggested that he might have more fully tapped the game aspect of the play on stage,[14] he apparently kept the action away from theatrical gimmicks, presenting another clean kill. In his first directorial effort, he also placed his trust in the actors, including Bob Hoskins. 'The rules came from the actors', he said at the time. 'Because they were so good and they've had so much experience, it wasn't me making absolute decisions, though I saw things that they were doing and pointed them out, and then tried to mould a little bit from what they were doing.'[15]

Like *The Tooth of Crime*, *Geography of a Horse Dreamer* concerns itself with Shepard's permanent occupation, 'visioning', and categorizes visioning as the artist's heroic, almost extinct role in a post-historic society, where the 'Mr. Artistic Cowboy here' cannot survive. Like the American buffalo, he is hunted and snared, his image is kept for coinage, and he is then left to 'dream about the Great Plains'.

In its focus on a hero as a curiosity, a sample in captivity of an endangered species, *Geography of a Horse Dreamer* takes itself far less seriously than does *The Tooth of Crime*. In *Tooth* the hero is a musician, a literal artist, an 'original man' in these 'last days of honour'. The true artist is forced to 'fence [his challenger] with the present'. The hero is fully aware of what this means as he takes on and lets himself be swallowed by a new-wave vampire artist, a 'master adapter' of present times who can break through a 'neutral field state' to fill himself with Hoss's personal vital energy, who can steal Hoss's sound, but, as Hoss knows, *not* his music. For, although the artist readily acknowledges sources and influences, what he *is* cannot help but remain the same.

In *Geography of a Horse Dreamer*, Shepard applies a much lighter touch in dramatizing the hero at the end of his rope. He locates the action of this play outside the realm of art, in the realm of business. The play fixes on one of the aspects of creativity that makes others envy it: success. To focus on the profit motive that diverts the artist from his calling, from his true sources of luck and power, and that makes him a target for moneymakers, Shepard shapes a fantasy out of two of his own London pastimes, dog-racing and betting. ' It's really a sort of romantic impulse, you know', said Shepard, 'being around the track, punters and all that kind of stuff – I like that world.'[16]

This play covers the same ground as does *The Tooth of Crime*. Cody, the lucky horse dreamer, has been kidnapped by thugs, who are greedy for his winnings. In their hold, he loses his visioning powers, but he later regains them in an altered state (now he predicts dog races). Evoking in its own action the logic of a dream, the play ends with a Wild West *deus ex machina*. His six-shooting brothers blast Cody, also dubbed Mr. Artistic Cowboy, out of his hotel-room captivity back to Wyoming, but, like Hoss, he is diminished. At the end, Cody has been robbed. He goes home minus something undefinable but essential, minus the great good luck, the art of the hero.

Cody's final speech contrasts with those arias of otherly animation so common in Shepard's plays that maroon characters in their reveries. Grounded as a hero, Cody, like Hoss, delivers the kind of inner-directed speech that will become Shepard's trademark for post-heroic characters such as Vince in *Buried Child*. Cody's inner-directed speech suggests that what has seemed (for a play by Shepard, at any rate) an unusually upbeat ending, is a fluke. Cody suffers a fate far worse than Hoss's. Hoss kills himself when he sees his powers diminished, his light dying. But Cody continues.

'You see the territory he travels in. He's perfectly capable of living in several worlds at the same time. This is his genius', observes the Doctor who has come to steal Cody's magic by cutting into his neck. Wounded at the site of his gifts, but with his hide saved by his brothers, Cody has a moment, a spot of time, when he sees into the life of things, when he experiences otherly animation. Earlier, whenever a glimmer of a winner came to Cody, it was expressed in *'another voice . . . as though he's been inhabited by a spirit'*. But in his last speech, it is Cody's own voice that speaks; and it speaks across a great divide. Reassured that he will be 'good as new', Cody clarifies his transformation. He will be good as new, but not in any ordinary sense, rather:

> In a sacred way. This day. Sacred. I was walking in my dream. A great circle. I was walking and I stopped. Even after the smoke cleared I couldn't see my home. Not even a familiar rock. You could tell me it was anywhere and I'd believe ya'. You could tell me it was any old where.
>
> (End of Act II)

The hero, although still open to epiphanic visions, is now lost inside himself. The dreamer whose gifts brought him fame and success now finds himself out of time, stuck in that space between waking and sleeping where the dream comes, where the vision and, as it is sung about in *Tooth of Crime*, where 'the feelin' slips away. / What's with me night and day is gone'.

With *Action*, Shepard takes new risks. He plants this play firmly in a world with no heroes, in a future world, possibly a post-apocalypse world, where food, water, shelter, and companionship are scarce commodities. Such a world has no room for vaults of heroic action or for nostalgia about personal indulgences. Its characters must instead focus on physical survival; and, when they remember the past, their stories must stand alone, like Beckett's *The Lost Ones* or like the novel Hamm narrates in Beckett's *Endgame*. Talk's function is whittled down to essences: strategies for getting and keeping physical necessities; remembrances to hold onto the Walt Whitman America that preceded this posthistoric time; and terse, resonant anecdotes with which characters aim to make sense of their present extreme situation.

The play is a quite conscious stripping away of all surface action, all surface character traits, all chit-chat, and all clutter. Shepard pares down his play to its title. He even resists including in his cast one or two of his old reliables, a couple of those old familiar standbys Shepard lists in a tongue-in-cheek *Rolling Thunder Logbook* entry as his 'Character References':

Alchemist/Magician/Preacher/Poet/Teacher/Medicine Man/Wizard/Saint/Demon/Witch/Gunfighter/Boxer/ Prophet/Thief/Cowboy/Devil/Assassin/Bride/Lover/ TruckDriver/Pilgrim/King/Emperor/Fisherman/Drifter/ Messenger/A Nobody/Priest/Queen/Shaman/Idiot.[17]

Action draws on Shepard's work with the Open Theatre and on his new experiences as a director to distil movement and character. In place of those all-purpose 'Character References' who have always served him well, Shepard chooses to envisage a world where none of them could breathe, a shelter against the cold inhabited only by two rugged men with shaved heads and by two practical women, all of them making provisions, scared, expecting the worst.

The pared-down language of *Action* is especially akin to the language of Shepard's compositions for the Open Theatre, narrative monologues that are at once intimate and archetypal, always simply phrased and inflected, following rhythms based on the natural pattern of breathing, and often concerned, as are many actors' exercises, with physical sensations and sense memories. The Teleported Man in *Terminal* remembers his dying in words that sound authentic as they describe the personal sensations of an out-of-body experience, even as those self-same words also echo a universal experience. 'Everything seemed timeless and space opened out and out. I'd never felt so free in my life', he says:

> Then suddenly I couldn't get back. I couldn't go on and I couldn't go back. I knew I was lost . . . the panic filled me. I was going to die in mid-air. Out of my body . . . I was being pulled toward the stars. Deeper and deeper in space. I searched for my voice but nothing was there. I tried to scream and nothing came out. No one was there to hear me or see me. I was absolutely alone. I longed to be human again. To crash to the earth and die like a man.[18]

Nightwalk's monologue, 'The House and the Fish', describes – in a voice in touch both with physical sensations and with deeper echoes of shared experience – stark images of the place of man in nature:

> In my house the night moves in
> The air's changed.
> The water moves in the pipes.
> Somebody's taking a bath.
> I see myself on a ship at night staring out to the lights on the shore.
> One of the lights is me.
> Me in my house.
> Me on the ship at night staring out to myself in the house.

Also, 'At the edge of the world it looks calm . . . At the edge of the world it holds me trembling', writes Shepard in 'The Traveller's Speech' for the Open Theatre's *Nightwalk*.[19]

A similar feeling of dread and foreboding at the edge of time permeates the minimal room of *Action*, which is furnished with a table prepared for a sparse Christmas celebration. Around this table gather Shooter, Jeep, Liza and Lupe to eat a turkey (possibly the last turkey), to drink water (possibly the last of the water), to smash some chairs (definitely the last of the chairs), and to 'do the best with what we've got'. As Liza describes their deliberate mode of behaviour about halfway through this one-act play:

> We'll have to do the best with what we've got. We're all eating now. At least we're eating. We'll have to gauge our hunger. Find out if we actually need food when we think we need it. Find out how much it takes to stay alive. Find out what it does to us. Find out what's happening to us. Sometimes I think I know, but it's only an idea. Sometimes I have the idea I know what's happening to us. Sometimes I can't see it. I go blind. Other times I don't have any idea. I'm just eating.

By means of pared-down action, then, this feeling of winding-down, accompanied by a heightened awareness of the severed connection between action and intention, is expanded to the level of world vision. In *Action*, as in Beckett's plays, all consciousness is pain.

Both in its location at the end of something and in its characters' deliberate manner of verbal and physical expression, *Action* comes across as a cool *Endgame*. Jeep can picture another time when they all felt and behaved differently, when they all really could concentrate on living instead of 'just . . . acting it out . . . just pretending'. The date at which *Action* is set is on the same Shepard calendar of future-present as are the dates for *The Tooth of Crime* and *Geography of a Horse Dreamer*, but the world presented in *Action* postdates them both. Lupe has a dim recollection of the days of mass entertainment and of something once called a 'community'. Jeep vaguely recalls that he 'exploded', and Shooter alludes to some event named 'the fall of the Great Continent'.

Something major, indeed, something so cataclysmic that it hovers in the air and defies discussion of its consequences, has happened to change them all. Whatever happened has pitched them all forward, unmoored them. When they speak to describe the world they inhabit, we see that Shepard has now found a way to imagine the bodies and habitat belonging to all those voices that I have elsewhere described in this book as lurching to the surface at moments of otherly animation in Shepard's plays. From *Action* on, the animation is no longer otherly; it is inner directed, deeply felt, projected only with the force supplied by wrenching, animal pain. The voice that makes the vitalizing connection between the present-time self (which is sensate, besieged by worldly desires, and floundering in attempts to hold tight to creativity) *and* the unmoored spirit (which is wise to impersonal cycles of destruction and regeneration) comes now from the character himself on stage; it comes from that space deep inside and back in time where the dream comes. This space is the only place where the hero, as Shepard imagines him from *Action* on – bereft of abstract meaning, haunted by dreams of meaning – can live.

Action is a formal expression of the parenthesis in which Shepard's new heroes will set up house and run amok, trying to fathom personal images and trying to connect themselves to a half-remembered scheme of things. Every gesture, every move, every spoken syllable seems at once freshly minted yet petrified, heaved with great effort by characters who seem freighted with an invisible but heavy history. Like the companions in Beckett's plays, and like the families who will inhabit Shepard's San Francisco plays, these survivors 'sort of . . . recognize each other' and can therefore find comfort for a while in not being 'completely stranded'. The play feels pressurized, like a space capsule, in which the characters, familiar lost ones in an unfamiliar place, must operate out of context, rediscovering words in a post-language, and rediscovering ideas in a vacuum.

The feeling of being perched 'at the edge of the world', where 'it looks calm' and yet 'holds me trembling', which runs throughout the hour it takes for *Action* to take its course on stage, is expressed primarily on a personal level of sense awareness. In that hour, we see what an enormous effort it takes for characters to call up and hold onto sense memories from a shared past that included such actions as putting food on the table, hanging laundry to dry, scaling fish, dancing a soft-shoe shuffle, sighting running antelopes, and drinking tap water. To recall such stuff, the characters rely on mnemonic devices: to suggest to himself, as does an actor, how running water sounds and feels, for example, Jeep uses an image of the Golden Gate; he also pours over his hand some of the freezing water he has drawn for the meal, concentrating intently on committing the moment to his memory. According to the stage directions, '*He keeps doing this over and over as though hypnotized by his own action.*'

Both Shooter and Jeep tell stories that resonate as allegories for a world without any a priori values, for a world in which all codes of symbolic meaning, all referents, are suspended or, worse, lost. Shooter talks about a 'walking stiff', a man betrayed and killed by his own body, which is now walking around 'vacant'. Also, while Lupe keeps on looking at her book and while Jeep keeps on pouring water slowly over his hand into the bucket (both Lupe and Jeep clearly locked in private dreams of personal meaning), Shooter stands on the broken-down armchair and '*directly to the audience*' he tells a tale of a moth whose mission to discover the meaning of a candle flame inside a window leads the moth to unite himself with the flame. This embrace with the flame brings the moth complete joy *and*, of course, it sears him in an instant. What can such an anecdote even remotely signify in a solipsistic world bereft of communally held assumptions about objective meanings and possible events? Shooter tells us that, 'The leader of the moths, who was watching from far off with the other moths, saw that the flame and the moth appeared to be one. He turned to the other moths and said: "He's learned what he wanted to know but he's the only one who understands it".'

Jeep's story is a personal one on the same theme as Shooter's tale of the moth. In the play's final monologue, Jeep does something as extraordinary as Kent's leap through the wall in *La Turista*. Jeep makes a leap inward rather than outward, and he makes a verbal leap that is as shattering as is his physical one. It is with this final speech that *Action* discovers and reveals the place inside whence originate all those voices of otherly animation, haunting and possessing Shepard's dissipated effigies of heroes in sudden and fleeting moments. He puts Jeep and the audience in touch with an other state of consciousness that is sensate and ancient, basic and primordial. In his final moments on stage, Jeep discovers and demonstrates as he re-experiences it that you cannot escape through the wall. You would just smash your head. There is 'no escape' that way. The only way out is by taking an 'inward leap' that results in losing the present social self to a more visceral, animal version of the self. Jeep exposes himself, as well as his natural and instinctual ancestors.

Jeep's animation, then, with his whole being taking on a

new colouration in performance, is not otherly. This new inner animation is accomplished by words and movement unfettered by convention and rising from the depths of consciousness in a manner akin to the acting methods developed by the Open Theatre. This animation is directly related to an actor's process of knowing, inhabiting and being inhabited by a character he plays; and this relationship between acting, speaking and being is one which Shepard will, upon his arrival at San Francisco's Magic Theatre in 1975, explore further in his work as a playwright/director with an acting ensemble. This is a focus on the actor as transformer, and on the artist as shaman, as Jack Gelber puts it in his introduction to the Applause edition of *Angel City*, another play in which Shepard would risk 'inner leaps' to yoke the actor's art to other creative and pure impulses. This focus is an outgrowth of the yearnings expressed by Shepard's characters since *Red Cross* to connect to the elements of earth, air, water and words 'as living incantations and not as symbols'. With *Action*, Shepard hones his dramaturgy around the vaulting, transformational capacity of words, 'always hovering' and 'ready to move'. 'Language', he writes, 'seems to be the only ingredient in this plan that retains the potential of making leaps into the unknown.'[20]

This ritualistic process of actor's animation goes behind the representational acting style that other directors have used to Shepard's repeated dismay when staging his plays. In his 1977 essay, 'Visualization, Language and the Inner Library', Shepard connects an actor's process, using sense and emotional memory, to the writer's process of 'diving back into the actual experience' so that information is given back 'as a living sensation':

This is very similar to the method-acting technique called 'recall'. It's a good description – I'm recalling the thing

> itself. The similarity between the actor's art and the play-
> wright's is a lot closer than most people suspect. In fact,
> the playwright is the only actor who gets to play all the
> parts. The danger of this method from the actor's point of
> view is that he becomes lost in the dream and forgets
> about the audience.   (Shepard, p. 52)

In this essay, Shepard connects the writer's process of jazz-
sketching with the process of a musician jamming. He
describes how his jamming with words as 'living incantations and not as symbols', whose power 'isn't so much in
the delineation of a character's social circumstances as it is
in the capacity to evoke visions in the eye of the audience',
has led him on occasion to feel his characters as an actor
might feel them:

> Language can explode from the tiniest impulse. If I'm
> right inside the character in the moment, I can catch what
> he smells, sees, feels and touches. In a sudden flash he
> opens his eyes, and the words follow. In these lightning-
> like eruptions words are not thought, they're felt. They
> cut through space and make perfect sense without having
> to hesitate for the 'meaning'.   (Shepard, pp. 53–4)

At the end of *Action*, Shepard begins to use the sister arts
of the potentially shamanistic playwright – ritualistic, cere-
monial acting and jazz music-making – to get language to 'cut
through space'. From here on, Shepard's characters reach for
this experience of transformation, which is the experience of
the felt life of the artist made actual. Shepard has connected
with this himself as a jazz sketching playwright:

> After periods of this kind of practice, I begin to get the
> haunting sense that something in me writes but it's not

necessarily me. At least it's not the 'me' that takes credit for it. This identical experience happened to me once when I was playing drums with The Modal Rounders, and it scared the shit out of me. Peter Stampfel, the fiddle player, explained it as being visited by the Holy Ghost, which sounded reasonable enough at the time. What I'm trying to get at here is that the real quest of a writer is to penetrate into another world. A world behind the form.

(Shepard, pp. 54–5)

At the end of *Action*, artistic transformation is made sensible on stage. By means of the actor's art, the play penetrates into another world that Shepard would later call 'the world behind the form', the 'looks-within' place in *Angel City*. In this way, the final monologue serves not to separate Jeep from his present world, but to unite him with it in a visceral, most elemental way. According to the stage directions, '*JEEP begins to move around the stage. The words animate him as though the space is the cell he's talking about but not as though he's recalling a past experience but rather that he's attempting his own escape from the space he's playing in. The other actions continue in their own rhythm.*'

What Jeep learns in this new state of deep animation is that his words can turn into sounds that can turn into animal moans. His movements can turn into shaking that can turn into stalking himself. His perception of the world can be savagely altered from within. Finally, he stands dead still before a Christmas tree with blinking lights, now an uprooted prop of petrified meanings, a thing that used to have symbolic and sentimental value, but is now vacated of such stuff, just there to be rediscovered, out of time, out of context. And finally, Jeep says: 'Everything disappeared. I had no idea what the world was. I had no idea how I got there or why or who did it. I had no references for this.' This state of deep animation into which Jeep moves at the end of *Action* is the destination of Shepard's next heroes, his post-heroes, his sons who journey homeward, backward in time, and inward to a level of deep consciousness.

In *Action*, Shooter describes an experience of gradual disorientation, accompanied by foreboding when the potential for transformation is felt. Transformation is dangerous. It is at once dreadful and exciting, for it brings with it the altered perspective on conventional expectations, behaviour, and being that comes from being drawn by the light, venturing inward, and losing what you had outside. At the start of the meal at the mid-point of this one-act play, Shooter tells himself quietly:

> Just because we're surrounded by four walls and a roof doesn't mean anything. It's still dangerous . . . Any move is possible. I've seen it. You go outside. The world's quiet. White. Everything resounding. Not a sound of a motor. Not a light. You see into the house. You see the candles. You watch the people. You can see what it's like inside. The candles draw you. You get a cold feeling being outside. Separated. You have an idea that being inside it's cozier. Friendlier. Warmth. People. Conversation. Everyone using a language. Then you go inside. It's a shock. It's not like how you expected. You lose what you had outside. You forget that there even is an outside. This inside is all you know. You hunt for a way of being with everyone. A way of finding how to behave. You find out what's expected of you. You act yourself out.

Action takes Shepard's audience back inside, where it is really dangerous. With this play, and with many of those to follow, Shepard's heroes relinquish what they had as outsiders. Drawn by the light, they go home, and they 'hunt for a way of being with everyone'. They learn a new language for living with blood kin in homes haunted by dead memories. They transform themselves from within, their own voices and bodies deeply animated by the journey inward.

From *The Tooth of Crime* on, Shepard shows that transformation can be heroic, therefore revelatory and perilous, a quieting reunion with the self rather than a means of escape from personality. From *Action* on, Shepard finds a way of making transformation a continuous action, an inner leap to a level of deep animation rather than a sudden vault to a level of otherly animation.

'No escape' is appropriately one of the last lines of *Action*. This play opens on a scared man sipping coffee, rocking, and looking 'forward to my life ... looking forward to uh – me ... the way I picture me'; and it ends with an 'inward leap', an inward escape route to a world for which no references exist. After writing and seeing this play produced at the Royal Court's Theatre Upstairs in 1974, Shepard returned home to America. The arc of action in Shepard's next set of plays will even more closely mimic the arc of a performance by a ritualistic actor or by a jazz musician, escape artists whose quests are similarly 'to penetrate into another world ... a world behind the form'.

5
'One Special Rhythm'

If everything could be sung to the standard rock and roll
progression – C, A minor, F, G chords – then everything'd be simple. How many variations on a single
theme. The greatest drum solo I ever heard was made by
a loose flap of tarpaulin on top of my car hitting the wind
at eighty. The second best is windshield wipers in the
rain, but more abstract, less animal. Like the rhythms of
a rabbit scratching his chin. Vision rhythms are neat like
hawk swoops and swan dives . . . And you call yourself a
drummer?

(Shepard, 'Rhythm', in *Hawk Moon*, Performing Arts
Journal Publication, pp. 63–4)

Shepard came back to America in quest of what he would
term in *Suicide in B Flat* a 'visual music'; his aim was to
experiment in the alchemy of theatre. His new plays would
be less overtly musical than *Melodrama Play*, *Operation
Sidewinder* or *The Tooth of Crime*. Instead, he now
composed plays such as *Angel City* – which is precisely

about the quest for the 'rhythm . . . the one, special, never-before-heard before rhythm which will drive men crazy' . . . *Suicide in B Flat* and *Seduced*. Now, Shepard's characters tend to be driven by inner rhythms, by a compulsion to break free of conventional beats so that private, unknown, dangerous rhythms might lurch to the surface of action as 'vision rhythms . . . like hawk swoops and swan dives'.

This was a period of transition for Shepard. No longer content to be a rock-and-roll playwright ('Mr. Artistic Cowboy' is what they sneeringly call Rabbit in *Angel City*), no longer content to parade myths across the stage or to celebrate kitsch Americana, Shepard's time abroad freed him from his early compulsion to clutter his stage with pop images, cruising, aimless action, baroque slang, and characters casually leaping into trance states. Now Shepard sought a new mode of drama, more akin to jazz than to rock music, more introspective and melodic, focused on what he terms in *Angel City* the ' "Looks-Within" place'.

Upon his return to the United States in 1974, Shepard began to seek a new way to escape from conventional characters and conflicts. Encouraged by his work abroad and by the influence of Open Theatre techniques stressing Artaud's ideas about 'affective athleticism', typified by Artaud's dictum that 'the actor is an athlete of the heart',[1] Shepard began experiments that might lead to a synaesthetic mode of performance, a way of making visual music and a way of inventing a concrete, physical language for the stage.

In quick succession Shepard had three premieres at regional theatres: *Angel City* at the McCarter Theatre; *Suicide in B Flat* at the Yale Repertory Theatre; and *Seduce*d at the American Place Theatre. All three of these plays ride on the success of *The Tooth of Crime* as a futuristic rock-music showdown, with the action of all three revolving around the kidnapping and ruin of more of Shepard's modern Fausts: a shamanistic screenwriter in *Angel City*, a jazz musician in *Suicide in B Flat*, and a Howard Hughes-like flyer in *Seduced*. However, the heart of these plays is not their subject, but their style. The war fought between an artist's creative drive and his worldly ambitions – that is, the war between his private voices and his American dreams – continues to obsess Shepard's heroes, but it no longer obsesses the playwright himself. Shepard quite consciously plunges into a new phase of playwriting in which he attempts to find physical equivalents for inner voices.

Shepard is, as he puts, 'burning bridges and entering new territory'. In a 1978 essay, 'Time', Shepard made a case for every play, whether a shorter work or a 'full-length, major opus', to be 'seen for what it is – a part of the gradually unfolding process of a playwright's total work'. In this same essay, Shepard noted that a writer's 'true aims' have to be 'continually re-evaluated'. In Shepard's view:

> If this re-evaluation is sincere [the playwright] has to come back to the point where he feels he knows nothing at all about the heart of what he's after. He knows a great deal about things like: timing, rhythm, shape, flow, character (?), form, structure, etc., but still nothing about the real meat and potatoes. So he begins again. He strips everything down to the bones and starts over. And in this is where he makes his true discoveries.[2]

If *La Turista* closes with a silhouette of an actor escaping through a back wall, *Suicide in B Flat* opens with an outline of a dead musician on the floor and *Seduced* ends with a dead man flying in his mind, silhouetted by moonlight.

In *Angel City*, Shepard mocks his old tune about the hero's drive and his seduction by success, all the while attempting to develop and sustain a new theatre vocabulary,

2. O-lan Shepard as 'Miss Scoons' and Austin Pendleton as 'Rabbit' succumb to the spell of movies in the premiere production of *Angel City* at San Francisco's Magic Theatre in 1976. Photo: Ron Blanchette, courtesy of the Bancroft Library, University of California, Berkeley.

here analogous to a filmic vocabulary. *Suicide in B Flat* is a sustained riff on gangsters and rubouts, always aiming for the scenic and verbal equivalent of jazz. With *Seduced*, Shepard attempts to defy gravity to evoke the sensations of flying, even soaring, by means of action and sound.

Angel City, however, marks a point of departure for Shepard. The language itself now becomes a signal of danger, of mysterious energies, of artistic, even potentially spiritual power. The quest of character is now to find one's own true voice or voices. For example, in a trance at the end of Act I of *Angel City*, Miss Scoons speaks in a kind of voice-over, linking her own situation to the one she shares with her bosses, the detached movie mogul, Lanx, and the enthralled Wheeler, a creative wheeler-dealer of the industry who literally has movies, a green pus of deforming power, in his blood. 'The urge to create works of art is essentially one of ambition', Miss Scoons says in that voice not wholly her own. 'The ambition behind the urge to create is no different from any other ambition. To kill. To win. To get on top.'

This link between an artist's drive and an ambition for power is at the heart of many of Shepard's plays. More profoundly than any of his earlier plays, however, *Angel City* faces Shepard's demon, his idea of live movies. In a relentless rhythm to match that of *The Tooth of Crime*, Shepard's rock-music showdown of epithets, *Angel City* explores the playwright's own cinematic imagination, his impulse towards a filmic vocabulary, rooted in myths about power.

Audiences at the 1976 McCarter Theatre production seemed most puzzled by Shepard's kinetic language with its sudden leaps from jargon to incantation. The play does, in fact, have a structural logic, but it is a language of film transplanted to the stage; the play jump-cuts from one image, one metaphor to the next, as if two films were being spliced together. Sometimes the effect is even more electronically disjunctive, as if a TV tuner or a jukebox knob were suddenly, fiercely being switched. Audiences at the McCarter production wondered, too, about the situation of the play, its plot, its structure (especially the shift from Act I to Act II), and they wondered about the green slime that eats away at Wheeler and finally oozes like blood out of Rabbit's medicine bundle depicting the West, the ' "Looks-Within" place'. In short, this play fulfils Shepard's expressed intention before he left for England, 'to write a movie for the stage'.[3]

To Shepard, movies surpass jazz, rock music, Westerns, science fiction and action comics as a drug, for movies include and intensify all the others. As Jack Gelber suggests in his introduction to the Applause edition of *Angel City*, Shepard is a shaman of theatre, a magician at a rite who is both the transformer and the transformed, turning his plays into trips, seeking shared transcendence through sympathetic action. He is also a self-styled hero, seeing in his audience that longing shared in a darkened theatre to project oneself onto the screen. Like Tom in Tennessee Williams' *The Glass Menagerie* (which opened in New York in 1945), Shepard knows why we go to the movies. When his mother accuses Tom of lying, because 'Nobody in their right minds go to the movies as often as you pretend to', Tom Wingfield lets loose a torrent of B-movie plots, gleefully projecting himself into all of them:

> I'm going to opium dens! Yes, opium dens, dens of vice and criminals' hangouts, Mother. I've joined the Hogan Gang, I'm a hired assassin. I carry a tommy gun in a violin case! I run a string of cathouses in the Valley! They call me Killer, Killer Wingfield, I'm leading a double-life, a

simple, honest warehouse worker by day, by night a dynamic *czar* of the *underworld, Mother*. I go to gambling casinos, I spin away fortunes on the roulette table! I wear a patch over one eye and a false mustache, sometimes I put on green whiskers. On those occasions they call me – *El Diablo!* (*The Glass Menagerie*, scene iii)

In *Angel City*, Shepard uses this kind of identification with packaged, mass-produced fantasies to a devastating end. He is a fan himself, scripting his plays to match the power of pop-culture myths. 'I love the Rolling Stones. I love Brigitte Bardot. I love Marlon Brando and James Dean and Stan Laurel . . . and Jesse James and Crazy Horse . . .' he once enthused in autobiographical programme notes.[4]

In *Motel Chronicles*, Shepard contrasts his fantasies about movies with his experiences of movie making as an actor. First, he writes of the hypnotic power of movies:

> *King Solomon's Mines* was the movie that most haunted me as a kid. I've never seen it since then but images from it still remain . . . The Rialto Theatre was dark and musky in the middle of day and I entered the world of the movie so completely that the theatre became part of its landscape. The trip to get popcorn up the black aisle with the sound track booming and the kids squealing in their seats was all part of the plot. I was in the cave of King Solomon at the candy counter. The 'Ju-Ju-Bees' were jewels. The ushers were jungle trees. Cheetahs roamed through the bathroom.
>
> I breathed African dust for days afterwards in a town of solid white folk.

And then, again in *Motel Chronicles*, Shepard poeticizes an encounter with the Star's stand-in on the last day of the

shoot of the movie, *Frances*, in Seattle in 1981. The local
girl is depressed, and her misery echoes Miss Scoons's
despair in *Angel City*, a despair at living a life, not living in
a movie:

> since this was her home town
> and she'd be staying right here
> while we'd be moving on
> and the agony of being just a local stand-in
> left behind
> in a town she ached to be out of
> was bearing down on her now
> with real force
> and it made me suddenly re-ashamed
> of being an actor in a movie
> at all
> and provoking such stupid illusions . . .
> I said look it's not worth it
> it's just a dumb movie
> she said it's not as dumb as life.[5]

This playwright who has always loved movies, who is now
himself an 'actor guy', then, is also scornful of movie
promises, and in *Angel City* these double feelings – his characters' Tom Wingfield-like yearnings for dream-machine
identities and his own recognition of the self-destructive
power of such yearnings – are cross-cut in a cinematic rather
than theatrical way.

The characters who inhabit Shepard's *Angel City* are all
outright spokesmen for or against the mosaic of promises
packaged on the West Coast, the ' "Looks-Within" place'.
Tympani, filling in on the drums, backing up fantasies
played out before him, is waiting for 'The rhythm . . . The
one, special, never-before-heard-before rhythm which will

drive men crazy.' A true child of the movies, Tympani knows the way the game is played. 'You won't go far', he tells the innocent newcomer, Rabbit. 'They've already busted up your buckboard and sold your horses. On foot you're as good as dead in this town. They'll swallow you whole and spit you out as a tax deduction.' Tympani not only knows the way the game is played, in a tough-talking slang of cowboys and industry; he also plays that game in earnest. In his Act I reverie, for example, Tympani '*shouts*', according to the stage directions, '*like a little kid to his mother upstairs*':

> I just wanna' go to the movies, Ma! I don't care about anything else! Just the movies! I don't care about school or homework or college or jobs or marriage or kids or insurance or front lawns or mortgage or even the light of day! I don't care if I never see the sun again, Ma! Just send me to the dark, dark movies!

In Act II, also, Tympani enters what the stage directions identify as '*a world of his own*', and, facing the audience, still lost in his own reverie of himself as a short-order cook in a diner, Tympani invites us to join him:

> What dya' say, just you and me, we leave the kids, get outa' the house, into the old Studebaker, leave our miserable lives behind, and join the great adventure of a motion picture? . . . What dya' say we just lose ourselves forever in the miracle of film? We nestle down, just the two of us, with a big box of buttered popcorn, a big cup of Seven-Up, a big box of Milk Duds, a giant box of 'Black Crows', and we just chew ourselves straight into oblivion?

Unlike his co-workers, Miss Scoons, Lanx and Wheeler, Tympani has always seemed distanced from his craft, ironic in his methodical drum beatings. Finally, however, Rabbit's guide to this underworld, indeed, *our* guide to this place, does succeed in finding that hypnotic rhythm – that is to say, as an artist he breaks through to find his original voice; and he, along with the others, is finally lost in it. With his seductive description of movie-house comforts, reminiscent of Shepard's journal entry on *King Solomon's Mines* and on how he lived life through the movies as a kid, Tympani shows how we, too, can be lost in its oblivion.

Lost in it from the start are Miss Scoons, Lanx and Wheeler. Miss Scoons seems to be the most vulnerable of all. She is a stereotyped sexy secretary with pipedreams of stardom. She is the most susceptible character on stage, the first to succumb to the hypnotic, frenetic drumbeats. When she falls into a trance, however – and she falls in and out of trance states even before Tympani hits on his mesmerizing rhythm – Miss Scoons speaks, according to the stage directions, '*in a kind of flattened monotone, almost as if another voice is speaking through her*'. In those moments of inner animation, with her back to the audience, Miss Scoons stares at the huge black screen that has devoured her, and in the middle of Act I she expresses the self-loathing that Shepard sees as the disastrous result of loving movies:

I look at the screen and I am the screen. I'm not me. I don't know who I am. I look at the movie and I am the movie. I am the star. I am the star in the movie. For days I am the star and I'm not me. I'm me being the star. I look at my life when I come down. I look and I hate my life when I come down. I hate my life not being a movie. I hate my life not being a star. I hate being myself in my life which isn't a movie and never will be. I hate ... Having to live in this body which isn't a star's body and all the time knowing that stars exist. That there are people

99

doing nothing all their life except being in movies . . .
People living in dreams which are the same dreams I'm
dreaming but never living.

The action of *Angel City*, at least throughout Act I,
suggests a home movie as well as a live movie, a play about
Shepard himself mythologized as the stranger showing up in
a wild place wanting power. The play opens with the arrival
of Rabbit Brown, a script 'doctor', at the plush office of a
movie executive who longs for a hit, a disaster-movie blockbuster:

LANX: You're not just another ordinary hack. You're
  supposed to be an artist, right?
RABBIT: Right.
LANX: A kind of magician or something.
RABBIT: Something like that.
LANX: You dream things up.
RABBIT: Right.
LANX: Right. So what we need in this case is a three-
  dimensional invention. Something altogether unheard
  of before. We have the story, the plot, the stars, the
  situation, but what's missing is this uh – this develop-
  ment. Something awesome and totally new . . . We're
  looking for an actual miracle. Nothing technological.
  The real thing.

The allusion here is to *Zabriskie Point*, which was to have
been the ultimate disaster movie for the nuclear age. Even
now, after having acted in numerous films, and after seeing
several more of his many screenplays and script outlines
realized on film, Shepard still sees the Hollywood system as
exploitative and anti-creative. ' "Collaboration" – that's the
word the producers use', he says. 'That means, don't forget

to kiss ass from beginning to end. That's basically what collaboration means in Hollywood terminology . . . I'd like to write, direct and make my own films. And I'd like to find a way to do that without being eaten up by the system. I'm certainly not willing to crawl around an office floor and beg and do 30,000 rewrites.'[6]

If Act I of *Angel City* may be seen as a movement towards immersion of all creative talent in the business of making movies, Act II may be seen *cinematically* as the nightmarish aspect of that process. Act II is connected to Act I by means of dream logic. For a while, the engine of the play ceases to move forward. Instead, the play moves inward, and Shepard attempts to find a physical equivalent for his by now trade-marked reveries, usually spoken by characters momentarily frozen in an attitude, lost in a vision. When Act II begins, all the characters, lulled into a trance by a rhythm that touches them all, are in worlds of their own. In Act II Miss Scoons, dressed as a nun, sings to herself as she scrubs the floor. Tympani, wearing a chef's hat and a white apron, cooks imaginary eggs. Lanx shadow boxes.

Rabbit and Wheeler, however, stand apart from the others, still working on the 'miracle', the disaster. Wheeler grows more and more desperate in Act II. According to the stage directions, '*His skin is a slimy green. He now has two fangs and extra-long fingernails. His posture is slumped over and painful. He seems to be having trouble breathing, and in general his health has depleted considerably.*' Finally in desperation, he confides in Rabbit; he lets him see the rushes of the top-secret film that wants a surreal climax. The play-within-a-play (the movie-within-a-live-movie?) is a stylized combat between '*two chieftains*', revealed as one male and one female, squaring off in the manner of '*Samurai warriors*', a kind of early cartoon version of Shepard's *Fool for Love*. Ironically, Rabbit finds this 'final duel in solitude' to be a cliché-ridden romantic depiction of the end of the world, when what is wanted, he says, is 'hard core disaster'. Still, its effect on him is marked. When Rabbit turns around to face the audience, adjusting his swivel chair (an executive leather lounger with a stick shift on the arm rest), he, too, is covered with green slime, and *'he has fangs, long black fingernails, and a long, thick mane of black hair'*.

Just what is that green slime that eats away at Wheeler and at his shaman script doctor protégé, Rabbit? And why does that same stuff pour out of the medicine bundle holding 'discovery . . . something deadly'? For starters, the slime is the standard seepage of horror movies, the malevolent force that can never be stopped, oozing its way across America in Roger Corman sci-fi-flicks. It is, too, a terrific metaphor for the power of movies in *Angel City*, where all movies are finally horror movies, and where all movies are finally disaster movies. That it is green might well have something to do with the colour of American money, but that it finally engulfs them all has more to do with Shepard's perception of film as a medium and as a theatrical force. 'I feel that language is a veil hiding demons and angels, which the characters are always out of touch with', Shepard has said. 'Their quest in the play is the same as ours in life – to find those forces, to meet them face-to-face and end the mystery. I'm pulled toward images that shine in the middle of junk.'[7] As in Nathanael West's *The Day of the Locust* and F. Scott Fitzgerald's *The Last Tycoon* (in which Stahr, the producer, Fitzgerald's title character, describes a moment of a girl burning her gloves and answering a telephone, and, when he is asked, 'What happens?' answers, 'I don't know . . . I was just making pictures'[8]), in *Angel City* Shepard makes pictures, pop images that shine.

Finally, like moving pictures, this city of angels and its

ubiquitous green slime are *deadly* 'images that shine in the middle of junk'. In Act II Wheeler calls himself 'An Angel in disguise . . . spawned somehow by a city . . . leaked out', and he cries, 'I HAVE A MILLION MOVIES! AND DO YOU KNOW WHERE THEY ARE! THEY'RE IN MY BLOOD . . . TRYING TO OOZE OUT AND TAKE ON A SHAPE THAT WE ALL CAN SEE!' Later, when Rabbit usurps his place, simultaneously catching his plague, Wheeler tries to reaffirm his own power. 'I'm in the business. I'm in pictures', he protests. 'I plant pictures in people's heads . . . and the pictures grow like wildfire. People see them in front of their eyes . . . Wherever they go I go with them. I spread their disease.' Movies fill his body; they shape his imagination. Rabbit, too, finally trades his creative energy for the commercial potential of a vampire art, a destructive, even demonic picture show. Like a drug, like a beat, like a chant of the secret self, movies flash dark news from *Angel City*.

If *Angel City* is a hybrid of filmic and stage devices, *Suicide in B Flat* is Shepard's attempt to meld language and music, and more daring, to meld *action* with musical form. Recognizing that dramatic form must, to a certain extent, stay 'within certain boundaries', Shepard came to see language as possibly 'the only ingredient in this plan that retains the potential of making leaps into the unknown . . . From time to time I've practised Jack Kerouac's discovery of jazz-sketching with words. Following the exact same principles as a musician does when he's jamming.' Shepard had always likened his playwriting to making music. 'When you write a play you work out like a musician on a piece of music. You find all the rhythms and the melody and the harmonies and take them as they come', he said in 1971.[9]

But in Shepard's opinion it was now no longer enough to have a 'great ear for language'. What this usually means, he argued, is that:

the writer has an openness to people's use of language in the outside world and then this is recorded and reproduced exactly as it's heard. This is no doubt a great gift, but it seems to fall way short of our overall capacity to listen. If I only hear the sounds that people make, how much sound am I leaving out? Words, at best, can only give a partial glimpse into the total world of sensate experience, but how much of that total world am I letting myself in for when I approach writing?[10]

Suicide in B Flat, subtitled 'a mysterious overture', grapples with this question. As Niles, the central character, explains, 'You talk to yourself and other people talk to themselves. I wonder where my voice is.' Throughout this play, actors playing jazz musicians accompany their Shepard-style soliloquies about art, identity and emptiness with riffs on their instruments. 'YOU'RE IN MY HEAD! YOU'RE ONLY IN MY HEAD!' yells Laureen, describing her own possible suicide while she bows her bass and Petrone mimes playing the sax, for example. When Niles finally confesses how he substituted a faceless corpse for himself to escape his identity and his calling, he raves, 'Are you inside me or outside me . . . Am I buzzing away at your membranes? Your brain waves? Driving you berserk? Creating explosions? Destroying your ancient patterns?' This speech is backed also by Laureen's mournful bass and piano music. According to Shepard's stage directions, '*The sound of snapping hand cuffs should happen in a moment of silence between the language and the music.*'

The plot of this play is a B-movie parody. Two detectives, Pablo and Louis, fifties-style Sam Spade-like gumshoes in the *film noir* mode, are investigating the murder(?)/ suicide(?)/disappearance(?) of Niles, a major jazz pianist and composer. At one point in this murder mystery, while a pianist plays a strong bass line and a saxophonist plays silent music (throughout he blows and mimes music making but no sound is heard), and while one detective wrestles with his own hand wielding a knife, Pablo puts forth his theory about Niles:

> His music was driving him mad. His improvisations were lasting for days on end . . . He forgot how to speak and only uttered noises of varying pitch. His gestures were all in slow motion as the shock of fast movement was too loud for his ears. He began to feel certain that he was possessed. Not as if by magic but by his own gift. His own voracious hunger for sound became like a demon. Another body within him that lashed out without warning. That took hold of him and swept him away.

One critic described the 1976 Yale production of *Suicide in B Flat* as something like 'a free-form jazz opus by Ornette Coleman to a text by Wittgenstein translated by Abbott and Costello'.[11] A revival of the play at La Mama in 1984, however, was more in touch with the play's core of music as action. Directed by George Ferencz as part of 'Shepard Sets', a mini-festival also including *Angel City* and *Back Bog Beast Bait*, this production rejected the notion of background music, the use of music as atmosphere. Instead, Max Roach, the renowned jazz drummer, composer, and one of the pioneers of be-bop, was called in to write a score for four jazz musicians and to help incorporate an abstract musical quality into the acting, too. As Ferencz saw it:

> Music's *there*, it's part of the chemistry, the makeup of the piece. The play sends out reverberations, and its images create resonances In musical theater, so often what's musically behind the actors is redundant. It does

the same thing they're doing and it supports them. A lot of times, the music in this production is counterpointing them, and that's tricky stuff; the idea is not to enhance the pieces, but to inform them, which is a different responsibility.[12]

Roach's contribution to the production included a score of modal late-fifties-style jazz (in the key of F minor, not B flat), and work with the actor playing Niles on how to convey the essence of a jazz figure 'as phenomenal as Art Tatum, as profound as Charlie Parker, as strong as Miles Davis, as eccentric as Thelonious Monk'. Roach integrated music into the production, keeping in mind Shepard's background as a drummer, and noting that 'Sam himself in his poetry was not just polyrhythmic. He had no bounds. He must be a super drummer, because rhythm sections have to accommodate any kind of situation . . . Sam's poetry is not just rock – it swings, it's avant-garde, it's oompah, it's all of those things.'[13]

Seduced, produced at the American Place Theatre in 1979, is Shepard's last lone-hero play. Although here Shepard puts aside the musical experimentation that shapes *Angel City* and *Suicide in B Flat*, he experiments with another aspect of dramatic form, the concept of transformations, the concept derived from his work with Chaikin and the Open Theatre that is premised on the potential power of an actor telling a story to revivify the events through language and gesture. In *Seduced*, instead of including lyrical passages that attempt transformations, as he has so frequently done in earlier plays, Shepard analyses and questions the process. He takes it to its logical end: the annihilation of self. At the end of *Seduced*, the central character loses himself so completely in a reverie of flying over a lost America that, even though at the very end of the play he is shot full of holes, he continues to soar 'high over the desert . . . invisible . . . a ghost in the land . . . no voice . . . no sound . . . a phantom they'll never get rid of', his silhouette outlined in moonlight. Hackamore's escape is complete. 'I'm dead to the world but I never been born', he chants at the play's end. 'I can move anywhere I want to now . . . My body's gone. You can't even see me now . . . Freer than life. Flying.'

This play's considerable humour derives from its parodic treatment of the legend of Howard Hughes's dying. Henry Hackamore looks like a *'cross between a prisoner of war and an Indian fakir'*, like 'something from another world'. As played by Rip Torn sporting an unruly mane of silver hair, with long white beard and glittering eyes, with finger-nails like corkscrews, the character physically resembled artists' renderings of the reclusive, paranoid, aged Hughes. The play is filled with references to the notorious Hughes obsessions: the Kleenex, the paper towels, the germs, the empire of wealth 'built . . . on nothin' but air! Thin air. Invisible. Tiny little invisible molecules. Jet propulsion!'

Like Hamm in Beckett's *Endgame*, Hackamore is practically immobile and implacable. 'I've lived through earth-quakes, disasters, corruptions, fall-out, wives, losses beyond belief', he snarls at his visitors. The absolute law is 'nothing from out there comes in here! Nothing! No life! Not sun, not moon, not sound, not nothing!' For Hackamore's greatest obsession is complete control of his environment, complete isolation with nothing but his visions, the pictures in his head. 'We can't allow penetration' (*Seduced*, Act I).

The play is set in some huge luxury Caribbean hotel, on an unnumbered high floor, in *'the* room . . . the inner-most chamber room . . . the secret nucleus that everything springs from . . . the Pharaoh's crypt. And lying in state, at the very heart of things, is the Pharaoh himself'. Hackamore's servant, Raul, periodically massages him, humours him, transfuses him with plasma, and plans getaways, each time closer to the United States, closer to Nevada, a world whose industries and wasteland both call to Hackamore.

Hackamore has made a deathbed decision. He wants to fly again. 'A man's got a right to die in his homeland', he reasons at the end of Act I, so he wants to fly: 'Straight to Nevada ... We're going to disembark in the blazing sun. We're going to appear out of nowhere. We're going to climb into sixteen black Chevrolets and drive straight out across the Mojave Desert.'

The action of *Seduced* revolves around Hackamore's intention to fly home, to escape through acts of memory and sheer will. He has instructed Raul to import two visitors, women in gowns and furs who Hackamore hopes will help him relive his past. Both Luna and Miami are dressed and coiffed as if time had stood still in the forties, when Hackamore knew them. Both are actresses, and what Hackamore wants from them is help in achieving his deliverance from the world at large, a world Hackamore shuns because of his paranoid conviction that it is 'wild ... undominated ... ravenous for the likes of us ... ready to gobble us up at the drop of a hat'.

This play goes beyond parody. Shepard's caricature of Hughes emerges as another Shepard loner seeking real escape through acts of transformation. He asks Luna and Miami for help in remembering, in 'bringing something back'. He wants them to tell him a personal story about Las Vegas, but, more than that, he wants them to 'get real animated ... almost like you were in a movie ... except more than a movie ... sort of re-living the experience', acting it out. The vision Hackamore seeks to bring back is the reality that preceded his amassing of wealth and power, and the usurpation of the land by him and by others like him.

Hackamore sees himself as 'the demon ... the nightmare of the nation', planting 'Hotels! Movies! Airplanes! Oil! Las Vegas', over-running the flat, barren spaces of the Southwest, which he still envisions as clearly as he did when he was a boy in Texas. His vision, revivified in this play, is, as far as 'the eye could take in', one of unspoiled open country:

> Enormous country. Primitive. Screaming with hostility toward men. Toward us. Toward me. As though men didn't belong there. As though men were a joke in the face of it. I heard rattlesnakes laughing. Coyotes. Cactus stabbing the blue air. Miles of heat and wind and red rock where nothing grew but the sand. And far off, invisible little men were huddled against it in cities ... I saw the whole world of men as pathetic ... Getting smaller and smaller until they finally disappeared. (*Seduced*, near the end of Act II)

In the late 1970s then, Shepard was in transition, breaking away from plays of personal escape to a world of connections with others: a family, a home, a communal rather than an idiosyncratic vision of the past. He was open to all kinds of theatrical experimentation having to do with musical rhythms and ideas of transformation. Among his minor experiments were *The Sad Lament of Pecos Bill on the Eve of Killing His Wife* (1976), a 'cowboy operetta' he composed with Catherine Stone as part of San Francisco's bicentennial project; *Inacoma* (1977), a work-in-progress about a woman hospitalized in a coma, created collectively with a group of actors at the Magic Theatre and with the San Francisco Jazz Ensemble; and *Jacaranda* (1979), a tone poem about love and need, to accompany a solo dance performed by Daniel Nagrin. For *Jacaranda*, Shepard suggested a score by Jelly Roll Morton, but Nagrin decided to record the script and dance to the language instead, for he felt that 'The words have not only a mounting meaning but they are a kind of music'. Shepard himself thought of his script as a catalyst and welcomed Nagrin's incorporation of it into a dance, saying, 'My work is not written in granite. It's like playing a piece of music. It goes out into the air and dissolves forever.'[14]

Inacoma is notable because it grew out of Shepard's continuing interest in the voices of dreams, memories and desire, voices that can escape the body, voices that make obsolete the idea of 'character' in the fixed sense. In the Magic Theatre programme notes, Shepard describes the starting point he provided for improvisations by the actors and musicians:

> All I could visualize was a hospital bed, the coma victim and creature-characters. Then various scenes would start popping up, all out of context and wandering in and out of different realities. The scenes were joined by sounds of breathing, the music, then back to sounds. I kept abandoning the idea of even starting to write something because the subject became too vast and uncontrollable.

Inacoma is also notable because it grew out of Shepard's continuing wish to consider drama a musical form. Aspects of the play such as the 'Demon Chant', and an incantation of 'Who is the person when the person's gone', reflect both Shepard's concern with questions of character and shifting selves *and* his background work with Chaikin and the Open Theatre collective productions of *Terminal* and *Nightwalk*. As he writes in the programme notes:

> I've tried to make use of every influence that has moved me. From vaudeville, circuses, the Living Theatre, the

110

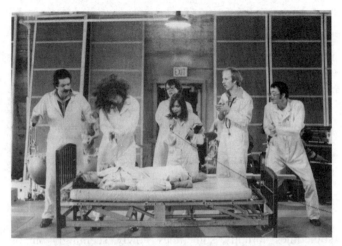

3. *Inacoma*, an improvisational ensemble piece scripted by Shepard with the support of a Rockefeller Foundation grant, premiered at the Magic Theatre in 1977. Photo: Ron Blanchette, courtesy of the Bancroft Library, University of California, Berkeley.

Open Theatre and the whole world of Jazz Music, trance dances, faith healing ceremonies, musical comedy, Greek tragedy, medicine shows, etc.[15]

Shepard's most significant experimental project was a dual collaboration with his mentor, Joseph Chaikin, on two pieces, *Savage/Love* and its companion, *Tongues* (1978). In his note on *Savage/Love*, included in the Bantam edition of this play, Chaikin writes that the subject of *Savage/Love* is 'the difficulty of expressing tenderness and the dread of being replaced'. The focus of the experiment was:

to choose the moments, and then to speak from within those moments. A 'moment' could be the first instant of

111

meeting the lover, or it could be the experience of lovers sleeping next to one another, with one a little bit awake watching the other one sleep. Unlike our approach to *Tongues*, I would improvise around or inside a moment; Sam would write. (p. 320)

A film of *Savage/Love*, performed by Joseph Chaikin, was made by Shirley Clarke, and it effectively communicates the haunting rhythms of the piece.

The complementary focus of *Tongues* was on improvisation akin to jamming. As Shepard writes in his note on *Tongues*, included in the Bantam edition (pp. 300–1), in this piece, he considered the focus to be on voices 'as attitudes or impulses, constantly shifting and sliding into each other, sometimes abruptly, sometimes slowly, seemingly out of nowhere. Likewise, the music is not intended to make comments on the voice but to support these changing impulses, to make temporary environments for the voice to live in.'

In *Tongues*, the piece for voice and percussion which Shepard both wrote and performed with Joseph Chaikin at the Magic Theatre, the Speaker faces head-on the hunger that 'knows no bounds', the hunger that is eating him alive. This piece abandons ideas of action, concentrating only on the incantatory power of rhythm and incremental repetition. Accompanied by what the stage directions indicate are the percussionist's '*gnawing rhythm*' and continuously sweeping circular arm motions, at the centre of this one-act performance piece the Speaker marvels at this unseen enemy, this nemesis with no name that gnaws at Shepard's heroes:

Nothing we find will satisfy it. Absolutely nothing. Whatever we find won't be enough. It will only subside. For a little while. It won't disappear. It will come back. It

4. Joseph Chaikin performed *Tongues*, at once conveying both stillness and energy, here in rehearsal, backed by Shepard and four other floating arms on tympani, in the 1979 production of *Tongues* and *Savage/Love*, co-authored by Chaikin and Shepard, at the New York Public Theatre. Photo: Sylvia Plachy.

113

will be stronger when it comes back. It will devour everything in sight when it comes back. It will eat me alive
when it comes back. It will be ravenous when it comes
back. It will devour me whole when it comes back. It will
go through all the food in the world when it comes back.
It will go through all the possessions in the world when it
comes back. It will go through all the sex in the world
when it comes back. It will go through all the power in
the world when it comes back. It will go through all the
ideas in the world when it comes back. It will go through
all the gods in the world when it comes back. When it
comes back there'll be no stopping it when it comes back.
When it comes back there'll be no appeasing it when it
comes back. When it comes back there'll be nothing left
but the hunger itself when it comes back. Nothing left but
the hunger eating the hunger when it comes back.
Nothing left but the hunger eating itself. Nothing left but
the hunger.

The acting style of Shepard's later plays can be based on –
indeed, driven by – the need to assuage this terrible hunger.
Also, the eerie light cast on a character's face as he investi-
gates the contents of an unreliable refrigerator figures
prominently in plays from *Curse of the Starving Class*
through *The Late Henry Moss*, as 'stockin' up the larder'
becomes a central activity.

Shepard has described *all* of his plays as musical, saying:

I like to look at the language and the inner rhythms of the
play, and all that to me is related to music directly. In *True
West* there are coyote sounds and crickets and things like
that. And the dialogue is musical. It's a musical, *True
West*. I think it's very related to music, the whole rhythmic

structure of it. Rhythm is the delineation of time in space, but it only makes sense with silences on either side of it. You can't have a rhythm that doesn't have silence in it. I studied for a long time with a drummer from Ghana. He was totally amazing. And I found out that, particularly in African music, every rhythm is related. You can play 4/4, 5/8 and 6/8 all together at the same time and at some point there's a convergence. Even though it sounds like all these things are going off in totally crazy directions that are beating up against each other, they'll always come back. That was a big revelation to me, that rhythm on top of rhythm always has a meaning. So the same is true on the stage. There are many possible rhythmic structures that an actor can hit, but there's only one true one. There's one moment that he has to meet . . . It has to do with an emotional relaxation, where suddenly the tension just goes and it's just *THERE*. I was a drummer for a long time and I realized that a lot of the time you're straining to keep the time. And then there are times when all that drops away and everything just . . . it all just rides together.[16]

So rhythm, movement and ensemble storytelling coalesce into an idea of 'one moment' of 'emotional relaxation' when the individual story reverberates on a universal level. When he got back from London, Shepard formulated a plan for creating a new theatre out of all the elements he used to do battle with and explode. The plan was based on the play-wright's interest in ensemble work, maintaining control of his own productions, and exploring these basic elements of drama – rhythm, movement and storytelling as revelation. His grant application, now in the Bancroft Library collection at the University of California at Berkeley, puts forth his aims:

115

For the past twelve years I have been writing plays and having them produced in a great variety of situations. These have ranged from Lincoln Center to obscure lofts and cafes in New York to the Royal Court Theatre in London and all the way back here to the Magic Theatre in San Francisco. I feel like I've gone more than full circle in my search for the right environment, and more importantly, the right director for my work. Sometimes in this search I have even gone so far as to allow a play to be totally dismantled and re-structured by a director or even to have sections of a play taken out of context and placed in a revue. . . . Except in rare cases I feel that all these attempts have failed to show me what I was looking for.

Last year in London, I took the opportunity to direct my own work for the first time. What I discovered was amazing to me. I suddenly found myself vitally interested in the work as a piece of theatre and not merely as a piece of writing. By stepping into the role of director I was actually stepping into the experience of the play. I was dealing with living people and not ideas. . . . The whole dilemma was right there in front of me. That one experience was so strong for me that when I came to San Francisco and got in touch with John Lion I insisted that I try it again with two new plays, *Action* and *Killer's Head*. Doing these two plays has led me further into the possibilities of directing my own work. I'm convinced now that the only way to grow as a playwright is to become directly involved in the production of a play in this way.

Starting from the nucleus of actors (five people) which I brought together for these two plays and adding three more actors to it, I would like to form a small company in conjunction with the Magic Theatre to explore ways and means to produce my own work. These would be small workshops and rehearsals, always working from the springboard of either a finished play or a play in progress. I would like to use these actors to investigate the most basic elements of performance such as voice, movement in space, music, narration, story-telling etc. . . .[17]

This vision of Shepard's would come to fruition at the Magic Theatre, where, sponsored by the Magic Theatre and by a $15,000 grant from the Rockefeller Foundation, he went on to do collaborative work on acting and interior monologues, notably *Inacoma* and, with Joseph Chaikin, whose Open Theatre first inspired him to do these kinds of theatrical explorations, *Tongues* and *Savage/Love*. The Magic Theatre would also become a home to Shepard, where he found a sympathetic artistic director, John Lion, and a director with a strong visual imagination for his family plays, Robert Woodruff. At the Magic Theatre, just across the bridge from his new family home in Mill Valley, Shepard would also begin to direct his own pieces in America.

6
'Dynamite in the Blood'

A short fuse they call it. Runs in the family. His father was just like him. And his father before him. Wesley is just like Pop, too. Like liquid dynamite . . . It's chemical. It's the same thing that makes him drink. Something in the blood. Hereditary. Highly explosive . . . The fear lies with the ones who carry the stuff in their blood, not the ones who don't.

> (Emma in *Curse of the Starving Class*, midway in Act I)

Shepard's plays of every period have sought to 'penetrate into another world . . . a world behind the form'.[1] In his youthful cruising plays, Shepard paraded all the myths of America across the stage. His early use of language and icons was baroque, decorative. In plays written after *The Tooth of Crime*, that is, in plays such as *Angel City* and *Seduced*, he grappled with a series of questions. Just what is a hero? Where does the imagination reside? What is an original voice? Where is, as he put it in *Geography of a Horse*

Dreamer, 'the space inside where the dream comes'? How does one hear that 'never-before-heard-before rhythm' sought in *Angel City*? The language of these plays strove for originality, for expressions of the inner, musical voice.

Shepard next turned to write what turned out to be a quartet of family plays: *Curse of the Starving Class, Buried Child, True West* and *Fool for Love*. These plays would gain him a wider audience and more conventional critical acclaim, because in them he harnesses his experiments with characters and voices to traditional plotting and structure. His technique becomes archaeological: characters move inward, and they dig deeper and back as far as they can, finally facing the family as 'an animal thing', rehearsing the making of myths about homesteads, blood ties and legacies.

The writing of these plays coincided with Shepard's move back to his Circle Y ranch in northern California's Mill Valley, and to his association, from 1975 to the mid-1980s, in some 14 productions with San Francisco's Magic Theatre. There, Shepard first found a place to experiment with ensemble pieces such as *Inacoma* and to work on language as an interior musical form in his collaborations with Joseph Chaikin on *Tongues* and *Savage/Love*. There he also found a home conducive to plays that, more and more, explored character rather than isolated images, plays that targeted the family, plays that would finally be so personally strong that Shepard would flinch from having others direct them.

From *Curse of the Starving Class* to *Fool for Love*, Shepard's scope is huge. 'I used to be a lot more interested in situations or just the sound of words, and what that did to characters', Shepard said. 'Now I'm interested in character on a big scale.' Talking about *True West*, for example, Shepard explained:

I wanted to write a play about double nature, one that wouldn't be symbolic or metaphorical or any of that stuff. I just wanted to give a taste of what it feels like to be two-sided. It's a real thing, double nature. I think we're split in a much more devastating way than psychology can reveal.[2]

Though they show his scope widening, Shepard's four family plays are precisely drawn, incorporating the home-sick, reminiscing blues caused by Shepard's increasing popularity as a movie actor during this period and his increasing involvement in film projects. Shortly after his move back to northern California, Shepard was asked to join Bob Dylan's 1975 Rolling Thunder Revue tour to script a screenplay of the concert tour, being filmed as the musicians went along. Shepard's *Rolling Thunder Revue Logbook* was published by Viking in 1977, and Shepard's brief appear-ances in Dylan's film that resulted from the tour, *Renaldo and Clara* (1977), marked his on-screen debut. Soon after, Shepard made a splash as a laconic doomed farmer in Terence Malick's *Days of Heaven* (1978), and from then on he was frequently on location making movies. Each of his journeys to shoot films led to introspection about love and family life, and about breaking boundaries to escape limits of personal memories, many of which are recorded in *Motel Chronicles*, Shepard's journal of this period.

Each of the film roles that Shepard, a very selective movie star in his prime, agreed to play, also touched a personal chord. *Days of Heaven* deals in biblical terms with timeless themes about the earth's cyclical fecundity, murder and retribution, and sexual and filial corruption in an Eden-like setting. In Daniel Petrie's *Resurrection* (1980), Shepard plays the wastrel son of an ultra-fundamentalist preacher, and his character ultimately goes berserk, frightened that the healing power of love might be demonic. In *Raggedy Man* (1981), directed by Jack Fisk, art director of *Days of Heaven*, Shepard plays the father who abandons his family to become a local hobo, a scarred shadow of his former self, a hermit hovering nearby but unrecognized by his wife and sons. In *Frances* (1982), the screen version of movie star Frances Farmer's career and self-destruction, which starred Jessica Lange, Shepard played an outsider, a fictionalized reporter who chronicled Farmer's bouts with directors, doctors and strangling family ties. And in San Francisco director Philip Kaufman's *The Right Stuff* (1983), Shepard, who himself much prefers trucks and trains to planes, got to play a hero's hero, Chuck Yeager, the test pilot who, taking off from the desert with the determination to break the sound barrier, kept 'stretching the outside of the envelope'.

Curse of the Starving Class is Shepard's first family play, a play revolving about the nexus of flesh and blood, the bonds that strangle the loner even as they embrace him with a name, an identity, a sense of belonging. The play champions the right of the predator to devour, with an important caveat. He must be hungry. He must need sustenance. Then he has the right to kill. The killing, however, is fraught with peril, for in killing he puts his own power of survival to a test. Sometimes the battle is grisly, unheroic: is it worth it to endure, if enduring means destroying everything weak which you hold dear? Must you sacrifice the guts of an innocent lamb to kill the coyote? Starting with *Curse of the Starving Class*, Shepard grapples time and again with nothing less than the fate of scavenging survivors. Talking about the engine of these plays, the director Robert Woodruff says, 'It's always something intangible. Call it what you will, but it drives the plays. It's inescapable. And Vince is sucked home to deal with that in *Buried Child*. We're not the

121

masters of our fate at every level. There's something that pushes us in directions we might not go otherwise.'[3] 'It's bigger than government, bigger than business, it's *bigger*', as Ella says in *Curse*.

Curse of the Starving Class strikes its audience at first as a zany comedy in the tradition of Kaufman and Hart's *You Can't Take It With You*. Its action revolves around Wesley, a sympathetic young man who tries to belong in a family of idiosyncratic misfits: Weston, a ne'er-do-well drunken, wandering father; Ella, an absent-minded, unstable mother; and Emma, a brilliant, wilful younger sister who harbours fantasies of hitting the highway, fixing cars, and writing novels on the side. But this play also has a darker side, reminiscent of *The Cherry Orchard*. Through neglect, bad schemes and debts to unsavoury thugs, this family are about to lose their California house to land developers. They will lose more than their house: 'the whole thing . . . the whole fandango! . . . the orchard! . . . the air! . . . the night sky!' Facing his future and his heritage in this broken house at the edge of America, at the start of Act II Wesley envisions the next step for this place. 'There'll be bulldozers crashing through the orchard', he says. 'There'll be steel girders spanning acres of land. Cement pilings. Prefab walls. Zombie architecture, owned by invisible zombies, built by zombies for the use and convenience of all other zombies. A zombie city! Right here! Right where we're living now.'

Curse goes deeper than social comedy or social commentary. Shepard says, 'I'm not interested in the American social scene at all. It totally bores me. I'm not interested in the social predicament. It's stupid. And . . . the break-up of the family isn't particularly American; it's all over the world. Because I was born in America, it comes out as the American family . . . It just seems an incomplete, a partial

122

way of looking at the play . . . That's not why I'm writing plays.'[4]

What draws Shepard's attention during this period is the mystery of character. When he conducted a four-week-long playwrights' workshop as part of the 1980 Bay Area Playwrights Festival, under the artistic directorship of Robert Woodruff, Shepard said that developing characters is a process of coming in touch with *voice*:

> Character is an expression of voice, the emotional tone underneath. If a writer is totally connected with the voice, it will be in the words . . . Dialogue and words don't invent characters. It's the other way around. Characters invent dialogue. The *mystery* is that you don't know what they're going to say next . . . Imagination only takes you so far, as far as your experience goes. It isn't a question of having to write about ourselves, but of contacting in ourselves the elements – forces and tendencies – that are characters.

The language and images that used to dominate Shepard's plays now take a back seat to character, a force he now wishes to reckon with. 'If you can connect with character', he told the assembled aspiring playwrights in 1980, 'you don't have to worry about the rest.'[5]

Also, Shepard's idea of myth becomes more complex than it was in his early plays, where myth simply meant a conjuring image, a prop or figure that resonated on stage. Now myth is connected to an expansive view of characters and archetypal emotions. Discussing the meaning of myth, Shepard now says:

> One thing it means is an ancient formula that is expressed as a means of handing down a very specific knowledge.

That's a true myth – an ancient myth like Osiris, an old Egyptian myth that comes down from antiquity. The thing that's powerful about a myth is that it's the communication of emotions, at the same time ancient and for all time. If, for instance, you look at *Romeo and Juliet* as a myth, the feelings that you are confronted with in a play like that are true for all time . . . Hopefully in writing a play, you can snare emotions that aren't just personal emotions . . . but emotions and feelings that are connected with everybody . . . So that you suddenly hook up with feelings that are on a very broad scale. But you start with something personal and see how it follows out and opens to something much bigger . . . Something that you can't pin down. Something where you say, 'I feel something here that's going on that's deeply mysterious' . . . If emotions that come up during a play call up questions, or seem to remind you of something that you can't quite put your finger on, then it starts to get interesting. Then it starts to move in a direction we all know, regardless of where we come from or who we are. It starts to hook up in a certain way. Those, to me, are mythic emotions.[6]

The family knot – and the mythic emotion it connotes – is central in *Curse*. A family marooned at America's western edge moves from careless waste and loss to mysterious self-destruction and to questions about the possibility of salvation. The house is falling apart; a drunken father has kicked in the kitchen door, an angry son urinates on the floor, a maggot-infested lamb is brought in for warmth, bags of artichokes are brought from the desert to fill the empty refrigerator. Each of these images is in itself witty and vivid: together they add up to what Shepard called something larger, something deeply mysterious. The kitchen door is gone; the natural world is moving in.

Finally, the family's blood-ties both to each other and to the long buried heroic past of this land haunt and destroy them. While his father extols the trite regenerative powers of a hot bath and 'a great big breakfast of ham and eggs . . . that table will deliver you', Wesley attempts a real ritual of redemption. Dripping wet and still naked from his bath, Wesley carries the lamb outside to slaughter it. He returns, still dazed, wearing his father's discarded rags, the clothes of a bum, and he raids the newly stocked refrigerator with a primitive hunger that knows no bounds. At the end of Act III Wesley explains the mystery of character and the legacy of transferred identity to his sister:

> I tried taking a hot bath. Hot as I could stand it. Then freezing cold. Then walking around naked. But it didn't work. Nothing happened. I was waiting for something to happen. I went outside. I was freezing cold out there and I looked for something to put over me. I started digging around in the garbage and I found his clothes . . . I had the lamb's blood dripping down my arms. I thought it was me for a second. I thought it was me bleeding . . . I started putting all his clothes on. His baseball cap, his tennis shoes, his overcoat. And every time I put one thing on it seemed like a part of him was growing on me. I could feel him taking over me . . . I could feel myself retreating. I could feel him coming in and me going out. Just like the change of the guards.

Emma sees it all clearly. As she put it, a short fuse 'runs in the family . . . his father was just like him . . . like liquid dynamite . . . something in the blood'. Ella, her mother, sees the mystery of it, too. Late in Act II, 'It's a curse', she says. 'I can feel it. It's invisible but it's there. It comes onto us like nighttime . . . And it goes back. Deep. It goes back and back

5. Kathy Bates played 'Ella', pictured here on-stage with Karen Tull as her feisty daughter 'Emma', in the 1985 revival of *Curse of the Starving Class* at the Promenade Theatre in New York. (Bates reprised her role in the 1994 film version of the play.) Photo: Carol Rosegg.

to tiny little cells and genes . . . Plotting in the womb . . . It goes forward too . . . We inherit it and pass it down again. It goes on and on like that without us.'

Curse has a mortgage-melodrama plot about a broken home, deeds and deals, bar room brawls and petty criminals planting bombs. And the play abounds with what we may now call Shepardesque images of food: the family prides itself on being hungry but not starving; Wesley's first monologue about his parents is accompanied by the sound and smells of his mother frying up some bacon and bread; a chicken raised as a 4H Club project is boiled for supper by mistake; the door of an empty refrigerator is periodically opened and slammed shut by hungry people 'hoping for a miracle'; there is a sudden bounty of artichokes; and then there are ham and eggs and coffee and 'a whole mess a' groceries in the icebox . . . just like Christmas'. But the plot and the images are all intensified and enlarged (overdetermined like a line of poetry) by our mounting sense of ill-fated characters and inner decay. With this family Shepard lays bare the animal nature of all our desires, the savage hunger at bottom of the need to belong among people. The father, who has 'lived apart . . . right in the midst of things' has a revelation at the beginning of Act III that 'the family wasn't just a social thing. It was an animal thing. It was a reason of nature that we were all together under the same roof . . . I started feeling full of hope.'

This play ends with a parable of an eagle and a tom cat 'fighting like crazy in the middle of the sky', the eagle's chest being torn apart by his prey, a cat who holds on tight even though the eagle is devouring him. Some instinct tells the cat that he can't let go or he will fall and die. Finally, as the story goes, 'both of them come crashing down. Like one whole thing'. This old family tale conjures up the tragic meaning Shepard gives to being bound together by blood: a

127

clawing animal hunger and an instinct to survive combine to look like an embrace, but they mean slow, gruesome death.

Buried Child (1979) is about yet another family of doomed 'hopers' tied to the land, to each other's secrets, and to a dream gone sour. This play takes the shape of a homecoming. Vince brings Shelly, his Los Angeles girlfriend, on a journey across America to his Illinois home, a place whose exterior reminds Shelly of a Dick-and-Jane-primer world, a Norman Rockwell world of turkey dinners and apple pie. Behind this American gothic façade, however, is, as far back as you can go, 'a long line of corpses . . . not a living soul behind'.

The home to which Vince returns, seeking recognition, is not the Paradise he remembers. Indeed, no one in this mutilated family of fathers and broken sons ever recognizes Vince, and none bears even the 'slightest resemblance' to the faces in the idyllic family portrait he described to Shelly on the drive home. Only Vince's father, the distracted, lonely Tilden, who has come back from New Mexico to dig 'right down to bedrock' in the backyard, looks closely at Vince and thinks he sees 'a face inside his face'. The fertility of the land has even gone awry, producing a sudden bumper crop of corn and carrots that no one recalls having planted. The land also gives forth a tiny, rotted, decomposed corpse – the buried baby of the title who is Vince's legacy.

Shepard once told the *New York Times* that this play no longer rings true for him, that it has all the melodramatic gimmicks of a 'Pulitzer Prize-winning play', which, in fact, it is. As Shepard put it, 'If I was gonna write a play that would win the Pulitzer Prize, I think it would have been that play, you know. It's sort of a typical Pulitzer Prize-winning play. It wasn't written for that purpose: it was kind of a test. I wanted to write a play about a family.'[7]

Audiences, however, continue to find *Buried Child* Shepard's most satisfying play, for several reasons, all of which have to do with the play's use of devices, echoing the structure and stage effects found in works of other modern playwrights. First, its imagery, characters, and family secrets all resound in an Ibsenesque way. As in *Ghosts*, secrets from the past enter into the metaphoric language and imaginative life of the characters, and the plot's resolution depends upon 'the sun . . . the sun', the 'miracle' of rebirth following a confrontation with the deceit and betrayals of the past. Second, its action and dialogue are suggestive and theatrical in an opaque Pinteresque way. The action of the play as a whole recalls that of Pinter's *The Homecoming*, with Shelly, like Pinter's Ruth, taking a lot of alternately funny and terrifying abuse from an assortment of family relations. And the stage business immediately before the black-out that ends Act II, Bradley's assault on Shelly – he wants her to shut up, so, exasperated, he orders her to open her mouth and then he rams his fingers in, stares at her, then pulls his hand out – recalls both in its intensity and implied violence the black-out assault on Lulu in Pinter's *The Birthday Party*. Third, the play's surreal comedy is familiar: Tilden's entrances in each act, his arms piled high with mounds of vegetables, burying old Dodge under corn husks and littering the house with carrot peel, seem like something out of an Ionesco absurdist play; and Shelly's visit in Act II, precipitating a loony family reunion, recalls the Student's journey to see the 'Mummy' of the girl he loves at the ghost supper in scene ii of Strindberg's *The Ghost Sonata*.

Finally, the secret of the play, the revelation upon which the plot hinges, recalls in its placement in the play and in its dramatic rhythm both Mary's anguished revelation at the close of O'Neill's *Long Day's Journey into Night* and Jamie's story of his train ride home with his mother's corpse on board in O'Neill's *Moon for the Misbegotten*. But, for O'Neill's characters, the secrets revealed are greater than their function within the structure of the plays: They are heart-wrenching confessions of souls in purgatory. The nature of the secret of *Buried Child*, however, is more of a device akin to the secret shared by George and Martha in Albee's *Who's Afraid of Virginia Woolf?* (It is not until *A Lie of the Mind* that Shepard confronts the world of his imagination as 'some mystery he doesn't even have a clue to. You can't save the doomed!') As in *Who's Afraid of Virginia Woolf?* where George and Martha's ritualistic verbal murder of their imaginary son rings tinny despite its considerable theatrical power, in *Buried Child* the plot is better served than is the play's premise – the premise being that recognition is *impossible* – by Dodge's third-act confession that he drowned and buried Halie's fourth son, born much later than the others and probably fathered by someone else, a baby deeply loved by Tilden, who himself feels, 'I had a son once but we buried him', a baby who proved defective, in slang terms, a 'vegetable'.

Even if it does work on its audience like a grandfather clock, very imposing and traditional, ticking away and occasionally chiming out the hour, still, on its own, *Buried Child* is a haunting play. In Act I we meet Dodge, a dying man in a baseball cap, marooned under a blanket on a couch in front of the TV. He hacks, sneaks smokes and swigs of whisky, and when he can stand it no longer he takes a handy pill, which knocks him out for a while. We also meet Halie, Dodge's wife, who for a while is a disembodied voice wafting down the stairs, nagging and remembering her youth while she primps herself for her outing with a local minister. Tilden, their oldest son, a hulking, somehow broken former All-American fullback, who has been in jail, has come home with a single intent, to unearth the past, and in Act I he harvests some sweet corn. Tilden tells Dodge, 'You gotta talk or you'll die . . . That's what I know. I found that out in New Mexico. I thought I was dying but I just lost my voice.' Another son appears in Act I. Bradley, who once chopped off his own leg with a chainsaw, shows up to give Dodge a haircut, with electric clippers that will nick the old man's scalp. Halie talks wistfully of a third son, Ansel, a basketball player and soldier who she believes was killed by the Mob. Not very inviting.

Most inviting in Act I is the on-stage world of this play, a world of shelter from the incessant rain. As Walter Kerr noted in his review of the New York premiere, something graphic holds our attention:

> In *Buried Child* it is the abrupt staircase that seems to vanish into nothingness, and the further curious nothingness of a useless corridor at the rear of the stage. We are in a run-down Illinois living room, possibly on deserted farmland; the entire back wall is a vast picture window; beyond it is an enclosed, purposeless passageway as clinically bare as a hospital corridor; beyond *that* is the exterior wall, with a door in it. Anyone entering or leaving must pass through a void. If the precise meaning of the added space is less than clear, a suggestive dimensionality is created – not in characters who remain cut-outs, but in the planes that extend their world.[8]

Vince, the 'prodigal son', and Shelly, his Los Angeles girlfriend who can fend for herself in a house full of eccentrics, arrive at the start of Act II and set the plot in motion. Planning just to stop by and say hello to his grandparents, Vince is really on the way to New Mexico to seek out a reunion with Tilden, the father he has not seen for six

6. *Buried Child* in its Magic Theatre production, 1978, depicts an American family in the heartland as ghostly shadows. Photo: Ron Blanchette, courtesy of the Bancroft Library, University of California, Berkeley.

years. Vince is surprised to find Tilden has also come home, on a parallel quest for self-discovery. As Dodge sneers at Shelly at the start of Act III:

> You're all alike you hopers . . . Full of faith. Hope. Faith and hope . . . If it's not God then it's a man. If it's not a man then it's a woman. If it's not a woman then it's the land or the future of some kind. Some kind of future . . . See, you're glad it stopped raining. Now you think every-thing's gonna be different. Just 'cause the sun comes out . . . Don't be so easily shocked, girlie. There's nothing a man can't do. You dream it up and he can do it. Anything.

When Shelly questions Dodge about his past, a past depicted in photos on the wall in Halie's room, Dodge stops her cold:

That isn't me! That never was me! This is me! Right here. This is it. The whole shootin' match, sittin' right in front of you ... How far back can you go? A long line of corpses! There's not a living soul behind me. Not a one. Who's holding me in their memory? Who gives a damn about bones in the ground?

As all Vince's illusions about home and family are stripped away, he is left with only the basic instincts of family duty, the will to survive together. At the end of Act III his disillusioning pilgrimage takes Vince back to a primal vision of his heritage – to a family identity he recognizes – revealed in his own image, reflected in his car windshield:

My face. My eyes. I studied my face ... As though I was looking at another man. As though I could see his whole race behind him. Like a mummy's face. I saw him dead and alive at the same time ... His face became his father's face ... And his father's face changed to his Grandfather's face. And it went on like that. Changing. Clear on back to faces I'd never seen before but still recognized. Still recognized the bones underneath ... Then it all dissolved. Everything dissolved.

This vision of Vince's is a breakthrough to a world without myths. His process in this play is archaeological, going back as far as he can by means of memory and imagination to understand his inheritance, and then deconstructing – here literally smashing – the myth. But, even though Vince hurls a whole bag full of empty liquor bottles on the porch and he cuts through the screen door when he returns to recount his epiphany, still he loses his freedom when he finally accepts all that Dodge wills to him – his tractors, his forsaken land and his unburied child. Finally, all this play's symbolism and brutality is left to weigh heavy on Vince's shoulders.

Roughly a decade and a half after *Buried Child* won the 1979 Pulitzer Prize, Chicago's Steppenwolf Theatre Company mounted a revival of this play that was such a huge success, it moved to Broadway. Working with the revival's director, Gary Sinise, who made a huge splash as director and performer in Steppenwolf's 1982 revival of *True West*, Shepard made judicious cuts. Also, extensive, though subtle, revisions (mainly tag lines added for emphasis) were peppered throughout the script – serving to rein in the zaniest speeches, to heighten suspense, and to clarify the subtext without affecting its action or characters. The revision also solved the plot mystery, clearing up what Hitchcock fans would call 'the maguffin' of the play: Whose baby was that? How did he die? And who buried him in the yard, setting in motion the forces of nature that would make new sources of nourishment ooze forth from the earth? As Shepard noted at the time, 'It's a lot clearer now, and the humour has been brought out.'[9] Thanks to these revisions, Shepard found himself in an odd category, nominated for a 1996 Tony Award as the author of the Best New Play on Broadway.

In rehearsal for the *Buried Child* revival, Gary Sinise reflected on how he knew from the start that Shepard's style was right up his alley. 'We were just a bunch of punks in the basement of a Catholic school', he recalled, describing the genesis of Steppenwolf. 'We would get really wild and crazy. We just loved to get really sweaty when we acted. And along came Sam's work. There was a lot of passion in what we were doing as a theatre company. And there's a lot of fire and passion in his work. Plus, its sense of humour is oddball, and we had a bunch of oddballs in our company. So we were able to attack the work with this vengeance that sort of cut to its veins.'[10]

Shepard's plays have become a touchstone for Sinise, who in film has made his own mark in two roles, as Lieutenant Dan Taylor in *Forrest Gump* and as Ken Mattingly in *Apollo 13*. Both of those characters are what Dodge in *Buried Child* would cynically categorize as 'hopers', would-be heroes cheated out of a mythic destiny, who undergo Shepardesque transformations as they reinvent themselves as ordinary men. From the start, Sinise found Shepard's plays 'free' him to explore a frenzied 'world of images and behaviour', where double nature is expressed in jazzy outbursts, and where manic behaviour leads to altered states. Sinise comprehends this world intuitively, and he found himself especially drawn to the 'inexplicable' moments when, without a clue, characters leap beyond the logic of their past, when they escape the notion of given circumstances, and the unfathomable happens.

The breakthrough production for Steppenwolf was Shepard's *True West*, the play that got critically panned in its first New York production at Joe Papp's Public Theatre where it was directed by Robert Woodruff and performed by Peter Boyle as Lee and Tommy Lee Jones as Austin. Back in Chicago, Sinise, who became Artistic Director of Steppenwolf in 1980, began to pursue the rights to the play relentlessly. 'It took me almost two years.' Clearly, it took what Dodge in *Buried Child* calls 'Persistence, fortitude, determination'.

Sinise remembers the day he got the rights to *True West*. 'I was jumping up and down, running around, screaming, "We're going to do *True West!*" ' When the production of *True West* transferred to New York in 1982, Sinise also played Austin, the middle-class screenwriter who dreams down the highway, opposite John Malkovich as his big brother, Lee, the volatile hermit who survives in the desert. The production was a revelation: a farcical trashing of a suburban kitchen by two brothers racing to exchange personalities, and ending in a photo finish. 'We focused on the humour and on the musical structure; it's just like a constant crescendo', recalls Sinise.

Readying the revival of *Buried Child* for Broadway in 1996, Sinise focused on ways in which behaviour in this play is yoked to the immediate needs of the character, encouraging the actor playing Vince (Jim True, replacing Ethan Hawke after the Chicago run) to stalk, manœuvre, ricochet around the old homestead. He also noted how Shepard 'revolutionized the way we looked at playwriting. Broke all kinds of conventions . . .' The momentum was building as Sinise counted off playwrights. 'John Guare, David Mamet, David Rabe – all those people have had success on Broadway. But Sam never had that kind of commercial venue for one of his plays.' Of course, praising *Buried Child* as Shepard's long overdue Broadway debut conveniently overlooks *Operation Sidewinder*, Shepard's desert epic with music, a renegade fiasco that puzzled and shocked audiences at Lincoln Center in 1970 and that led to an unprecedented number of disgruntled subscribers, and to Shepard – who called it 'a total disaster' – escaping to England.

Nevertheless, Sinise's theory about *Buried Child* applies as well to many of Shepard's plays. Sinise sees Shepard as an artist always at the edge, a liminal playwright always challenging conventions. 'I think maybe *Buried Child* was ahead of us back in the '70s', said Sinise, 'and now audiences have been changed and jostled, so a broader audience may come to appreciate this play in a way that they couldn't back then. It mystifies and entertains you at the same time.'

The mystery of *Buried Child*, while suspenseful, goes far beyond the stuff of melodrama, suggesting a miracle, or at the very least, a natural phenomenon, as the rains come, and a young man disappears behind his own face, which he finally recognizes as a reflection of his legacy. Sure, the play can be as funny as *You Can't Take It With You*, but it can also jolt us when slapstick turns to violence, and when a quirky family turns out to haunt its own home. As Sinise observed while rehearsing the revival, 'This play was written as an experiment. It's not written to be an O'Neill-esque family drama. Things turn; sharp corners get taken.'

True West (1980) focuses again on the integrity of the land beneath suburban developments and on the strangling yoke of the family. But now Shepard merges these concerns with his earlier interest in the creative artist *qua* escape artist.

This is a rather delicate play. It can come across on stage as a sombre *pas de deux* showdown between rival brothers, as it did in the New York Shakespeare Festival production at the Public Theatre, when Robert Woodruff's Magic Theatre production was recast and redirected by Joseph Papp, where Tommy Lee Jones and Peter Boyle filled Austin and Lee with a simmering rage that coloured every ridiculous stunt they pull on one another – from stealing one another's jobs to stealing one another's dreams. But in the hands of deft performers and directors who take a lighter approach, as when Sinise and Malkovich of the Chicago-based Steppenwolf Company performed this play (in the version that has been videotaped for public television), or when the edgy John C. Reilly and Philip Seymour Hoffman alternated the roles in a Broadway revival in 2000, or when Bruce Willis played a tough but lost Lee in an Idaho production taped for Showtime in 2002, *True West* affects its audience with an inspired silliness. Taking sibling rivalry to the limits,

Austin and Lee are, after all, ridiculous in their murderous frenzy. What is there for them to destroy but their mother's plants and her Formica countertops? What is there for them to steal but toasters and two-bit ideas for movies? The emotions are huge, but the stakes are small, so in *True West* Shepard can entertainingly mock his own vision of the land of plenty jerry-built adjacent to the desert, the first populated by feuding families, the second by predatory animals.

Two brothers, one a screenwriter and the other a petty thief just back from the desert, turn their mother's suburban California kitchen into a primal arena where they square off in a showdown of identities, weighing their value systems one against the other. Here, as in *Buried Child* and in *Curse of the Starving Class*, the love and need for family is depicted as a primitive, almost atavistic impulse; and an idea of Paradise and salvation can be conjured up by simple, homely pleasures: 'the smell of toast . . . and the sun's coming up . . . It makes me feel like anything's possible.'

True West is a geometrically designed exploration of 'what it feels like to be two-sided . . . it's a real thing, double nature'. The situation faced by Austin and Lee, Shepard's 'odd couple', is an American equivalent of the Teddy–Lenny battle in Pinter's *The Homecoming*. In Pinter's play, Teddy, a professor of philosophy at an American university, returns to make peace with his father and brothers, still at home in London's East End. Instead of making peace, Teddy finds himself back in the old rut of one-upmanship with his brother Lenny, who is a violent, acid-voiced pimp. In Shepard's play, Austin, a screenwriter, in search of some peace and quiet to help him get his latest project off the ground, agrees to housesit for his mother in a quiet Pasadena suburb. Instead of peace and quiet, Austin finds himself confronted with Lee, the brother who followed their father's path into the life of a desert drifter and derelict.

True West has also been called a 'West Coast *Endgame*', because 'there is a level, and not so far beneath the surface, at which his brothers can claim kinship with Beckett's Hamm and Clov: ravenous body and troubled mind, each incomplete in itself, interdependent yet doomed to be hostile.'[11]

Comparisons with Pinter and Beckett enrich our appreciation of Shepard's play rather than diminish it. Shepard does not simply Americanize the modern homecoming, the modern symbiotic /destructive couple. For him, especially in *True West*, America is not just a geographic location; it is a state of mind. As John Lahr writes in his *Automatic Vaudeville*, 'The vagueness in the land is what punishes his brothers. They are infected by the twin emotions of the West: primitive self-sufficiency and modern luxury . . . The standoff is between two mythic psychopathic styles of American individualism: the killer instincts of success and crime.'[12]

The opening stage directions of *True West* indicate that this play is less concerned with plot machinations than with large questions of character and doubleness. After calling for a suburban California kitchen, Shepard cautions that:

> *The set should be constructed realistically with no attempt to distort its dimensions, shapes, objects, or colours. No objects should be introduced which might draw special attention to themselves other than the props demanded by the script. If a stylistic 'concept' is grafted onto the set design it will only serve to confuse the evolution of the characters' situation, which is the most important focus of the play.*

The action of *True West* revolves around Lee's notion that anything his kid brother with the college degree can do, he can do too. This petty thief, sensing that his stories would be great movie material, tries to write a 'true-to-life' pulp Western for the movies. After all, Lee decides, if he makes a Hollywood deal he can be just like his hotshot brother, 'gettin' paid to dream. Ridin' back and forth on the freeway just dreamin' my fool head off.' Austin gets caught up in the competition as well. Even while protesting, 'There's no such thing as the West anymore! It's a dead issue', Austin yearns to connect with his brother and with his long-gone father. He would like to live the life of the rugged antisocial individual, the self-sufficient life in the Mojave Desert that he has romanticized since his youth.

Rekindled sibling rivalry leads Austin to stealing toasters on a bet, getting drunk, and trying to strangle Lee with a telephone cord. Between the brothers there is constantly a murderous tension, objectified by the off-stage yapping of coyotes killing pets from suburban yards and by the repeated fade-out of scenes with the two brothers silhouetted motionless, Pinteresquely sizing each other up.

While entertaining us with funny dialogue about formula movie Westerns and suburban Paradises, *True West* is about taking clichés seriously. It asserts the truth behind clichés. The old-time chase that Lee envisions as the climax of his Hopalong Cassidy-like movie, for example, reflects the fear felt by the brothers, each scared of the other's secret self, each wary of the part of himself he sees in his brother's eyes. In Lee's movie, the rivals would:

> take off after each other . . . What they don't know is that each one of 'em is afraid, see. Each one separately thinks that he's the only one that's afraid. And they keep ridin' like that straight into the night. Not knowing. And the one who's chasin' doesn't know where the other one is taking him. And the one who's being chased doesn't know where he's going.   (Act I, scene iv)

Where they are going in *True West* is unknown, emotional territory. The centrepiece of this nine-scene play is scene viii, a showdown that ends with a deal. When the scene opens it is, according to the stage directions, '*very early morning, between night and day ... no crickets, coyotes yapping feverishly in distance before light comes up.*' Their mother's once-gleaming-clean kitchen (not a tealeaf in the sink, Lee recalls), is a shambles, all of her house plants – the plants she misses so much that she will cut short her Alaska vacation to return to them – are neglected, '*dead and drooping*', while Lee and Austin see how they measure up in each other's place. Both men are drunk, and the kitchen is littered with squashed beer cans and empty whisky bottles. Lee has been frustrated in his attempt at writing an outline of his screenplay, which he convinced, or perhaps coerced, Saul, the Hollywood producer, to back for him in the course of an early-morning golf game.

As the scene opens, Lee is methodically smashing the typewriter with his golf club and dropping pages of his script into a burning bowl on the floor of the alcove. (Perhaps Lee would do better with a tape-recorder! Or, if Shepard would approve an updated staging, perhaps with a laptop!) Lee is further frustrated by his inability to deal with the telephone in this scene. Trying to find some woman, Lee calls the operator, crashes through drawers in search of a pencil, and then rips the phone off the wall when the operator hangs up. 'This is the last time I try to live with people', he swears. 'I can't believe it. Here I am! Here I am again in a desperate situation! This would never happen out on the desert. I would never be in this kinda' situation out on the desert.' The reckless behaviour in the pristine kitchen by Lee, the proverbial bull in the china shop, the Huck Finn who cannot abide women and the civilization they require, gives this scene a giddy quality of dislocation and abandon, like a concert by the rock group The Who, who would smash their instruments on-stage.

Meanwhile, Austin has been more successful at his complementary attempt at breaking and entering. He has lined up a whole bunch of stolen toasters on the sink counter, and in the course of scene viii he polishes them all, drops slices of bread into each one, and, as they pop up, butters and stacks them, gradually filling the theatre with the smell of toast. Austin's giddy sense of accomplishment further infuriates Lee, who blurts out, 'What is this bullshit with the toast anyway! You make it sound like salvation or something. I don't want any goddamn toast!' Austin's response is synaesthetic; it is a writerly response to the smell of all kinds of toast from burnt to 'golden fluffy'. 'It is like salvation, sort of', says Austin. 'I mean the smell. I love the smell of toast. And the sun's coming up. It makes me feel like anything's possible.' When Lee suddenly explodes, knocking the platter of toast out of Austin's hands, scattering buttered slices all over the floor, and he starts to circle Austin, crushing pieces of toast in his wake, Austin simply begins to gather the toast from the floor and to restack it on the plate, even the crushed pieces.

The scene ends with a pact. Austin confesses that his yearning to exchange places is sincere. He really does want to learn to live on the desert. It is through Austin that we can sense what Wesley and Emma are fighting against in *Curse of the Starving Class*, the progress that homogenizes the landscape and razes the past. Like Vince in *Buried Child*, Austin keeps feeling cheated out of homecomings and connections, and, like Travis in Shepard's screenplay *Paris, Texas*, Austin wants to wander away from a technological age and bourgeois responsibilities, down a dusty highway, back to a simpler time suggested by sepia photos and old postcards:

There's nothin' down here for me. There never was. When we were kids here it was different. There was a life here then. But now – I keep comin' down here thinkin' it's the fifties or somethin'. I keep finding myself getting off the freeway at familiar landmarks that turn out to be unfamiliar. On the way to appointments. Wandering down streets I thought I recognized that turn out to be replicas of streets I remember. Streets I misremember. Streets I can't tell if I lived on or saw in a postcard. Fields that don't even exist anymore ... There's nothin' real down here, Lee! Least of all me!   (Act II, scene viii)

Lee seizes his chance. He offers a deal. 'You write me up this screenplay thing just like I tell ya', he tells Austin, conceding that Austin may also embellish his work, functioning like Rabbit in *Angel City*, using all his 'usual tricks and stuff. Yer fancy language. Yer artistic hocus pocus'. And then 'I'll sure enough take ya' with me to the desert'.

The final scene of *True West* opens on a '*ravaged*' stage. It is mid-day. There is no sound, and there is blazing heat. All the debris from the previous scene, '*bottles, toasters, smashed typewriters, ripped out telephone, etc. . . . is now starkly visible in intense yellow light, the effect should be like a desert junkyard at high noon.*' In this scene Mom returns, and the brothers fall back on old patterns. Austin has kept up his side of the bargain – for lack of a typewriter, he has written out by hand the script dictated by Lee of 'Two lamebrains chasin' each other across Texas'. But with Mom's return Lee suddenly feels suffocated by the possibility that he might become part of 'this town', that he might 'sell [himself] down the river', so he tries to make a quick getaway. It is Austin who finally goes berserk, who ends the play trying to strangle the brother – and the shadow of the father – who wants once again to betray him by escaping to

7. Gary Sinise as 'Austin', a screenwriter with a deadline, and John Malkovich as his wastrel brother, 'Lee', attempt to murder each other in their mother's suburban kitchen in the Steppenwolf revival of *True West* at the Cherry Lane Theatre in New York in 1982. Photo: Martha Swope.

the desert, who hopes once again to leave him behind to fend for himself in a world where any kind of connection with other people, or with real space and time, where any kind of deeply felt recognition, is impossible.

Like Shepard's other family plays, *Fool for Love* is set on the edge of an American wilderness. But this is a bleaker landscape than the others. This hinterland ('this is not a black Mercedes Benz type of motel', says May) harbours no orchard (as in *Curse*), offers no escape from the suburban sprawl (as does the desert in *True West*), and yields no bumper crop of corn and exhumes no secrets unknown to the characters (as the buried child in *Buried Child* astounds the on-stage family as well as the audience). This untamed land yields not comforts, but bullets and consuming flames.

Once and for all, with Eddie and May, Shepard attempts to shatter the dreams of kinship that sustain his characters in other family plays. Country-and-Western music sets the mood of this piece (the play opens and closes to Merle Haggard tunes), which is itself 'a love ballad' about the relationship between men and women. Why country music? 'Because, more than any other art form I know of in America', says Shepard, 'country music speaks of the true relationship between the American male and the American female.' And what is that? 'Terrible and impossible.'[13]

In a monologue called 'Savage', performed at the centre of *Savage/Love*, Shepard captures the cynicism and the 'terrible and impossible' obsessive need at the heart of *Fool for Love*:

YOU
Who makes me believe that we're lovers
YOU
Who lets me pretend
YOU
Who reminds me of myself
YOU
Who controls me
YOU
My accomplice
YOU
Who tells me to lie
YOU
Who is acting as though we're still in the first moment
YOU
Who leads me to believe we're forever in love
Forever in love.

In a *Motel Chronicles* entry dated Los Angeles, 23 November 1981, Shepard writes, 'I've about seen/all the nose jobs/capped teeth/and silly-cone tits/I can handle/I'm heading back/ to my natural woman', and he describes feeling 'the demonic attachment of a man for his only woman'.

London critics dubbed *Fool for Love* a 'motel room *Phèdre*'[14] because its plot of incestuous desire and destruction is acted out in May's sparsely furnished motel room – an iron bedstead and Formica table with two plastic chairs suffice – at the edge of the Mojave Desert. (For the screen version of *Fool for Love*, directed by Robert Altman, and which featured Shepard himself as a sneering, seedy version of Eddie, a stuntman past his prime, Shepard as screenwriter 'opened up' the play to include the motel parking lot and rusty playground, too, as well as flashback images to accompany the memory monologues.)

In this play, Shepard for the first time constructs a home-coming without hope, a homecoming without a home. The play is set in the most transient, insubstantial, yet quintessentially American dwelling: the roadside motel. This setting is by now as familiar to Shepard audiences as it is to admirers of Edward Hopper's paintings, and its felt meaning has deepened in later plays. Indeed, a theatre company could do a season of Shepard plays set in motel rooms: in *Red Cross*, *La Turista*, and *Cowboy Mouth*, some of his early image-splattered plays, as in Jean Claude van-Itallie's *Motel*, the unmade motel bed is a catch-all for social commentary on the American experience, with disposable images strewn across it helter-skelter; in *Geography of a Horse Dreamer* and *Seduced*, two of Shepard's plays that question myths of the hero, the hotel is the only place a chameleon-like hero en route from one nowhere to another can call home; now, in *Fool for Love*, and, as audiences will see in *Sympatico*, too, Shepard is deconstructing myths.

Ruby Cohn writes in reference to Shepard's family plays, in *Fool for Love* Shepard uses the motel setting to dramatize 'a tragic America, mired in sin'. If we do not get too bogged down in notions of sin, we can agree that this play, more than any other, supports Cohn's suggestion that the family plays may be Shepard's attempt at tragedy in an American idiom.[15]

Eddie, May's high-school sweetheart who also turned out to be her half-brother, is now a stuntman, and he has come back for the umpteenth time in the fifteen years of their stormy relationship. Pursued here by the unseen, irrational, furiously jealous 'Countess' who will later shoot out his windshield and set fire to his horse trailer, Eddie tries to persuade May that they are 'forever in love'. While Eddie clings for a while to his delusions of a quiet country life with May among horses in Wyoming, his hardened half-sister and sometime lover shows not even a vestige of hope for this one version of the American dream that recurs in Shepard's plays of this period. 'I got everything worked out. I been thinkin' about this for weeks', says Eddie, when he shows up and tries to get May to rejoin him. 'I'm gonna' move the trailer. Build a little pipe corral to keep the horses. Have a big vegetable garden. Some chickens maybe.' But May is finished with this dream:

> Wyoming? Are you crazy? I'm not moving to Wyoming. What's up there? Marlboro Men? . . . I hate chickens! I hate horses! I hate all that shit! You know that. You got me confused with somebody else. You keep comin' up with this lame country dream life with chickens and vegetables and I can't stand any of it. (Opening of Act I)

By the end of *Fool for Love* both May *and* Eddie are finished with all their dreams, finished with all the versions of reality – all the lies of the mind, as Shepard would come to call them in his next play – that they have conspired to create over the years. The action of *Fool for Love* is a wrenching-free by Eddie and May from their shared history, a breaking of the 'pact' they have made with themselves and with their father, the family pact to fictionalize and prettify the past by means of lies of the mind.

There is much talk about 'realism' in *Fool for Love*, a play that includes in its cast of characters a decidedly non-realistic convention: the Old Man, big as life in his rocker, with his whisky and his Stetson hat and his conversations with his son and daughter, exists only in their minds. The Old Man puts forth his definition of the realistic mode early on. Pointing to an imaginary picture on the wall, he tells Eddie that it is a portrait of Barbara Mandrell, the country singer. 'Would you believe me if I told ya' I was married to her?', he asks Eddie. 'No', says Eddie. Then the Old Man explains: 'Well, see, now that's the difference right there. That's realism. I am actually married to Barbara Mandrell in my mind.' Later, Martin arrives expecting to take May to the movies. (Martin is May's hapless beau, a man who does yard maintenance work, really a rather awkward stage device, like Peter in Albee's *The Zoo Story*, a human prop who appears so that Eddie and May have someone to whom they can unravel their tale.) Later, in *Fool for Love* as Eddie toys with and tries to bully Martin, Eddie embellishes the Old Man's definition of truth and reality:

EDDIE: Well, you could uh – tell each other stories.
MARTIN: Stories?
EDDIE: Yeah.
MARTIN: I don't know any stories.
EDDIE: Make 'em up.
MARTIN: That'd be lying wouldn't it?

148

EDDIE: No, no. Lying's when you believe it's true. If you already know it's a lie then it's not lying.

In *Fool for Love* the scenic image of the motel – with its unmade bed with four posters suitable for lassoing, with its doors suitable for slamming, and with its dirty window suitable for letting in the glare of unwelcome headlights – takes on an Artaudian dimension as poetry of the theatre, serving as a concrete, physical language to fill the stage. Shepard's ultimate family play is set in a motel where archetypal conflicts and tragic emotions can be hurled full force around the stage: a woman bows her neck interminably; later, she hugs the walls, maintaining, according to the stage directions, *'this complete embrace of herself with crossed arms as though holding the one who's gone . . . her body weeps'*; and a man crawls around the room because there is 'less tension' close to the ground. The action also includes several 'suspended moments of recognition' during the Old Man's monologues. According to the stage directions, *'The door is amplified with microphones and a resonator hidden in the frame so that each time an actor slams it, the door booms loud and long'*, and the headlights that *'slash across the audience and then dissolve'* should be *'two intense beams of piercing white light and not "realistic" headlights'*.

In its intense focus on the irresolvable relation between the sexes, in its spare, homely setting, and in its use of props, sound and lighting effects to heighten reality, this play recalls Strindberg's *Miss Julie*. Like *Miss Julie*, *Fool for Love* is driven by the felt presence of the absent father, who in Shepard's play quite literally hovers beside the action. As John Lion, artistic director of the Magic Theatre, writes:

the draft I finally saw had Eddie, May and Martin in it but not the 'princess'. This was odd to me, because we had

149

auditioned about a hundred actresses for the part of the 'princess', script unseen. This draft, draft 11, also didn't have 'the old man' in it, but the story was essentially there. I was convinced it would play like gangbusters, but it somehow seemed 'square'. (I don't mean the attitude, I mean the shape.) It was pretty linear, unusual for Sam, and I remarked on it. 'Maybe it needs a three-quarter circle surrounding three points of the square', I said. Three weeks later, we had the completed script, with 'the old man'.[16]

When Eddie and May finally, at the end of *Fool for Love*, retell their complementary versions of the father who kept a secret, wandering back and forth between two women, neither of whom could live without him, they confront their father with the fact of Eddie's mother's suicide. The Old Man rises from out of his rocker and moves between Eddie and May, appealing to his son to speak on his behalf. 'That's the dumbest version I ever heard in my whole life', he tells Eddie. 'She never blew her brains out . . . Tell her the way it happened. We've got a pact.' But this time Eddie breaks the pact, betraying the Old Man, and freeing himself:

EDDIE: (*calmly, to the Old Man*). It was your shotgun. Same one we used to duck hunt with. Browning. She never fired a gun before in her life. That was her first time.

THE OLD MAN: Nobody told me any a' that. I was left completely in the dark.

EDDIE: You were gone.

THE OLD MAN: That's right, I was gone! I was gone. You're right. But I wasn't disconnected. There was nothing cut off in me. Everything went on just the same as though I'd never left.

Instead of reinforcing the Old Man's version, though, Eddie keeps his eyes glued to May's, both of them renouncing the Old Man's hold on them and thereby managing to free each other from the pact too.

Using hyper-real props and sounds in a claustrophobic setting in *Fool for Love*, Shepard creates stage images of hopelessness, images of power sapped, possessions gone. Two silhouettes remain from this play. The after-image of the woman, despairing and desperate, derives from an episode dated October 1978, Homestead Valley, California, that Shepard records in *Motel Chronicles*:

> She was sitting on the bed with all the curtains drawn, her legs crossed under her and her head hung down between her knees. Red hair hiding her face. I knew she wouldn't attack me. I wasn't afraid of her physically. I touched her head. It was stiff. As though she'd been in that position for hours or days. The lap of her skirt was wet. Her nose and eyes were running but she wasn't sobbing. Her eyes were deeply inside like she'd seen the last she wanted to see of Real Life. I tried to hold her but it was ridiculous. She was locked in position . . . I rubbed her neck. It felt like wood. She made a sound. I asked her something else but she was incapable of words. (*Motel Chronicles* [City Lights] p. 76)

In *Fool for Love* this image of the worn-out woman weeping, the nape of her neck exposed interminably, stays with us long after the battle of the play is over. Later, she will slam herself against walls, and she will become a blur of a woman packing fast, cramming her clothes into a battered suitcase while muttering, 'He's gone'. The other silhouette that remains from this play is that of a stuntman – a make-believe cowboy – lassoing bedposts instead of livestock.

151

The spine (the vector of action) of *Fool for Love* is expressed in such stage images and movements as well as in the taut language of the play and in the repeated ear-shattering slammings of the door. (Shepard not only wanted to wire the walls of the set for reverberation; he also had four speakers placed under the audience.) In *Fool for Love*, in sharp and painful contrast to other Shepard plays, the central characters do not, in the end, achieve the object of their obsession. Rather, they have to ' let it go'. Indeed, actors might say that the spine of *Fool for Love* – its super-objective, the infinitive phrase that expresses the thrust of its action – is to 'let it go'.

Shepard's period of drama about desperate hopers, begun with *Curse of the Starving Class*, now reaches a turning point. Eddie and May will be followed by more tired travellers in *A Lie of the Mind*, *States of Shock*, *Simpatico*, *Eyes for Consuela* and *The Late Henry Moss*, all of whom must also grapple with letting go of what is long gone or never was for real. In these plays, rusted tools and shoeboxes of old photos will keep getting discarded, refrigerators with nothing in them but whisky and jalapeños will keep getting restocked, and old scores will keep getting settled. Still, they cannot 'let it go'.

Shepard's focus on such characters may even be seen in the independent film work in which he becomes engaged now, such as his screenplay for Wim Wenders' bleak depiction of a blacktop odyssey in *Paris, Texas* (1984) and his role as the unmoored engineer in Volker Schlondorff's film version of Max Frisch's *Homo Faber*, also called *Voyager* (1991). In *Silent Tongue* (1993), which Shepard both writes and directs, the agony of letting go and the grip of dead on the living is expressed most directly.

We are left with characters who wish to let go of hope, who finally extricate themselves from family ties, and who end up alone, desperate and hopeless.

7
'Destination': Emotional Territory

Maybe I should make a fire. Would you like a fire? I'll make a fire . . . Maybe I should just take a walk with no destination.
Maybe I should stay in one place and stay put and stop making up reasons to move.
Maybe we could both have a conversation. Would you like to have a conversation?

>　　　(Shepard, *Motel Chronicles*, entry date 14 January
>　　　　　　　　　　　1980, Homestead Valley, California)

DESTINATIONS: From some place to some place. But in between is where the action is . . .
Notice the way the moon beam shining on the water chases you. Chases you. As though you were the only one. No escape. I'm taking you to a special place.

>　　　(Shepard, 'The Curse of the Raven's Black Feather',
>　　　　　　　　　　　　　　　in *Hawk Moon*)

In December 1985, shortly before his three-and-a-half hour *magnum opus*, *A Lie of the Mind*, opened – at the Promenade Theatre on Broadway on 76th Street, about thirty blocks uptown from the traditional 'Broadway' theatre district, but, none the less, on Broadway – Shepard mused, 'You don't write a play out of a sense of wanting to interpret an idea. You don't have a thesis that a play is an explanation of. The play is an adventure in the same sense that acting is an adventure. You're going into unknown territory. And you find pieces and bits here and there of what you're searching for.'[1]

At the time he was working on it, planning also to direct it, Shepard considered *A Lie of the Mind*, like its companion piece, the screenplay for Wim Wenders' *Paris, Texas*, to be his most ambitious venture into unknown territory. 'I guess I'm always hoping for one play that will end my need to write plays', he said.

> Sort of the definitive piece, but it never happens. There's always disappointment, something missing, some level that hasn't been touched, and the more you write the more you struggle, even if you are riding a wave of inspiration. And if the piece does touch something, you always know you haven't got to the depths of certain emotional territory. So you go out and try another one.[2]

A Lie of the Mind does get to the very depths of certain 'emotional territory'. It is a play of devastation, a play that travels across America, a road play with no destination, even as it is a tragedy with a precise destination, a special place of fire and ice, a place of the mind from which there is no escape.

Although, if pressed to be succinct about it, Shepard could categorize *A Lie of the Mind* as 'a love ballad . . . a

154

little legend about love',[3] this is really a major play, a dirge for all that has come before. It feels as though it must be the last play of a cycle, the end of something. The play is a coda; it journeys through all the old territories and methodically destroys them all. Language and mobility disappear, the hunger and pleasures of food are gone, the family stories, secrets and memorabilia are demystified, purged of their power to hold people together. (*In Buried Child* the yearning to unearth the past, to belong some place, to recognize the self behind the face, drove Vince to that vision-in-the-windshield of himself disappearing into all that possessed him, into that vision of ruin beneath the plenty, the rotten bones beneath the bumper crop. In *A Lie of the Mind*, when you unearth the past, it is a box of ashes under the bed.)

There is a new yearning here, a resolve to burn it *all* down: the kitsch Americana, the dust under the bed, the boxes of snapshots and Western souvenirs, the mobile of miniature fighter jets circling over a man's bed in his mother's house, a place the man has long since outgrown. Even the American flag is just one more rope lassoing us to received meanings of character, land, family and identity. No more 'poetic rodeos', as Skeetz put it in *Man Fly*, Shepard's modern *Dr. Faustus*. No more 'hopers' as Dodge dubbed them in *Buried Child*. No more myths. *A Lie of the Mind*, though most directly about violence, is Shepard's gentlest play: it begins as an aftermath. It embraces desolation. All that is left is organic, atavistic: the red moon, the fire, the wind, snow, the earth, love.

Now, in *A Lie of the Mind*, Shepard does what Eddie and May wanted to do in *Fool for Love*: 'let it go'. Here, in this large-canvas play that puts all the others in perspective, Shepard deconstructs the myths of his whole oeuvre, really finding the emotions beneath the surface of a civilization and its codes of behaviour, its structures for belonging, killing and myth-making. When the aphasic Beth tries to locate her brain in the geography of the body, she points to her belly. Emotion is the only solid touchstone; emotion is the only truth. The 'whole fandango' (as Shepard put it in *Curse)* stretches across the stage. It is a roadmap of all Shepard has ever shown us before, but with no names, like a prehistoric land, before myths came up. In this regard, it is a play purer than *Action,* which implied in place of present-time reality a futuristic no man's land. Here, the music is blue-grass, with sentiments and feelings of love, betrayal and the land expressed most simply, directly, almost sweetly, rather than ironically by means of rock music, metaphorically by means of jazz, or incidentally by means of the country music that respectively characterized the first, second and third phases of Shepard's playwriting.

The pacing is Shepard's slowest and most deliberate. This is a winding-down; man is no longer revved-up, breaking through walls, as in *La Turista*; or backtracking into a ritual of rebirth that doesn't work, as Wesley does in *Curse;* or criss-crossing the country to get back to an idea of home in a roadside motel, as Eddie does in *Fool for Love.* This play strives, as did *Action,* for a starkness and purity of character, a whittling away of extraneous detail to suggest essential urges of survival.

The animatronic gestures and vocal tracks of characters like Miss Scoons in *Angel City,* or Mom in *True West* – creating parodies akin to the robotic creatures that populate Disneyland as complacent residents of highly efficient homes-of-tomorrow – are also banished from *A Lie of the Mind.* Shepard's shape-shifting characters used to mock ideas of characters frozen into family versions of such Disneyland Ubermarionettes, harmless, flexible mannequins with computerized voices and movements, and with eerily doll-like features. They conjure up a particularly

American horror-movie vision of future: humanoids as plastic shells vacated of individual will and personal anguish (as depicted in pop films such as *Futureworld*, *Stepford Wives*, *Invasion of the Body Snatchers* . . .).

Shepard specifically uses animatrons in his parody of a commercial for desert land developments in Antonioni's *Zabriskie Point*; and he has a character poke fun at the idea of invading 'zombies' building zombie cities in *Curse of the Starving Class*. Elsewhere in Shepard's work, animatrons can serve as metaphors for his befuddled heroes, who find themselves bereft of creative impulse and desire, stuck in neutral with no gear shift in sight, like Shepard's kidnapped, enchanted horse dreamer, or like Hoss in *The Tooth of Crime*, waiting to be gunned down in his *Westworld*-like showdown with the well-oiled machine, Crow. Such animatron-heroes are locked into their behaviour patterns. They must operate solely on the basis of appearances and received symbolic meanings. The only way to break out is to destroy the circuitry, to tear down the whole structure, as in *La Turista*.

A Lie of the Mind grapples with the question of man destroying his own animatron existence, his own zombie version of a doppelganger, and his own myths of consistent, verifiable personality. The silhouettes of this play, in Peter Brook's sense, are basic and overwhelming: man wanders under the moon on some unmarked road, and he crawls in the snow to some shelter. In this regard, the use of the upper stage and back of the theatre in the first scene, and the use of centre-stage, untouched until the end of the play, are innovative.

A Lie of the Mind may seem episodic and rambling because its tempo is slow, one might say, languid. Yet this is Shepard's clearest expression of pining and keening for the

157

loss of love and for the lost sense of self that was based on that shared love: a double loss that is inexplicable and humbling. The play is clear and, for Shepard, relatively gimmick-free, in its plot, idea, structure, characters and their distinctive voices, imagery and spine (or vector of action). All are expressed simply and directly.

The plot of this play concerns Jake and Beth and their respective, relatively symmetrical families – Jake's in California, stage right, and Beth's in Montana, stage left. (Each family includes a mother who lives in the past and a brother who wants to save and make sense of their lives. In addition, Jake has a spirited sister and his dead father's ashes, bomber jacket, war medals and flag; and Beth has a deer-hunting salt-of-the-earth father.) After the first scene, in which, in the New York production, Jake makes a desperate phone call from a booth on a highway, located on an upper level, to his brother, who is seated behind the audience, the action ricochets back and forth between the two camps, stage right and stage left.

When the play opens, Jake has beaten his wife so severely in a jealous rage over her involvement with acting in a play and possibly with her leading man, that he has left her for dead. Delirious and inconsolable, he makes his way home to his old bed and his mother, but he is repeatedly visited by visions of Beth in his mind's eye. Meanwhile, Beth, brain-damaged from the beating, recuperates and yearns for Jake, first from her hospital bed and then from her parents' home in Montana. Jake later tries 'to get to Montana in [his] underpants with an American flag wrapped around [his] neck', travelling by night. Both are heartbroken, and their severe pain and longing, which neither attempts to conceal, serve to embarrass, infuriate and finally illuminate the other characters, driving everyone to extreme acts: Baylor shoots Frankie, Jake's kid brother, who has come to Montana to find out 'what happened with Beth', causing Frankie's leg to go gangrenous while he languishes helpless on their living-room couch; Lorraine and Sally, Jake's mother and sister, burn down their house and all the memories of love and desertion in it; Mike, Beth's brother, beats and enslaves the contrite Jake when he comes to Montana to acknowledge to Beth 'I love you more than this life'; and Baylor, Beth's father, gives her mother, Meg, the first real kiss Meg believes she has had in twenty years.

The idea of this play is a distillation of the ideas about strangers expressed in Shepard's family plays: the futility of questioning motives, because man is capable of anything ('It's nothing but a man. A stranger. Some stranger', says Meg); the family as an expression of the animal instinct for survival and comfort ('He's not gonna hurt us. We're related . . . Strangers he'll hurt. Strange women. Outsiders he'll hurt. That's guaranteed. But not us. He knows us', says Lorraine); and the impossibility of recognition. As Beth, rediscovering language and syntax, reassures Frankie:

> Your whole life can turn around. Upside down. In a flash. Sudden. Don't worry. Don't worry now. This whole world can disappear. Everything you know can go. You won't even recognize your own hands. (*A Lie of the Mind*, Act II, scene iii)

The structure of the play, with its ellipses and allusive parallel actions, linking memory and desire, mimics Beth's condition of aphasia. Elsewhere, in the ensemble poetic work *Inacoma* and in *Motel Chronicles*, Shepard has written movingly about the need to reinvent the self through a new language, a language to counter despair after a catastrophic event in the brain. The final entry in *Motel Chronicles* is a straightforward account of the therapy required by his mother-in-law after she suffered a cerebral haemorrhage in 1979:

> She would sit and stare at the floor in front of her. Her head limply tilted to one side. She would cry silently, her whole face distorted in a grimace of pure grief as though she was mourning the loss of her own life. A life dimly remembered . . . A Speech Therapist showed her different objects . . . Some she named with nouns of her own invention. Sounds. Some she misnamed but came close – like 'keys' she called 'locks', 'books' she called 'bucks'. The therapist told us she was suffering from something called Aphasia where the comprehension of language symbolism becomes jumbled. In other words, she may recognize an object but not remember the name for it . . . It's been exactly a year to this day . . . She still falls silent and sits and stares into space for long periods of time. She refers to her past as the time before she was 'blown away'. (*Motel Chronicles* [City Lights] pp. 137, 142)

In A Lie of the Mind, Shepard uses aphasia not for realistic effect, as Arthur Kopit does in *Wings*. Rather, he uses it to create a dramatic structure that reflects an inner experience of reality. He uses it to evoke what Joseph Chaikin explored in his work after his own survival of a catastrophic cerebral event and which Chaikin poetically called 'thought music'.

'Language has to be discovered, not structured,' Shepard told playwrights enrolled in his 1980 Bay Area Playwrights Festival workshop. 'There are modes of expression lying dormant and every once in a while something is triggered and they become accessible to us. We need to learn how to open that channel.'[4] Both the language and the structure of *A Lie of the Mind* open that channel. When her brother reprimands the slowly recovering Beth for her stream-of-consciousness conversation, Beth explains softly to Mike that 'If something breaks – broken. If something broken – Parts still – stay. Parts still float. For a while. Then gone. Maybe never come – back. Together. Maybe never.' After he, too, has been beaten and broken, Jake's journey back to Beth leads him to a final understanding of a simple point. All the stories about the whys and wherefores of family life and betrayal slip away, and his head is clear, his concentration fixed on the one still point left in the wake of all this family havoc. To Beth, *'very simple'*, he says, 'These things-in my head – lie to me. Everything lies. Tells me a story. Everything in me lies. But you. You stay. You are true. I know you know. You are true. I love you more than this life.'

Not only Beth, then, but all the characters of *A Lie of the Mind* speak in voices that reflect their inner instead of outer experience, accumulating into a quite coherent image of that reality, the vivid, tangible reality to which the Old Man in *Fool for Love* (who is himself a reality conjured out of the other characters' memories and imagination) refers when he assures his son, 'That's realism. I am actually married to Barbara Mandrell in my mind.' 'Now don't start imagining things', Sally warns her mother at the very end of Act II of *A Lie of the Mind*. 'There's nothing imaginary about it', says Lorraine. ' I can see it'. And, when Sally asks Jake what's wrong, he tells her:

There's this thing – this thing in my head. This thing that the next moment – the moment right after this one – will blow up. Explode with a voice. A scream from a voice I don't know. Or a voice I knew once but now it's changed. It doesn't know me either. Now. It used to but not now. I've scared it into something else. Another form. A whole other person who doesn't see me any more. Who doesn't

161

even remember that we knew each other once. I've gotta' see her again.

According to the stage directions, suddenly, from the other side of the stage, in her realm, Beth screams his name '*from out of the darkness*', giving lie to Jake's belief that he is lost to her since the beating.

The imagery of this play, like the plot, idea, structure and characters, is graphic and unembellished. As the characters rid themselves of the familiar Shepard imagery, literally setting fire to the house filled with 'all the junk', the play is a liberating affirmation of hopelessness. 'Doesn't matter now', says Lorraine as she plans her own getaway. Her disappearing husband, Jake's father, whom he saw die in the road, run over while drunk, in a race from bar to bar which Jake himself engineered, was 'one a' them hopeless men. Nothin' you can do about the hopeless', she says philosophically. 'I know one thing for sure', she says, looking around Jake's room:

> All these airplanes have gottta' go . . . All the junk in this house that they left behind for me to save. It's all goin'. We'll make us a big bonfire. They never wanted it anyway. They had no intention of ever comin' back here to pick it up. That was just a dream of theirs. It never meant a thing to them. They dreamed it up just to keep me on the hook. Can't believe I fell for it all those years.
> (Act III, scene i)

If Shepard strives for his usual visual effects, he does so only at the end of Act I with two powerful images. In his boyhood room, Jake blows a soft puff of his father's ashes up into the beam of a spotlight, with the earnest intensity of a child wishing as he blows out a candle. Across the stage, we see Jake's obsessive vision of Beth. '*She is simply his vision*', according to the stage directions, half-naked, oiling her body, primping herself for the lover he suspected, not for Jake. The abandoning father and the unfaithful wife, worlds apart, both have a permanent hold on Jake's mind.

Elsewhere, the pervasive imagery is of healing and cleansing and natural forces. In other Shepard plays, food, especially breakfast, usually helps a situation – from *Cowboys*, which extols the pleasures of breakfast, though *Curse of the Starving Class*, which times reveries to synchronize with the frying of bacon, through *Buried Child*, where Shelly offers to cut up carrots for Tilden and to cook bouillon for Dodge, to *True West*, which serves up hot buttered toast as if it were 'salvation'. Even in the squalor of *The Late Henry Moss*, a neighbour's soup will bring some measure of solace. In *A Lie of the Mind*, however, food is no longer a cure or a redemptive offering. On his side of the stage, Jake spits out his mother's cream-of-broccoli soup; and later on, on Beth's side of the stage, Beth can't even make coffee, and her mother rejects Baylor's deerstalking. 'It doesn't make sense . . . it's not necessary', she tells her husband. 'We're living in the modern world. We've got the grocery store just four miles down the road. We don't need to kill animals anymore to stay alive' (Act III, scene ii). Healing and cleansing can now only be accomplished by natural forces – the heat of fire in Jake's world, the cold of snow in Beth's. More than anything, Lorraine wants a wind, 'one a' them fierce, hot, dry winds that come from deep out in the desert and rip the trees apart. You know, those winds that wipe everything clean and leave the sky without a cloud. Pure blue. Pure, pure blue' (Act III, scene i).

Everyone in this play is 'desperate to get out of [his or her] situation'; everyone in this play is capable of making a desperate move. The spine of *A Lie of the Mind* – that is, its vector of action – is to make sure 'we're not gonna' have any place to come back to', because, as Lorraine says, striking the match, 'Who's comin' back?' As the play ends, the blaze set by Jake's mother is suddenly visible in the mind's eye of Beth's mother, who stares into space and envisions 'a fire in the snow' an oxymoron of nature, like the mating of men and women.

Around the time he wrote *A Lie of the Mind*, Shepard was drawn more and more towards film-making. The playwright who once aimed to write 'movies for the stage' devoted himself for a time primarily to writing plays for the movies. Shepard's *Motel Chronicles* inspired director Wim Wenders with its vignette of a man walking off the freeway and disappearing into the desert. The collaboration that grew from this vignette became *Paris, Texas* (1984), winner of the Grand Prize at the Cannes Film Festival.

Paris, Texas haunts the viewer with luminous set pieces and revelatory monologues that bear Shepard's stamp: a loner staggers out of the desert and he staggers out of silence; the stranger/brother/uninvited guest presents his hosts with his idea of a thank you gift – a row of shoes, polished and buffed, lined up on a ledge, gleaming in the sun; a man and his long lost woman confess fears and obsessions, each trapped alone and apart on either side of a one-way mirror in a brothel. With his work on the concept and the shooting script of *Paris, Texas*, Shepard proved himself capable of translating his vision of dusty roads and lost connections into a cinematic language of images.

In the more ponderous and quirky *Far North* (1988), the first film both written and directed by Shepard, characters' situations and desperate quests are starkly defined. In *Far North*, a rural Minnesota clan, 'thick with women', grapples with memories of men and with the question of revenge

164

against the horse that threw their patriarch. Recalling the more expansive mythologizing of *A Lie of the Mind*, *Far North* cross-cuts between a hospital and home, and leads its characters into the woods, under a full moon.

Like the screenplay of *Paris, Texas*, in which a man, stunned at the breakup of his violent, obsessive marriage, wanders across Texas and becomes a mute bum, going nowhere, and men and women can barely communicate through a one-way mirror, *A Lie of the Mind* goes to the bone, stripping away metaphors and traditional ideas of character and conflict. Conflict is not a contest of character with character; it is within man's own nature. Instead of characters, or even voices ('tongues'), Shepard now creates persons of the drama on-stage, fluid, worn and purified as are Beckett's persons, going from one nowhere to another in their minds, bound in limbo by nature, by the only true reality, the inner reality, the reality of tides, and of passion, which is two-sided, both creative and destructive ('savage/love'), and of the one true other. 'You're the only real thing', says Jake, crawling through the snow beneath a red moon to the bruised wife who half-remembers him. 'You disappeared . . . I love you more than the earth.'

Shepard had always been a playwright to be reckoned with, but now he became a playwright and film-maker devoted to shaking up the status quo and to sounding the silent voices of women as well as of men. Notably in *Far North* and *A Lie of the Mind*, Shepard began to move deeper into this area of exploration, and he began using yet another mode of language to do it. He was now using what Hélène Cixous identifies in 'The Laugh of the Medusa' as the language of women, the language of the 'body'.

According to Cixous, women 'write the body' to speak their subjectivity:

> By writing her self, woman will return to the body, which
> has been more than confiscated from her, which has been
> turned into the uncanny stranger on display.[. . .] Censor
> the body and you censor breath and speech at the same
> time. Write your self. Your body must be heard.[5]

America has always feminized (i.e., humiliated,
fetishized, disempowered) artists. Hence, at its best, since he
became famous as a film actor who writes plays and whose
life-companion is a movie star, Shepard's place in the public
consciousness became something like that of Arthur Miller
or of F. Scott Fitzgerald's Gatsby. Regardless, the public's
interest in movie-man Shepard's fame became vulgar and
intrusive. In this context, at best, Shepard found himself
treated like Madonna. As his 15 minutes of fame (the
amount of time Andy Warhol once predicted would be allot-
ted to each of us) ebbed, in the befuddled mind of the public,
Shepard became someone who might be married to Dolly
Parton. (He isn't; he just played her husband in *Steel
Magnolias*.) Of course, this tabloid style attitude is inappro-
priate in a discussion of Shepard's plays. Yet even in
Shepard criticism, gossipy 'fan's notes' and personal
remarks occasionally surface, objectifying Shepard as physical icon, much as women are objectified by the male gaze.

Now, surely such nonsense had been rolling right off
Shepard's back for years. It just reinforced his common
sense conviction that it is wise to keep a low profile. He has
always written mainly for himself, ignoring, as must a
woman artist, the 'cultural negation of her status as a speaking subject'.[6] But it *must be* an eye-opener for an artist to
experience his public persona as feminized object (body)
rather than as male subject (mind).

Shepard's style has *always* privileged the body. In his off-
off-Broadway days at LaMama, or so the story goes, he used

to practise the drums while he wrote plays, stressing the physical rhythm of writing over the words that came through. From the beginning of his theatrical career, writing has been a physical act.

Like Hélène Cixous, then, Shepard believes we must 'write the body' in order to possess it. To reclaim the self, that 'uncanny stranger', it is necessary to find a personal, visceral language. With the character of Beth in *A Lie of the Mind*, Shepard found a way to depict just such a quest to banish the mind/body problem from cultural consciousness. Battered and brain damaged, the aphasic Beth heals as she gropes towards a new idea of a 'woman-man' and towards a new ungendered physical language to be apprehended sensually.

In his 1992 interview with the author, included at the end of this book, Shepard, a self-described 'lucky [. . .] renegade artist', certainly did *not* describe himself as a feminist. In fact, he anticipated the ways in which his remarks on this topic might be taken out of context, and repeatedly demurred at describing his new work in feminist terms. When pressed, however, he did allow that he had become interested in how 'the female side of things', the 'female force in nature [. . .] relates to being a man. You know in yourself that the female part of one's self as a man is, for the most part, battered and beaten up and kicked to shit just like some women in relationships. That men batter their own female part to their own detriment. And it became interesting from that angle; as a man what is it like to embrace the female part of yourself that you historically damaged for one reason or another?'

Keeping in mind that until *A Lie of the Mind*, Shepard's most fully realized female characters had been Miss Scoons, the bimbo mesmerized by movies in *Angel City*, and Emma, the pre-teen rebel resisting womanhood in *Curse of the*

167

Starving Class, it is astonishing that the 1985 journey play, *A Lie of the Mind* and its companion piece, the family reunion film *Far North*, derive their strength and laughter from women. Plenty of Shepard plays had been set in the kitchen, but until *A Lie of the Mind* and *Far North*, Shepard's women were mainly functional rather than essential: so the cook had always been invisible, the hunger never sated.

For Shepard, the danger had always been that 'everything disappears'. But since he made cinematic use of the visual emblem of a one-way mirror, fusing a male and female face, blind to each other, lonesome twins behind the heavy glass, in the saddest moment of his *Paris, Texas* screenplay, Shepard had begun to seek a new theatre language in which to express the yearning for and recognition of the sexual Other, an atavistic proto-language, a Chaikinesque 'theatre music'.

In this context, *A Lie of the Mind*, which Shepard directed as a 'love ballad' in late 1985, can be considered as a major turning point in his positioning as an artist who devotes himself to depictions of love as a hunger. With this play Shepard was first trying to take 'the female part', to see and 'embrace' things from the woman's perspective. More radically than before, in *A Lie of the Mind* Shepard creates a new stage language, returning to the battered, objectified and silenced female subject a voice of her own. It is a highly physical language, yet one that aims at dissolving the splits between conflicting and mutually exclusive genders, in an approach towards a concept of love not based on power and submission. In light of new wave feminism, this play can be appreciated as it could not have been when it first opened in New York. *A Lie of the Mind* could, in fact, be staged as a gender journey, on the road to gentleness and hope.

'You're gonna try to get to Montana in your underpants

with an American flag wrapped around your neck'? This is Sally's question to Jake, her violent brother, as she watches him don their dead father's medal encrusted World War Two flight jacket and embark on a journey across a no-man's land toward his personal landscape of redemption: a vision – a lie – in his mind of Beth, the wife he has abused beyond recognition, a beaten, broken, healing woman. Sally's question, which she poses with a mixture of incredulity and resignation, conjures up 'this whole thing', this whole slapstick tragedy of treacherous families and the minefield of love in *A Lie of the Mind*. Sally's question, which hangs fire like the vibrating sound made by a blue-grass musician as he plucks the 'A' string on his fiddle, should get a laugh from the audience, for its quirky, quizzical tone is true to the play's atmosphere of laissez-faire lunacy, its eccentric talisman-laden behaviour, and its presentation of action as a dangerous mission into unknown enemy territory. After all, Jake is dead serious. He will embark, half hero/half naked fool, and travel by night to arrive at what Shepard likes to call 'emotional territory'.

More than anything else, *A Lie of the Mind* depicts the journey from male to female consciousness, rendered literal by the geography of the original production's stage picture of ramps and platforms at varying heights and levels. Jake, and his brother Frankie, who functions as a gentle extension of Jake, his peacemaking scout, his redemptive double, travel across the landscape of the stage.

Shepard's casting of the original production could be read as shorthand of maleness: Harvey Keitel played Jake as an obsessive man, intense as a searchlight. His American flag, unlike the one he wore in the 'renegade' young playwright's *Up to Thursday* more than two decades earlier, was now bereft of symbolism. Keitel, who can project on-stage the quality of a world-weary hand grenade of a man, now

169

used the flag organically as an essential cloth to cover his nakedness in the snow. Playing Jake's softer brother, the man to redeem men in a woman's gaze, the man who functions here to soften and blur the edge between genders, was Aidan Quinn, who can project on-stage the very gentleness for which Beth expresses yearning.

The opening stage direction calls for an '*impression of infinite space, going off to nowhere*'. The action of the play moves back and forth for a while, like a male/female crossfire, mutually exclusive languages echoing across a great divide of dialogue, alternating between Jake's family home, finally abandoned and burned to the ground by the women who are 'desperate to get out', to 'go in a whole different direction', and Beth's family home, finally reclaimed by women, and wrenched open to the possibility of including a man other than Jake, but bound to him by blood, in a new family to be constructed.

A Lie of the Mind charts a simple pilgrimage. The voyagers are a man who finds stillness, silhouetted by the moon in the snow, and a woman who finds a voice, and rejects the old truth, the old love, choosing instead the gentler Frankie. The voyage is characterized by the hopelessness of life without love, by the feeling of death that love's absence brings, and by the yearning to invent new patterns, to escape the past.

If this sounds maudlin, and vaguely country-western, that is because it is. What saves the play from becoming a sentimental tear-jerking ballad about an abusive but contrite jealous husband is its relentless mockery of men and their fetishes: their games of war, their medals, their guns, their prey, their trophies, their spoils, their domestic tyrannies. If the main quest in the play is to construct a concept of love that is not also a concept of power, then a corollary quest is to redefine maleness in a way foreign to the neglectful,

bullying, domineering, and abandoning fathers of both Jake
and Beth. Most surprisingly, the play mocks love, a cornball
notion concocted by self-serving men. 'Love. What a crock
a' shit. Love! There's another disease', sneers Lorraine,
Jake's mother, as she remembers Jake's Dad, his meanness
'like hidden snakes', and his disappearances 'like an appari-
tion'.

In *A Lie of the Mind*, then, Shepard favours the female
side of the hunt, putting a feminist spin on all of that macho
paraphernalia of wilderness survival. The self-invention of
men in nature, stalking, with equipment and camouflage,
supplies and strategies, is demythologized and mocked.
Male characters get tracked, shot, beaten, humiliated, and
stripped bare, that is, treated like women. Their journey is
from a safe hearth to an open space with nowhere to hide.
The man of *A Lie of the Mind* finally crawls towards a
recognition that 'These things – in my head – lie to me.
Everything in me lies'. He finally reconciles himself with
the female perspective, with nature, with what Jake sees in
Beth, something 'true'.

Throughout two-thirds of the play, Jake believes he has
killed Beth, and Beth believes that she is either dead or
mentally mutilated beyond repair. Both are convinced that
this time, they have gone too far. They are past redemption.
At first, Jake stumbles through the darkness, from one
phone booth to another, from one motel to another, across
America's anonymous blacktop landscape in 'You-Name-It-
U.S.A.' By the end of Act I, Jake has found his way home,
back to his mother, his sister, and his plastic memorabilia.
They are all here, ready and waiting to lie for and to justify
Jake; here are his women, the mother and sister who love
him unconditionally, feeding and swaddling him, rationaliz-
ing his temper as his maleness, his father's temper, his
father's 'animal sound'. And here are his 'model airplanes

and bombers' hovering above him, while below, his father rests in a box of ashes in the dust under the boyhood bed.

Withdrawing in sympathetic despair after beating Beth senseless and leaving her for dead, Jake sees a series of images of Beth in his mind, all of them sensual and more real than anything he experiences with his body. These visions are a kind of haunting – 'a lie of the mind' – that is, paradoxically, the essence of love as fire, consumed by its own bed of ashes.

Jake's mind drifts to Beth at key moments in Acts I and II. He won't 'let go of her'. 'You never did see me, did you, Beth?', he says, staring right through his sister, seeing instead a woman in his mind. 'Just had a big wild notion about some dream life up ahead. Somebody who was gonna save yer ass.' At the end of Act I, Jake sees Beth '*naked from the waist up*', surrounded by blue silk and satin, '*seductively*' oiling her chest and shoulders from a small bedside bottle. When Jake blows into the box of his father's ashes downstage, he scatters some, and in a soft puff of ashes, this vision – which once drove him over the edge – vanishes. Towards the end of Act II, Jake sees a more startling, less predictable flash. He sees Beth gently tending his wounded brother, wrapping her soft shirt around Frankie's gangrenous leg.

Jake's quest in the play is to seek out the source of the mirages, to see as a mystic sees, that is, to conjure up the dead-living-murdered Beth that completes him, that makes him 'one whole thing', and to let it go.

Just as surely as Gogo and Didi, Beth and Jake are tied. For both Jake and Beth, the greatest fear is losing the other. The first words Beth struggles to say are 'He killed us both', 'Nobody can stop him in me', and 'He's my heart'. And although Beth sees no parallel vision of Jake's struggle, she has complementary senses. She hears the voice that is Jake's voice (in the outcry of Jake's brother, mistaken for a deer and wounded in the thigh); she smells the sex of men in her father's flannel fishing shirt; and she feels Jake near when he is outside, beaten in the snow.

But Beth knows the terror, and the big joke that is the secret about love: 'This whole world can disappear. Everything you know can go. You won't even recognize your own hands' (Act II, scene iii).

In the course of the play Beth invents a new language, a counter-language to romance as submission to a stranger. Jake senses this happening at the end of Act II. That is when he feels the urgency of the situation. He plots his 'escape' from his kin to 'travel by night' to Beth's homestead in Montana. But 'there's this thing – this thing in my head'. This thing in his head is a premonition of imminent combustion, when someone he used to know will explode into 'another form'.

'Another form.' This is the only thing Jake sees that is not couched in lies and self-delusion. And with this phrase Jake sees the possibility of escape for himself, too. So the hopeful grace note struck at the end of this play even includes him. He loses his language, his male lexicon of conquest and contrition as the mode of interaction with women. He is speechless. He is also bereft of the use of women as objects to be bartered, tokens of a system of exchange between men. In the final moments of this play, the women are energized by the fire, the moon, the earth, the cold. It is the men who take each other's place, who exchange positions, like hostages in the snow.

Beth's injury-induced aphasia has caused her to create language in a new key, an essential 'thought music' derived from Chaikin's theories and experiments, and shaped by Shepard's quest to discover new 'modes of expression lying dormant'.[7] Now, through Beth, it is a female language that emerges, like the ancient script called *'nushi'*, or 'women's writing', invented in the mountains of central China over a thousand years ago.

Robin Morgan describes *'nushi'* in her book, *The Word of a Woman*:

> It was a totally female language. [. . .] Researchers had uncovered hundreds of stories, poems, songs, and letters written over the past millennium in a unique script invented by rural women for their own secret use [. . .] because they were forbidden to learn standard writing. [. . .] This female language was an underground code – an act of rebellion in conception, and utterance of rebellion in content.[8]

And it is a kinesthetic language. It is the concrete, visual language of signs to be apprehended sensually. It is a language of the body that binds Beth to nature, to the earth and the moon. It is a slippery dream language, hard to come by and hard to hold on to, and in succeeding at doing both, Beth has become a woman shaman, capable of encircling and catching dreams.

Such spiritual connections, and Beth's transformation and transformative power, are clear in the centrepiece of the action, Beth's pantomime of men and women, a dance of gender she performs with her father's oversized flannel fishing shirt. 'Look how big a man is. So big. He scares himself. His shirt scares him', Beth giggles. Then she puts the shirt on, pumps her chest up, closes her fists, sticks her chin out and struts, laughing at her new self. 'Shirt brings me a man. I am a shirt man', she jokes. Next, Beth turns to Frankie, asking him to play, too, at this gender reversal. 'You could pretend to be in love with me. With my shirt. You love my shirt. This shirt is a man to you. You are my beautiful

8. Amanda Plummer, as the damaged and recovering 'Beth', and Aidan Quinn as 'Frankie', her wounded brother-in-law, ponder questions of gender in the premiere production of *A Lie of the Mind*, directed by Shepard at the Promenade Theatre in New York in 1986. Photo: Martha Swope.

woman. You lie down.' Finally, she suggests what will turn out to be the only hope of this play, that Frankie become Jake, the 'other one. . . . Just like him. But soft. With me. Gentle. Like a woman-man' (Act II, scene iii).

In the interview appended to this book, Shepard said that he, too, felt:

> That was one of the big changes . . . that the women suddenly took on a different light than they had before. Because before it felt so sort of overwhelmed by the confusion about masculinity, about the confusion about how these men identify themselves. That sort of overwhelmed the female. There wasn't even any room to consider the female, because the men were so fucked up.

175

You spent the whole play trying to figure out what these men were about, who had no idea themselves. But then, when the women characters began to emerge, then something began to make more sense for the men, too.

Shepard's women refuse to disappear in this phase of his playwriting. In fact, it is quite the contrary in *Far North*, where instead the men have all 'disappeared', leaving a world of women with unloaded shotguns and uneaten mountains of biscuits, wild horses and sepia-toned photos of lovely young mothers waving goodbye.

Shepard's next original film was *Silent Tongue* (1993), about a faith healer in the Wild West, a woman who cannot speak, but who holds power inside. Like a 'woman-man'.

8

'Ghosts and Sacrifices'

No – Look – I – I am an ordinary man. Just a plain old everyday average ordinary American man. I come from an ordinary background. Generations of ordinariness. There is nothing – absolutely nothing inside me that can even begin to comprehend this stuff . . . I simply want to return to the *known world*. Something safe and simple. My wife, my children. My house. My car. My dog. The front lawn. My mobile phone! The Internet! . . . Tangible things in the real world! . . . I don't want to be dealing with madness now. Ghosts and sacrifices! Superstition and visions. We're approaching the milennium here! Things have moved beyond all that. Don't you have any concept at all of the outside world? The global perspective? The Bigger Picture! . . . We're on the verge of breaking into territories never dreamed of before . . . So we don't have to be lost out here – totally lost and – wandering – without – without a clue – where we stand – in the scheme of things. Just completely – cut off.

(Henry in *Eyes for Consuela*, Act II)

After *A Lie of the Mind* in 1986, it was a long time between plays for Shepard's audience. At the off-off-Broadway houses that served up Shepard's mile-a minute excursions in the 1960s, we had watched his heroes bounce dreams off the walls, even break through the rear stage wall in *La Turista*. Between 1970 and 1975, Shepard wrote a series of energetic war plays, setting battles in a no-man's-land of the mind. He experimented formally with variations on this idea of a *High Noon*-style showdown – writing the broad-canvas *Tooth of Crime*, the stripped down *Action*, and the internalized *Killer's Head*, as well as *Geography of a Horse Dreamer*, a play in which a cowboy hero is kidnapped by thugs who want to cash in on his mysterious (though waning) power to predict winners at the races. With this production, Shepard, who had grown weary of watching other directors 'shape' his plays, first decided to try his own hand at it. At San Francisco's Magic Theatre, the regional theatre that became home to Shepard's dysfunctional American family cycle in the 1970s, we listened to stories of betrayal, abandonment, and self-destruction, echoed by sons and brothers hoping to find a way out. Probably the most keenly awaited Shepard play up until this point had been *Fool for Love*, his 'motel room *Phèdre*', an explosive doomed lover's quarrel, which followed hard upon his Pulitzer Prize-winning homecoming play, *Buried Child*.

Then, in 1991, Shepard was back. After a hiatus from the stage while Shepard wrote screenplays and prose, *States of Shock* opened and ran at the American Place Theatre. It depicted a Beckettian dynamic of power, but it was widely dismissed as a political portrait of a power-mad military man.

With the notable exception of *The War in Heaven*, an Angel's monologue co-authored with Joseph Chaikin, *States of Shock* was Shepard's first full-length play since *A Lie of the Mind*, the three-hour 'love ballad' that played out a full

178

shuffle of brothers and sisters, fathers and daughters, mothers and sons against a cold, bleak, Montana landscape. Not
only did *States of Shock* mark Shepard's long overdue return
to playwriting, it also marked a turning point in Shepard's
work. His cycle of family plays had been put to rest with *Lie
of the Mind*. With *States of Shock*, Shepard returned to his
original beat: the American psyche – its aggression, hunger,
rowdy humour, and legacy of whimsical sacrifice.

States of Shock also heralded Shepard's return to home
ground: The American Place Theatre, shepherded by Wynn
Handman, had always served the playwright well, allowing
him freedom to experiment with form and acting styles. It
was here, after all, where Sam Waterston had ripped through
the fourth wall in *La Turista* years ago, and where Rip Torn
had later tried to fly in *Seduced*. The musicians behind a
scrim at this premiere production of *States of Shock*, who at
crucial moments would pound their way towards oblivion,
and who would punctuate every toast to 'the Enemy' with a
drum roll, also went way back with Shepard: the same sound
designer and composer had wired the San Francisco Magic
Theatre for reverb to accentuate those slamming doors in
Fool for Love; a percussionist had first collaborated with
Shepard on the ensemble piece, *Inacoma*, in the early 70s.
The rear-projected strobe-light show was designed by the
usually more subtle Anne Militello, who memorably lit the
fire in the snow and Harvey Keitel's broken plea for love in
Shepard's *A Lie of the Mind* in 1985. Director Bill Hart
harked back to the prehistoric Shepard plays of the free-
associating 1960s, the off-off-Broadway *Cowboys #2* and
the silly *Shaved Splits*. For his return to the New York
theatre, Shepard insulated himself from strangers.

The setting of *States of Shock* is vintage Shepard. Danny's
diner is indicated minimally by red vinyl banquettes and two

Formica tables, with no flashing neon or jukeboxes. The two tables, dressed with the familiar American roadside-diner salt shakers and glossy menus, seemed to be floating out of time and out of space in the original production, enveloped by a concave movie screen. The resonant set of this play recalls Tennessee Williams's microcosmic bar in *Small Craft Warnings* and O'Neill's last chance saloon in *The Iceman Cometh*. And both the action and the setting of the play recall *The Wild Ones*, in which the classic American café is invaded by Brando as Johnny. ('What are you protesting?' Brando is asked. 'What've you got?' is the surly answer. A generation later, the question was the same, and so was the answer.)

States of Shock depicts 'marooned but invincible' characters who stop at a 'family restaurant' where they have a food fight while awaiting the 'impending doom' of chemical warfare. It is an often hilarious, uneven, and special-effect laden play: unsettling and galvanizing. The 80-minute, one-act has the Shepard signature of whiz-bang action, sentimental invocations of American heroes of yore, ear-piercing sounds, primary colours, and otherly animation. And the play is energized by Shepard's by now copyrighted version of American slanglish; his patented patois, culled from car culture, cowboy movies, and home cooking. With words, once again, Shepard's characters fight for power and for turf. As in *Tooth of Crime*, arguably Shepard's greatest, most enduring play, language is a weapon, a signal of danger, mysterious energy, and power. So reading the menu and ordering a banana split are desperate acts of hostility and of hunger in Shepard's café. 'We were generated from the bravest stock. The Pioneer. The Mountain Man. The Plainsman. The Texas Ranger. The Lone Ranger. These ones have not left us to wallow in various states of insanity and self-abuse. We have a legacy to continue. . . . Here's to them and to my son! . . . THE ENEMY HAS BROUGHT US TOGETHER', argues the Colonel.

The play's premise is: 'a catastrophe must be studied from every possible angle . . . the exact configuration . . . Study every detail, every nuance; let nothing escape your scrutiny.' The catastrophe in question is perpetual war fever and the destructive instinct. Men sacrifice their sons. There is no end in sight – no way out – until the last image when the play shapes itself into a silhouette of power and potential freedom: Accompanied by a melancholy tune, old as the hills, sung by a chorus of war casualties, a son can murder his nemesis and free himself from war, from phantom pain, from flashbacks, and from states of aftershock.

The play opens with the off-stage sounds of artillery and airfire, explosions behind the scrim. Percussion and rear projections of planes, helicopters, and the lights bombard us and surround the actors. Shepard time-capsules us in a flash, catapulting the audience back to the world of his early plays, where he shamelessly conjured the apocalypse as a Fillmore East light-show. Now, as then, the rules of narrative go out the window. Shepard supplants them with the sur-logic of a drumbeat, a drum.

Thunderous drumming and strobe lights are meant to punctuate the action of the whole play, and they bracket the action. Enter the Colonel on a mission to debrief the 'lucky' Stubbs, a young disabled veteran in a wheelchair, blowing the whistle he wears round his neck with ear-piercing fervour. All the wars since the Revolution are on the Colonel's back. His layered uniform, a piece of military found-art, is a souvenir of all soldiers – from his Revolutionary War dress uniform to his Robert E. Lee cavalry sabre to his Vietnam combat boots and camouflage – and all combine to give us a sense of hopelessness: we will never escape this world of war. And all the wounds of war are projected onto Stubbs, who stopped a bullet, possibly friendly fire, which burned a hole right through his soul leaving him crippled with a gory scar at his solar plexus. 'When I was hit . . . America had disappeared . . .' says Stubbs. Later he accuses the Colonel with a memory: 'I remember the moment you forsook me, the moment you invented my death . . . when you left me. That left a hole like I never felt.' Gradually it seems as if all the enemies since Truman's time are poised to attack, hovering above and outside the lonely family diner where the Colonel and Stubbs run for cover.

So much for plot. The montage of uniforms and the vagueness of the situation keep this play from being mired in historical incidents. The customers at Shepard's heart-of-darkness coffee shop are all outright spokesmen for or against the urge to fight and win. According to the relentless Colonel, 'We are here to toast the death of my son and have a nice dessert . . . the enemy had brought us together . . . Without the enemy we're nothing!' Reprising his ode to aggression, the Colonel posits a world in which 'Fear takes a back seat to confidence . . . I fly on the wings of my own initiative.' For him, war is the ultimate expression of the life force. According to Stubbs, the remnant of a soldier whom the Colonel plans to interrogate and then to resurrect, 'How could we be so victorious and still suffer this terrible loss?' He tries to understand, 'No way of knowing the original moment. – Maybe Abraham, Judas, Eve – best way is to kill all the sons . . . Fill every river. Every hole in this earth. . . . Let us go down screaming in the blood of our sons.' But the Colonel will never let go. 'Sacrifice needs a partner.' We may be 'marooned', he howls towards the end. But 'we're invincible'.

Pivotal to the premiere New York production, of course, was John Malkovich, the quintessential Shepard actor: He hit the stage with a demonic gleam in his eye and with an awry timing and idiosyncratic phrasing that can make set speeches sound like inspired jazz solos. To a certain extent, Malkovich was reprising his performance as the malcontent anarchist of *True West*, but he was now using that dangerous energy to play the opposite role here – the control freak who has the most at stake in maintaining the status quo. Careening around the stage, Malcovich again proved himself to be a uniquely unselfconscious and mischievous performer. Whether miming the climbing of a wall, balancing coffee cups, slurping up a banana split, whipping a surrogate son, leaping for joy when he found a bottle of painkillers, or suggesting an escape to Mexico while dancing a marimba, there was no stopping him. His broad slapstick performance lifted this play's weighty metaphors off the ground, like a tornado.

As in plays written decades earlier, the ironically envisioned hero, here Malkovich's Colonel, was clearly the motor of this play, and as in most plays by Shepard, that motor runs on fear and anger. The actor's balletic gestures were always intentionally one-half step out of sync with his language, and his character's potential for violence was always palpable, even when he strained with sweet reason. Thanks to Malkovich, the Colonel's absurd demonstration that 'the human body is a complex machine that can be trained through repetition and practice', along with his tips on how to balance hot liquids, were passed along with a juggler's grace and a lunatic's obsessiveness to the hapless and flustered sole surviving waitress, who puzzles over the invasion incredulously, 'When the first missiles struck, I studied the menu . . . I worshipped the menu. I thought the menu would save me', she remembers. Wiser now, shaky but alive, spilling coffee and clam chowder as she gingerly serves her customers, she knows better. She knows her limits and her powers. When all else fails, she can cha-cha and sing the blues.

Ever since he worked on the script for Antonioni's *Zabriskie Point*, which climaxed in a sudden apocalypse in the desert, with typically American detritus – coke bottles, cereal boxes, and furniture – floating slow-motion through space, Shepard has been drawn to the firecracker as a *coup de théâtre*, the explosion as a climax. *Fool for Love* leads to a crazed Countess blasting a motel at the edge of the Mojave to smithereens. Similarly, here, in *States of Shock*, Danny's homestyle diner will finally be hit by chemical weapons, but first the wreckage and the carnage will be fully felt and internalized. Rather than stop the action, as they sometimes did in the past, in *Shock*, Shepard's soliloquies are highly physicalized: they drive its kinetic language forward.

States of Shock was a another breakthrough for Shepard; it took him out of his rut of 'thicker than water' plays, and back to his strength as a playwright: his uninhibited histrionic imagination, capable of writing what he calls 'movies for the stage', and his sense of theatrical jazz – building rhythms that mimic and influence states of mind. Supported here by improvising actors and percussionists, Shepard wrote monologues like drum solos, finding what Tympani in *Angel City* longed for, 'a never heard-before rhythm'.

States of Shock is no less than Shepard's *Endgame*, with Nagg and Nell somewhat heavy-handedly humanized, stuck together but mutually isolated, ignored, and unhappy at their table, awaiting their clam chowder. White Woman and White Man play opposite the Colonel and his son, who are Shepard's Hamm and Clov. But in Shepard's *Endgame*, Hamm and Clov are reversed. Hamm pushes the wheelchair and Clov awaits his painkiller, his release, his turn to play. Such allusions do not diminish the effect of *States of Shock*;

they merely show the high stakes for which Shepard plays, the quality of the company he keeps as an artist. Shepard does not simply Americanize the endgame lost of old; the doomed survivors debating strategy; the hunger, hope, pain, and cosmic jokes that grip us and won't let go; the symbiotic/destructive couple, and the perpetual enemy whose existence defines us. In *States of Shock*, Shepard puts America on-stage, not just as a geographic location, but as a state of mind. This play goes beyond issues – it is not simply a reaction to the first Gulf War or to any one war – to deal with something mysterious, mystical, and perversely funny.

Like all his work and major revivals since 1986, when Shepard himself directed the 1986 New York premiere of *A Lie of the Mind* with Geraldine Page, Harvey Keitel, Aidan Quinn, and Amanda Plummer, *States of Shock* was well served by its actors and production team. Since then, we have also seen *Simpatico*, which premiered in 1994 with Ed Harris and Fred Ward in roles later to be reprised by Nick Nolte and Jeff Bridges on-screen; *When the World was Green*, a collaboration with Joseph Chaikin for the Olympic Arts Festival in Atlanta in 1996, later included as part of an entire season devoted to Shepard's work at the Signature Theatre Company in 1996–7; a 1998 Manhattan Theatre Club production of *Eyes for Consuela* directed by Steppenwolf's Terry Kinney and a revival of *Buried Child* featuring Ethan Hawke and directed by Steppenwolf's Gary Sinise; *True West* on Broadway in 2000 with John C. Reilly and Philip Seymour Hoffman alternating as the brothers; and *The Late Henry Moss*, which premiered in San Francisco directed by Sam Shepard himself in 2000 with a cast including Sean Penn and an even more than usually bedraggled Nick Nolte (whose performance the previous year in the film of Russell Banks' *Affliction* provided yet more evidence of his ability to connect with the damaged

185

and damaging volatile fathers and sons who stumble and wander in Shepard's world, too). The New York premiere of *The Late Henry Moss* in 2001 was also steered by Shepard veterans, directed by Joseph Chaikin, and featuring performances by Ethan Hawke, Arliss Howard and James Gammon. In each instance of new production or major reproduction of his works in recent years, in fact, Shepard has chosen collaborators on whom he, a stage auteur, can rely to augment his highly personal vision.

Simpatico, billed as Shepard's first major play since *A Lie of the Mind*, took over a year to open in New York. It was tentatively announced by producer Lewis Allen for a January 1994 Broadway opening, probably under the auspices of the Broadway Alliance. The cast was to include Jennifer Jason Leigh and Frederic Forrest, as well as Ed Harris, in leading roles. But the Broadway plans fell through, as did financing from the independent producer for a limited run at the Public Theatre. Still, a new Shepard play causes a buzz. So finally, the New York Shakespeare Festival, headed by George C. Wolfe, agreed to produce the play at the Public on its own.

Simpatico runs three hours and centres on the consequences of painting oneself into a corner, the aftermath of making a name. In a series of two-character scenes, two tired and anxious has-beens hark back to an old racetrack swindle and a double-cross, a pivotal moment when they 'bottomed out' and made irrevocable choices. Vinnie and Carter are the Gogo and Didi of Shepard's oeuvre, Shepard's usual suspects, the bum and the regular guy who long ago took desperate measures and reinvented themselves according to some harebrained idea of escape: freedom or success.

In the New York premiere, Ed Harris, looking like a weathered choirboy, played Carter, whose 'yuppie Protestant aura' and attaché case belie his sense of guilt,

186

betrayal, and isolation. Harris had the plum role in the show. His character undertakes the most rigorous journey in *Simpatico*. Like Vince in *Buried Child*, like Austin in *True West*, and like Wesley in *Curse of the Starving Class*, among others, Carter strips away layers of self in a desperate attempt to know more about his true nature. But unlike his predecessors in more optimistic plays written previously by Shepard, Carter finds his attempt to perform a psyche-switch with his raggedy man doppelganger to be doomed.

Discussing his role in *Simpatico* and his long association with Shepard's heroes with the author of this book in November 1994, Harris poignantly conveyed Shepard's hero's ability to seem at once at home and out of place anywhere in America. Harris was completely absorbed in the production of *Simpatico* at the time of this interview. He pointed out that Shepard prefaced an earlier version of the script with Beckett's line, 'You're on earth. There's no cure for that.'[1]

Asked about the title of the play, given that the word 'simpatico' is itself never used on-stage, even though the characters are all connected and bound together, Harris said:

> I think the closest it gets is when I am in the last scene, when Carter [Harris's character] has kind of totally unraveled and lost everything, as far as he's concerned – and almost his mind, but not quite – and his body is just kind of quivering. He says to Vinnie, 'Maybe we could start over again. Maybe we could start up with the claimers again.' And Vinnie says, 'No, it's past that.' And Carter says, 'Yeah, but, well, we had a partnership. We had a real partnership, didn't we? We had a feeling between us. We were like a team.' And that is the closest it gets to the word ever being used, '*Simpatico*'.

Sam even actually thought about having my character

say the word, and Bill Hart, the dramaturg [director of *States of Shock*], said, 'no, Sam, you don't want to do that'. But it has something to do with the symbiotic kind of thing with these two guys. I don't tend to get too philosophical about it. (Harris, p. 14)

By the time he began rehearsals for *Simpatico*, Harris already had a long history of collaboration with Shepard. As Harris recalled in our 1994 interview, it began when he 'did *Cowboy Mouth* at a little theatre in L.A. I think it was the Pilot Theatre, actually. That was back in '78 or something, and then I did *True West* down at the South Coast Rep, down at Costa Mesa in California, which is the first time I met Sam. That was about 1981, I guess. I played the writer, Austin. I loved that play. I think we had a really good production. We just ran for three weeks' (Harris, p. 14). Although the story goes that the role of Eddie in *Fool for Love* was written for Harris, his version of the collaboration is more modest. 'He was going to write the play whether I existed or not . . . I think he wanted me to play the guy. But . . . I don't think the playwright writes something for someone. I think they write the play because they have to write the play. They might have some people in mind that they really see in the role, but that's a little different' (Harris, p. 14).

Nevertheless, Harris is often described as the quintessential Shepard interpreter on-stage. Indeed, when Shepard himself was asked to identify Shepardesque actors (in the interview that ends this book), he said he admired John Malkovich and Ed Harris, because of their contained energy. While his two signature Shepard roles do share 'contained energy' as well as a fear of tension at a reunion, Harris distinguishes Carter in *Simpatico* from *Fool for Love*'s Eddie in a matter-of-fact way. 'Eddie's younger, he's more vital, and he's living his life. He's living what he believes in. This guy', he notes, focusing on Carter's objectives and intentions, 'is trying to live something else. This guy is so full of shit it's scary' (Harris, p. 15). Asked about his own intensity and that of *Simpatico*'s Carter, Harris cut to the chase – the unravelling of character:

> One of the things I'm working on in *Simpatico* is trying to contain it a little bit more. I think Carter is very contained until he starts to unravel, and it's the whole process of when . . . how he falls apart . . . I tend to want to fall apart a little bit sooner than is necessary. So, I'm working on that. [laughs] It's fun to just kind of let go and go 'Baahh'. So I'm just trying to gauge it a little bit.
>
> (Harris, p. 14)

Acknowledging that much of Carter's unravelling occurs when he is off-stage, Harris continued to analyse the character's objectives and behaviour. 'Enough happens to him up to the end of the second act, where hopefully you can imagine what might have taken place in the ensuing day and a half or whatever, till you see him again.' Between Act II, scene iii, and the next time we see Carter, in Act III, scene iii, the actor could imagine a whole forgery of a life unravelling:

> Well, first of all, he finishes the bottle of whiskey, and then he's isolated there, and he has a major anxiety attack. He doesn't know what's going to happen. He doesn't know what to do. And in his mind, he's so paranoid, he can't go back home. He can't go out. He tries to sleep. He starts shaking. He starts getting cold. His muscles start tensing up on him. He thinks he's going to die. His heart starts racing. He's just flipping out. And

after all that goes on, he doesn't get any sleep. The booze thing probably passes, but that has some effect, but he says, 'It's not that'. It's like, 'I don't know what's going on with me'. Basically, he's unravelling . . .

The problem with Carter is that he's living a lie. He has attempted over the past 15 years to put this whole episode behind him. Unfortunately, he's living with his wife, who used to be his best friend's wife, and he's been taking care of this guy for 15 years who represents where Carter came from. But he's managed to change his lifestyle. He's very, very wealthy; he moves in high circles and he is a powerful man.

Once he makes the decision to come out and help his friend, then he just starts spiralling down into this world and he just can't get out of it. All of his intentions are not working . . .   (Harris, pp. 16, 15)

Simpatico is set in what appears, at first, to be familiar Shepard territory. There are some expectations raised in the audience when the play opens on the dilapidated motel room, with the unmade bed, the sink and the pile of dirty laundry. But Carter is quite different from *Fool for Love*'s Eddie, and it is through Carter, that we experience the arc of *Simpatico*. Carter is the only character in the play with no home base on-stage. He never knows where to put his coat, where to sit down, or even if he can stay. When he does stop, he feels, as Harris put it, 'caged'. We even see the set diminish as walls disappear from scene to scene. As Ed Harris noted in rehearsal, 'The room is disappearing as Carter is evaporating.'

For Ed Harris the playwright's tough resolution of the action raised an important issue for performance:

I was talking to Sam about the last scene, and I said, 'Isn't there a moment where he accepts what he's done wrong? That he admits some kind of guilt or that he confesses in some way to himself?' And the closest he gets is saying, 'We made a couple of mistakes, a couple of bad mistakes. I admit that.' But he's not really acknowledging . . . Part of his problem is he doesn't even know why he's shaking. He's totally flabbergasted. He has no idea that it's because as a human being, everything that he stands for has been taken away from him and he's got no center. If he could just acknowledge that he's lied, that he's cheated, that he's hurt people, and ask for some kind of forgiveness or something, that in itself would give him some kind of peace or some kind of place to recollect himself and then go get on with whatever else might be out there.

Sam said, 'I'm sorry. I'm not letting this guy off the hook.' I didn't ask for a speech, I just asked for the notion that there was some internal realization that this guy had of what had happened to him, why this was happening to him, Sam said, 'No, the guy's blind.'   (Harris, p. 15)

But Shepard does give us a stage image at the end of Carter, having discovered it is 'a late day for regrets', shivering in his underwear, wrapped in a borrowed blanket, surrounded by a mound of money. It is a final image reminiscent of that which ends *A Lie of the Mind*. But it is now merciless. It looks as if Carter, increasingly uncomfortable in his forged identity, attempts to strip it away and escape from it. He is hoping for something – some sort of transformation – that he is never going to get. He mentions the fact of having the daring to 'make a radical move . . . a force of nature . . . and everything shifts, carries its own momentum'. Now he is attempting another radical move. He says, 'I'm done with sleeping and waking.' But no one will cooperate. As Ed Harris noted in rehearsal for the role, 'But he's also not making any moves. He's not making any radical moves. His radical move was to blackmail this commissioner and get away with the money that he had in terms of the rip-off he was doing on the racetrack, get down to Kentucky and build on that and become a multi-millionaire. That was his radical move, and it's paid off' (Harris, p. 16).

The final scene, according to Harris, is 'pitiful':

> It's a desperate measure ... Sam's obviously saying something in there about a certain place he's come to. There's a certain something that settles in. You know that radical moves ain't going to lead you anywhere, necessarily. They may have in the past, but you got to start dealing with what you got and who you are, and what's really true about something. Quit pretending, you know?
>
> We all do certain things that ... put you in another zone, that you've now separated yourself from some place of innocence ... There's a sense of that to this guy, that he has done that so many times, that he doesn't have any connection with who he was, really. There's a glint, there's a faint thing in there. He remembers alfalfa bales and he remembers watching this horse, which won the Kentucky Derby, trot up and down the fence line there. There are things he recalls about the past that touch him in some way, but it's not enough to bring him back.
>
> (Harris, p. 16)

By the end of *Simpatico*, Carter is 'stuck ... there's a certain helplessness that overcomes the guy, because there is nothing to do'. Finally, anticipating Henry in *Eyes for Consuela* and Earl in *The Late Henry Moss*, two other shells of men trying to make amends in the bold later plays, haunted by guilt that they cannot appease at play's end, Carter is unforgiven.

As ever, with *Simpatico*, Shepard seeks to 'penetrate into another world . . . a world behind the form', but now, he cuts no slack for a lost soul marooned in a roadside mirage. As we have seen throughout this overview of his work, he has never minded leaving his characters in the lurch, waiting and pathetically hoping to switch gears from one mode of being to another one. In his reckless early plays of the 1960s, such as *Icarus's Mother, Red Cross*, and *Operation Sidewinder*, Shepard celebrated American myths while his would-be heroes flailed around. His use of language and icons was baroque, decorative. Then, Shepard's plays from the early 1970s, such as *Tooth of Crime, Angel City*, and *Seduced*, grappled with just what is a hero, where does the imagination reside, what is an original voice, where is, as he put it in *Geography of a Horse Dreamer*, 'the space inside where the dream comes'. The language of these plays strove for originality, for expressions of the inner, musical voice, and the plays were also original in their refusal to tie up loose ends in any way remotely connected to conventional dramatic notions of insight or salvation.

But then, a series of American gothic dysfunctional 'family plays' followed. They revolved around domestic secrets, recriminations, revelations of character, and the quest for forgiveness. Shepard's quartet – *Curse of the Starving Class, Buried Child, True West*, and *Fool for Love* – gained him a wider audience and conventional critical acclaim. In them he harnessed his experiments with characters and voices to traditional plotting and structure. In this series of plays – and in the dramatic apotheosis of this series, in the raw, icy and unyielding scape of *A Lie of the Mind* – his technique became archaeological. In these plays, characters move inward, and they dig deeper and back as far as they can, finally facing the family as 'an animal thing', unearthing and demystifying myths about homesteads,

193

blood ties and legacies. These are the plays for which Shepard is still best known.

Nowadays, except on college campuses, where, arguably, Shepard rivals Shakespeare as the most frequently produced playwright, most of his early and later plays – those revolving around stranded and befuddled ghostly shadows of the men they meant to be, unsuccessfully attempting to settle scores and ruminating – are widely ignored. There are countless productions each year of the family plays such as *Curse of the Starving Class* and *Fool for Love*. But where are the productions of *States of Shock*, or of *Simpatico*, or of its 1970s predecessor about the pitfalls of gambling and crooked racetracks and dreams of cashing-it-in gone awry, *The Geography of a Horse Dreamer*? After all, at the time of its premiere in 1974 at the Royal Court Theatre with a cast including Bob Hoskins and Stephen Rea, *Geography of a Horse Dreamer* drew a great deal of attention thanks to its linguistic inventiveness, its period paranoia, and its hero's Faustian reverb. Today, this play has been virtually forgotten in America. But its central concern with an artist's need to disappear, and its driving fantasy of predicting winners, are both still the trademark twin dreams of talent and luck prevailing, even in the theatre. Luckily for Shepard's audience, these trademark dreams prevail at New York's uncompromising and modest Signature Theatre, which, although it did not put *Geography* on its calendar, did include revivals of *Tooth of Crime*, *Action*, and *Killer's Head* in its 1996–7 season devoted to Shepard.

According to James Houghton, the founder and Artistic Director of the Signature Company, he first approached Shepard about the possibility of working together in 1992, when Shepard directed his own *Simpatico* at the Public Theatre. Courting Shepard then became mainly a question of timing because from the start, as Houghton recalls,

Shepard expressed enthusiasm at being involved in overseeing productions of his plays in retrospect and 'in context'.[2] Ironically, too, for a playwright whose very *signature* has been characterized by the graffiti which he himself has slapdashed haphazardly around the edges of every play, Shepard expressed a new desire to look back and possibly rework moments when, dramaturgically, as he might phrase it, he 'shot himself in the foot'.

All Signature seasons shape up according to the playwright's preferences, and so the Signature season placed an emphasis on Shepard's newest collaboration with Joseph Chaikin, as well as afforded him a chance to achieve with *Tooth of Crime* what he did with Steppenwolf's revival of *Buried Child*. Shepard's new-found interest in dusting off and revising some of his classics may have been attributable in part to his advancing years (at this juncture, 1996, he was, after all, 52 years old), but even more to his intervening experiences as the writer and director of two cult films (given limited distribution, a.k.a. box office bombs), both of them horse-operas: first, *Far North*, which depicts a tale of loopy female revenge against a horse with a will of its own; and second, *Silent Tongue*, in which mystical female shamanism overwhelms a world made cynical by medicine show charlatans. Also, 1996 marked the publication of his quasi-fictional vignettes in *Cruising Paradise*, suggesting another potential route for Shepard to take, away from the collaborative crap-shoot of the performing arts. *Cruising Paradise* signalled Shepard's emergence as an economical, elliptical storyteller, especially keen in tales like 'Winging It' (a stinging account of his use of 'impulses' and 'instinct' in his role in *Homo Faber*) at making self-deprecating observations about what passes for acting in movies.

At this point, Shepard seemed ready to concede two points he used to argue against: (1) sometimes art *is* permanent, not disposable; and (2) if you show something to an audience, you should expect them to look at it; therefore, it is wise to show them only what they need to see. So Shepard, who used to aim to transpose the cinematic language of jump-cuts, flashbacks, split images, voiceovers, soundtracks, dissolves, and special effects into 'movies for the stage', now, thanks to having dealt with the specific requirements of film-making, and having found a particular narrator's voice – wry, detached, and resigned – for his short prose pieces, had become a much more meticulous playwright, interested in eliminating some of his beloved detritus, the ambling, and the rambling that he used to toss in on-stage for atmosphere and for fun.

Despite hopes to the contrary, the only new work to make it into Signature's season was *When the World Was Green (A Chef's Fable)*, the product of Shepard's most recent collaboration with Joseph Chaikin. And even this was not a world premiere. This piece had premiered at Atlanta's Seven Stage company as part of the 1996 Olympic Arts Festival, where scalpers hawked tickets to sold-out performances. Alvin Epstein, the mime and vocal gymnast who had originated the role of Lucky in *Waiting for Godot* in America, played the Old Man, the Chef whose destiny is revenge and violence as abrupt and relentless as Woyzeck's, but who seeks salvation in 'some companion', some invisible partner' at the end of the journey. Chaikin described this play as a series of interrogations in a cold prison cell where an old man, together with the young woman who questions him, 'feed an ancient hunger', and 'end the killings', making peace with the feuds of the past.

In conversation at the time of the New York production, Chaikin generously credited Shepard with much of the writing of *When the World Was Green (A Chef's Fable)*, noting that here, as with *Savage Love*, they disagreed on the title

196

(Chaikin's title is the one now in parenthesis), but many of the speeches have the resonance, rhythms, and images that call to mind Chaikin's own bell-like voice and awe-struck phrasing, a voice and phrasing that Shepard himself mimics perfectly when he gives public readings, including excerpts from *Tongues* and *Savage Love*. It was Chaikin, after all, who wrote in *The Presence of the Actor*, 'The question is how to use the voice, not to refer to a condition, but to enter it.'[3]

Since his stroke in 1984, which left him struggling with aphasia, Chaikin had directed, taught, and performed/read, but this play, which both he and Shepard saw as 'political', marked his first new written collaboration with Shepard in over a decade. In it they grapple with a question Chaikin raised in a letter to Shepard before his stroke: 'Interrogation. Interrogator', he wrote in 1983, referring to 'The Grand Inquisitor', a section from Dostoevsky's *Brothers Karamazov*. 'Who's asking and who's replying is part of the choosing of questions and replies. Still, what are questions which resonate or surprise or bring us back to human continuity? . . . To win or lose/To get into heaven/or not.'[4]

On the back of Chaikin's 1983 letter, Shepard's notes mention 'stranded' characters. How appropriate, then, that book-ending a double bill with *When the World Was Green (A Chef's Fable)* at the Signature Theatre was *Chicago*, one of Shepard's first plays, dating back to 1965, a reverie of a character stranded in a bathtub. Chaikin directed this revival, for it was a sentimental favourite of his, a reminder of simpler times gone by, when a character could be named simply after the actress who inspired her creation. It is also what Shepard used to call one of his 'cavorting' plays, an image and idea of character that spills across the stage. As such, it is an example of what, in *Presence of the Actor*, Chaikin says 'attracts people to the theatre': 'a kind of discomfort with the limitations of life as it is lived, so we try to alter it through a model form'.[5]

Other plays produced in that Signature season were what Houghton dubbed a 'leaner and meaner' version of *Tooth of Crime*, directed by longtime Shepard collaborator Bill Hart and with new music and lyrics supplied by T. Bone Burnett; and a triple bill including the 1983 tongue-in-cheek operetta, *The Sad Lament of Pecos Bill on the Eve of Killing His Wife*, plus two keepers from the seventies, *Action* and *Killer's Head*, which was first performed at the American Place Theatre in 1975, in its first incarnation featuring Richard Gere as the condemned man who monologizes before his electrocution; the revival featured a series of well-known actors, each playing the role for a limited number of performances. The Signature also advertised a new 'full length' play by Shepard, but this new play did not materialize until 2001.

This new play would turn out to be *The Late Henry Moss*. As Shepard has described the genesis of this play, 'Actually, I started writing the play 10 years ago [in 1992], then I put it away, sent it to the archives unfinished. Jim Houghton, who runs Signature Theatre, wanted some new material so I got a hold of it. I reread it and I still wasn't sure. Joe Chaikin [and others] liked it, so I started work on it again. It had a good first act, but I virtually rewrote that, and then I did an entirely new second act.' By that time the Signature season had ended, so after a workshop directed by Chaikin in New York, Shepard took the script to the Magic Theatre, because of his 'great history there'. Asked about the stellar casting of the premiere production, he said, 'Sean [Penn] was the very first actor I went to. I just went straight to the top. When he said yes, the rest fell into place.'[6]

What did not fall into place was critical response. The

lukewarm response to this play seems the norm now for a playwright who used to be lauded. Indeed, a similarly unenthusiastic response greeted Shepard's other new play of recent years, the 1998 Manhattan Theatre Club production of *Eyes for Consuela*, from the story 'The Blue Bouquet' by Mexico's Nobel laureate Octavio Paz. This production, directed by Steppenwolf's Terry Kinney, drew hostile sneers from critics who seem to have tired of Shepard, much as critics in the past grew tired for a while of Miller, Williams, and Albee, three other great American playwrights who earned the scorn of critics for nothing less than the crime of becoming known for a singular voice, a singular view.

In Shepard's case, with *Eyes for Consuela* that singularity of vision has to do with his consistent motifs, which appear here, once more with feeling: (1) the chasm between men and their ideas of mysterious, unforgiving women, making what he calls in *Simpatico* 'radical moves', lamenting broken pacts; (2) the wasted tourist on a bender, seeking escape, meeting up with some dangerous characters; (3) the savage potential just beneath the surface of civilization once you get off the beaten path, once you expose the otherly self beneath the mask of social behaviour; and (4) a ghostly figure as a fulcrum of action, depicted in a style indebted always subtly – and here, quite directly – to the tradition of magic realism.

Eyes for Consuela takes its hero on a 'heart of darkness' vacation. Leaving behind the failure of his marriage and a laundry list of disappointments, Henry, the world-weary, rumpled American, carries his well-worn suitcase to a hotel in the Mexican jungle. There, sleepless and agitated, he goes walking into the jungle in the dead of night, ignoring the sensible advice of the one-eyed hotel keeper. Alone in the jungle, Henry encounters a bandit with a machete. The bandit has a proposition to make. He wants to gouge out

Henry's blue eyes so that he might offer them as a sacrifice to the ghost of his own dead wife, the implacable Consuela whose still-fettered spirit, like that of the Mother in Yeats's *Purgatory*, 'animates the dead night'. In exchange for his blue eyes, which would release Consuela from her purgatory, the bandit offers Henry the possibility of a reconciliation with Henry's wife back home. What a familiar bundle old Rabbit from *Angel City* is unpacking here! In it are all the usual Shepard subjects: a 'radical move', a broken pact, the potential for a sudden burst of violence, a homesick dislocation from everyday life, and a ghost of a woman ensnaring a worn-out man with the hope of redemption. The suspense of the play revolves around the desperation of Henry, a man lost in a fable. How far gone is he? How far could he go?

Such questions aside, it is easy to take pot shots at a play like *Eyes for Consuela*, for it spurns irony. Shepard is earnest still about those implacable shape-shifting ghosts and the price they demand from desperados baffled by the demands of women.

Similarly, *The Late Henry Moss* spurns irony. Here, Shepard depicts the territory of siblings haunted by a dead father who stubbornly sticks around, his body literally present on-stage. As in Edward Albee's *Three Tall Women*, a central character here is a lively and talkative corpse. But that is where any resemblance to Albee's genteel confrontation between multiple selves ends. Rather, like a nightmare we cannot shake off, the play is recognizable but strange. It harks back to other plays by Shepard where a split psyche is objectified as two distinct siblings, or where self-fulfilment is thwarted by the weight of memory, or where an exasperating old codger refuses to stay dead. Shepard's persons of the drama here, as in many of his plays of every period, may be considered ghosts. It is set in the dilapidated cramped

Shepard setting that always proves surprisingly indestructible no matter how much wreckage occurs in the course of the action.

The Late Henry Moss depicts yet another volatile family reunion, unravels yet another mystery, and features yet another life-force woman making pronouncements about men: 'Henry Jamison Moss; Dead. Deceased. Causes unknown' is how she characterizes old Henry in an obituary he decries as premature. All this adds up to a bona fide Shepard nightmare of a homecoming to a haunted house, predators and prey circling, mayhem ensuing.

The play opens with a dreamy invocation: a tango danced by a dead man, partnering Conchalla, the Woman who may hold some answers. The play that follows, a long-winded three-hour opus, is also a tango of sorts, a series of engagements and entanglements, interrogations and accusations, embraces and releases. After the preliminary tango ends, we see Earl Moss, played in the San Francisco production by Nick Nolte, seated at his dead father's table in a New Mexico adobe hut, where he has been keeping vigil for three days, drinking and smoking; while his younger brother, Ray, played by Sean Penn in the first production, faces the dead man's body upstage and swings a wrench. Before the play's end, the brothers will engage in a brutal fight, and the loser will wipe up the floor.

In some ways, this play might also be described as a Shepardesque fishing expedition. When the play opened, Shepard himself had doubts about whether this play would fly. 'I was worried about the brother thing', he said. 'I thought, "Jesus, who wants to see this again?" '[7] The brothers have converged after a long-standing parting of the ways, and now, Ray tries to solve the mystery of the old man's death as they scratch at old wounds about the dead man's abandonment of their family. Ray and the audience

9. Sean Penn, as the suspicious 'Ray', confronts Nick Nolte as 'Earl', his hungover brother, as they hold a vigil in the kitchen of their dead father, while Cheech Marin, as 'Esteban', keeps stirring his soup in the premiere production of *The Late Henry Moss*, directed by Shepard at the Magic Theatre in San Francisco in 2000. Photo: Anne Militello.

grow suspicious about the possibility of foul play after hearing conflicting stories about the old man's death from Earl, a neighbour named Esteban who always brings soup, and a cab driver who took Henry and Conchalla on a fishing trip. The fishing trip itself, called up in a flashback, is presented as some sort of rite-of-passage after which Conchalla takes a bath on-stage. During her bath – in a scene drenched in nostalgia both for those who fondly remember Shepard's *Chicago* and for those who fondly remember Freud – Conchalla taunts Henry about the size of his fish as she seems to give birth to and then eat that little fish which she and the late Henry Moss caught on their expedition.

The play had two major productions, first directed by the

author in San Francisco with Sean Penn and Nick Nolte, and then, directed by Joseph Chaikin in New York with Ethan Hawke and Arliss Howard embodying the brothers bereft of filial connections. On both coasts, the play was a huge hit at the box office, of course, because of the star power of the performers and the event-status of the premiere. As documented in Michael Almereyda's cinéma vérité account, *This so-called Disaster: Sam Shepard Directs 'The Late Henry Moss'*, Shepard's focus in rehearsal was on the play's autobiographical resonance. The 'so-called disaster' of the documentary's title is how Shepard's father referred to the family he abandoned for a derelict life in the desert.

Watching *The Late Henry Moss* feels something like keeping a vigil. It returns to Shepard's most obsessional narrative: the homecoming of grim, ferocious, cursed brutes to a ghostly habitat; but it finally rejects Shepard's most insistent idea of performance in plays of other periods: that otherness, escape and salvation are possible through memory, fantasy, the natural world or in trance-like states. At the end of *The Late Henry Moss*, Earl is back where he started. His legacy is isolation and regret. There is no escape.

Epilogue: In America

Time and again Shepard's plays strike us with their prismatic nature and with the variety of the languages of critical discourse they invite, each one a highly structured yet personal way of entering into a dialogue with the plays themselves. Shepard is a collector of languages of the stage; his plays can embrace them all. We might even go so far as to suggest that the vector of action in his plays has to do with escaping from the perpetual prison of language, that his characters yearn for nothing less than to demolish words and to speak in 'tongues'.

A conventional literary analysis of Shepard's plays is certainly valid, for his texts are thick with myth-making and memory, and his overdetermined poetic language always rewards us with revelations about psychologized characters buoyed by the imagination, perplexed by the nuances of speech and action, and hopeful about the symbolic valence of the world they inhabit.

However, as this study has stressed, to approach Shepard's plays on their own terms, we need to recognize their essential nature as theatrical vehicles, the engine of which is performance. To sight-read Shepard's plays – that is, to experience them as compositions of time, space, and action energized by actors on-stage – textual analysis alone does not suffice.

This is not to discount Shepard's words. His characters are often, as he himself has phrased it, 'marooned with language'. His plays yield terrific sure-fire speeches for actors. Asked, while in rehearsal for *Simpatico* in 1994, how he approaches language in a Shepard play, in contrast to a play by, say, Mamet, Ed Harris replied:

> If you use it, you don't have a better pal up there than Sam's language. The rhythm that he writes in and the words he chooses to use and the way he puts them together: If you just stood up there and just said the words, you'd be fine . . . 'Sparse' is a great word [for it]. You can't run over it. But it's not supposed to be bela-bored, either. There's a rhythm to it and there's certain key words that are important: 'Used to watch a horse named Swaps trot down the fence line with his neck bowed and his tail cocked high' – if I can't say those words and conjure up, not only for myself but for the audience, some picture of something, then I'm not very good at what I'm doing. (Harris, p. 17)

We used to say that an actor is someone who wants to play Hamlet. Nowadays, auditions are veritable Shepard-fests, overrun by frenetic young actors who have prepared mono-logues from Shepard's plays. Even scholars cannot resist quoting at length from Shepard's loopy arias.

But the critical strategy here has been to chase Shepard into the 'unknown territory' of the form and felt meaning of his plays in performance. So it may be best to end by taking the playwright's cue. In the tradition of Yeats, whose plays for dancers sought to penetrate to levels of 'deep consciousness',

Shepard's project has always been somewhat mystical. His quest is to invent a theatrical non-linear counterlanguage, true only to itself, but akin to the languages of music, dance, and painting. Yeats calls tragedy 'an art of the flood' which has the potential to bring us to a 'moment of exaltation . . . of dreaming'. At this point of reverie, character evaporates. Yeats writes:

> Tragic art, passionate art, the drowner of dykes, the confounder of understanding, moves us by setting us to reverie, by alluring us almost to the intensity of trance. The persons upon the stage, let us say, greaten till they are humanity itself.[1]

Using what Joseph Chaikin called 'word music', Shepard's plays foreground pitch and rhythm, challenging the adequacy of conventional language to evoke states of emotion. Chaikin writes:

> The theatre, insofar as people are serious in it, seems to be looking for a place where it is not a duplication of life. It exists not just to make a mirror of life, but to represent a kind of realm just as certainly as music is a realm. But because theatre involves behaviour and language, it can't be completely separate from the situational world, as music can. But much passes between people in the theatre which is intuitive and not at all concrete, having nothing to do with data. It's like marking off territories in which to enter together . . . There are zones in us which know more than we think they do. The secret is knowing how to listen to them.[2]

And like dance, too, Shepard's plays require actors to articulate action kinaesthetically, to move towards the potential of transformation and surrender. As Chaikin continues, 'Our wishes are modified by what it seems possible to attain. The whole spectrum of imagination humbles itself to what is available to understand. We must unmask and be vulnerable all over again.'[3]

Shepard's language of scenography is also highly suggestive and allusive. His plays offer a field day for set and lighting designers, both of whom might begin work on his plays by posting desert-scapes by Dali and Hopper on their drawing boards. And like René Magritte's 'La Réponse Imprévue', a painting of a door with a gaping black silhouette cut through it, Shepard's plays – from *La Turista* through *Suicide in B Flat* through *Curse of the Starving Class* and through *A Lie of the Mind* to *The Late Henry Moss*, which unfolds with a father's rotting corpse upstaging the action – all tend to reposition our relationship to familiar stage pictures by means of a personal vocabulary of colour, spatial relationships, and scale. Shepard's plays direct us in new ways of seeing, positing new strategies for escape with 'no destination'.

Sam Shepard, the gentleman farmer/horseman/cult *film noir* character actor past 60, is himself now a homo faber. He prefers to labour over his prose and his screenplays (perhaps occasionally taking a break to check the day's racing forms), refining and distilling the images that are by now his personal hieroglyphs of art as 'a way to inhabit a life',[4] a way to redeem and to forgive, and a way to chart new territory.

In November 2000, 17 years after *Paris, Texas*, Shepard was once again collaborating with Wim Wenders and T. Bone Burnett on a new screenplay, with the working title *In America*. When filming was targeted for 2003, the title had become *Don't Come Knocking*. Discussing their process, Wim Wenders described how they 'try to assess a common territory, to imagine characters. To start thinking about the situations we would put them in, to dream up an itinerary.' Wenders remarks on this odd choice of phrase himself:

> The itinerary! I guess we both like being on the road so much that we never even questioned where this new story would take place: on the move. . . .
>
> We would never jump ahead. We would have no idea where our story would take us. No 'dramaturgy'. No forced ending. No storytelling recipes. No formulas. That's the way Sam will write the script, scene by scene, from now on. A process that in itself feels more like going on a journey than writing a film. I wonder whether we'll manage to write an ending this time. All I know is, like on any other real journey, being on the road is more important than arriving at the destination.[5]

In 2002, Shepard published another collection of short stories, *Great Dream of Heaven*, that stands on its own. Stories collected here would be short-changed if they were to be considered simply as glosses on Shepard's plays. The stories are like Cartier-Bresson photographs, focusing on what Cartier-Bresson called 'decisive moments', spots of time when the felt meaning of relationships is crystallized in a serendipitous composition of shadow and light.

Among the haunting epiphanies of spent, cynical narrators still capable of further disillusionment in *Great Dream of Heaven* are: a wink in 'The Remedy Man' that signals 'there might be grown men in this world who actually get a spark out of life and somehow manage to dodge the black hole my father had fallen into'; the moment in 'Conception', when 'I caught a glimpse of my dad disappearing'; a sudden cold insight in 'It Wasn't Proust', when 'I think she was just waiting for someone to come along so she could unload her whole story'; and the realization of betrayal, when 'your luck just turned and that was it' and you were forced to 'recognize the terrain . . . this panic of aloneness' in the title story. Among the many powerful images of grief, disengagement, and rue are the moment in 'Coalinga ½ Way', when 'he sees himself from a distance now, as though looking down from a great height, like the hawk's point of view'; and the moment in 'Blinking Eye' when an injured hawk suddenly attacks its rescuer, and she panics. 'She wants to break down badly. She wants to fold up completely and have all this disappear. She dances in tight circles in the middle of the empty highway.'

A standout among these stories is 'An Unfair Question', a subtle tracking of a 'very, very unhappy' man put upon by women, avoiding skirmishes in the kitchen by doing an errand and attending a party, but drawing the line when it comes to showing his shotgun to an intrusive female guest in the basement. In the huge, almost empty parking lot of Rainbow Foods, the narrator remarks upon his disengagement, how 'a sudden great feeling of freedom and aloneness swept over me'.

As we have seen in this study, over more than four decades in the theatre, some dramatic signs have become recognizably Shepard's, particularly foregrounded male figures abandoned and abandoning, beaten and flailing, rootless yet homeward bound. In *Buried Child*, Dodge scoffs and calls them 'the hopers'. At his best, Shepard's focus is on the mystical, the timeless, what he would call 'ancient stuff', the battles to dust that mark us as doomed, and the tragic emotions deeper than language. Never a playwright to harness himself to a single political stance or to a specific cause of action, Shepard keeps his eye on the horizon, depicting archetypal quests for love or fame or power or redemption.

At his best, too, Shepard reaches for the musical value of

language, for the connection between sound and sense beyond words. 'I feel that language is a veil hiding demons and angels, which the characters are out of touch with', he said early in his career, and this statement has become a touchstone in this consideration of his oeuvre. 'Their quest in the plays is the same as ours in life – to find those forces, to meet them face to face, and end the mystery. I'm pulled toward images that shine in the middle of junk.'[6]

In plays like *Tooth of Crime*, *Geography of a Horse Dreamer*, and *Seduced* – and now in the no-man's-land diner of *States of Shock*, the off-the-map last resort of *Eyes for Consuela* or the flea-bags of *Simpatico* and *The Late Henry Moss* – Shepard allows that heroes exist, usually in American pit stops, in the Gatsby ash-heap, in blindingly illuminated Edward Hopper roadside settings. 'Hopefully the greater view has to do with the land, history, time and the fabric of America', he told The *New York Times* in 2002. In reference to 'the politics of feeling' in his works, he said, 'It's the artist's obligation to convert one's experience of the time we're living into forms of expression. Otherwise, what are you doing?'[7]

If Shepard's dispossessed and possessed heroes all fall, they also soar by means of poetry and hallucinatory stage pictures. In one of Shepard's earliest off-off-Broadway plays, *Up to Thursday*, a young and callow Harvey Keitel appeared draped in a facile symbol: an American flag. More than two decades later, *A Lie of the Mind* ended with the same offbeat actor, Harvey Keitel, draped again in the American flag. The image was no longer facile; like the flag itself in the situation presented on-stage, the image had become functional, reduced to its essence. It had become organic; it had become the 'the fire in the snow' to which *A Lie of the Mind* was headed.

The same logic can be applied when approaching other familiar Shepard totems, as restless shades from his earliest work wend their ways toward stasis in another 'zone in us'. As Shepard continues to 'dream up an itinerary', the past infiltrates new work and becomes organic. Think of how the relationship in *The Rock Garden*, the stage picture of *The Holy Ghostly*, the anecdotes of *True West*, and the nagging dead father rocking in the corner of *Fool for Love* all infiltrate and resound in the endless interrogation of the 'family stuff' in *The Late Henry Moss*. Think of the fireworks of *Icarus's Mother*, how they resonate in the stylized violence of *Action*, in the domestic demolition derby of *True West*, and in the fevered pitch of the assault that shakes the walls of *Fool for Love*. When, in *States of Shock*, the bombs finally hit, and the surviving spectre of a soldier dons his gas mask, we hear the playwright's guffaw and his rueful warning: 'Lock onto an image or you'll be blown to KINGDOM COME!!'

Well, I keep seeing this stuff and it just comes a-rolling in.
And you know it blows right through me like a ball and chain.
You know I can't believe we've lived so long and are still so far apart.
The memory of you keeps callin' after me like a rollin' train. . . .

There was a movie I seen one time, I think I sat through it twice.
I don't remember who I was or where I was bound.
All I remember about it was it starred Gregory Peck, he wore a gun and he was shot in the back.
Seems like a long time ago, long before the stars were torn down.

(Lyrics to 'Brownsville Girl', by Bob Dylan
and Sam Shepard, 2001)[8]

'Silent Tongues': An Interview with Sam Shepard

[This interview took place in Virginia in August 1991. It was first published in *The Village Voice*, 4 August 1992, with a front page banner headline reading 'Sam Shepard Speaks: A Rare Interview with the Cowboy Playwright'. A shorter version appeared as ' "Emotional Territory": An Interview with Sam Shepard' in *Modern Drama*, 36 (March 1993) 1. The abbreviated version included excerpts pertaining to Shepard's theatrical style, use of stage imagery, concepts of rhythm, myth, voice and transformations, and his continuing sense of character as fluid.]

Sam Shepard feels incredibly lucky. He often says so, and he often laughs. His gift for writing is one he accepts; he never expects to run dry and will easily discard work that strikes him as gone awry; his gift has delivered him from his demons. His demons – 'actual demons' he used to feel in the air and in his life – have mercifully left him in peace. He has escaped. Shepard makes a good living as an actor now, and is more and more comfortable in that skin, but still, this

212

family man, gentleman farmer, and rodeo and racing aficionado shies away from public recognition. He has absolutely no interest in self-promotion. Throughout our lengthy interview, he never even mentioned the most recent films in which he had been featured: Volker Schlondorff's *Voyager*, a film adaptation of Max Frish's *Homo Faber*, in which he played the engineer; *Bright Angel*, a film of Richard Ford's Rock Springs stories; or *Thunderheart*, in which he co-starred with Val Kilmer. He guffawed at a stranger's mention of *Defenseless*, a romantic thriller in release at the time of our visit and in which he played a taciturn and persistent police detective.

On film Shepard cultivates the brooding, sombre, firm-jawed presence that has been his forte since *Days of Heaven* and *The Right Stuff*. But in the flesh, he exudes mischief and a relaxation of spirit. In frayed denims, with his signature widow's peak obscured by a new 'Lazy Riding' cap, Shepard sank incognito into a chair.

'Drowning in coffee' and chain-smoking, Shepard has a gritty, twangy voice that is a dead ringer for Richard Farnsworth's. He looks brittle and almost frail, ready to play the remembered father in *Fool for Love*. But even in his raggedy man getup, his hawk face and lanky frame are easy to spot. 'Aren't you Sam Shepard?' asked more than one hesitant admirer. 'Naw,' he said, moving fast out the door to a dusty pickup truck that rambles down the blacktop to the sounds of Bonnie Raitt's blues.

Trying to maintain some degree of privacy, Shepard consistently turns down requests for interviews. Even his polite refusals have become fodder for quotes. Once, when asked to be interviewed for a *Vanity Fair* profile of Jessica Lange, he declined. 'I've decided not to talk', *Vanity Fair* recounted him saying. 'I've taken too many risks in that area and been burned too many times. I'm not going to put myself out like that anymore, particularly when it has to do with something private.'

But in our interview for this book on his work, Shepard graciously talked at length about myth, character, music, food, and women in his plays; his influences in the theatre and his method of writing and revising; his work as a film director and prose writer; the Gulf War; broken pacts and emotional territory. When I told him that I had packed several blank tapes, Shepard joked, 'That's in case we really get rolling, right?' Right. 'You're going to regret this when you play it all back,' he warned, and roared with laughter. No regrets.

Apologetic whenever he hears himself sounding 'esoteric' or 'intellectual', he is, of course, both despite his poker face and laconic manner. With Shepard, famous for 'burning bridges' and 'escaping' to 'new territory', every conversation is a discovery. He is, after all, the most original and vital playwright of our age.

Shepard's first major American interview appeared in *The Village Voice* in 1975, under the headline 'The Most Promising Playwright in America Today is Sam Shepard'. He has made good on that promise. The following 1991 interview, appropriately enough, also first appeared in *The Village Voice*.

CAROL ROSEN: Starting with some of your most recent stage work, I thought the piece you did for Joseph Chaikin, *War in Heaven*, was very beautiful.

SAM SHEPARD: You know the history of that thing? We started in Boston before his stroke and did a lot of work up there and then that fell through. Then after the stroke, we just started back up again and completely redid it. I think it was the second or third week of his rehabilitation, right after that, when he still could hardly speak at all.

ROSEN: There was something so beautiful about watching him speak, because this is one of the purest voices in the theatre.

SHEPARD: Oh yes, he had a great, great voice . . . He still has enormous ability to put meaning in his voice.

ROSEN: Given Chaikin's highly specific way of working with actors, and given his importance to your work, have you as a director developed your own particular way to communicate with actors? Is there a Shepardesque actor?

SHEPARD: When I started, with the first play I ever directed in London, I was terrified of the situation because I'd never done it before. So I immediately conferred with two people who I thought were the best directors in the world. One was Peter Brook and the other was Joe [Chaikin]. When I went in, I found myself sort of trying to imitate certain things from their points of view, but discovered that it was futile, that you have to deal with the actors you've got right in front of you and find out what the experience is like: directing. You can't use a formula to approach it.

ROSEN: What kind of actor are you drawn to?

SHEPARD: I like actors who are incredibly courageous and enthusiastic. I don't like sulking actors. I don't like actors who I have to pamper or who I have to go through a big song and dance with to come at a very simple thing. I like actors who are pretty much their own person and don't need a lot of care. It's a waste of time. I'd sooner start out with somebody who already is his own person, and not only that, has a combination of enthusiasm and courage. And intelligence. I don't want to work with dumb actors. Because I've found the essence of comedy, great comedians, is intelligence. Maybe sometimes they come off very stupid, but they're the smartest actors.

ROSEN: Like Chaplin?

215

SHEPARD: Or like Buster Keaton.

ROSEN: Yes, but are there 'Shepard' actors? With a look on their faces like anything can happen?

SHEPARD: I think John Malkovich is a good example: extremely intelligent, fearless, and enthusiastic. Just does not give a shit about how this fits into somebody else's idea of what it should be, just goes for ideas that are completely off the wall. They may be wrong but he'll go for them.

ROSEN: Marlon Brando is just such an actor. In *Far North* [Shepard's debut as director of a film he had scripted], I felt you needed Marlon Brando as the father.

SHEPARD: I asked him. And he considered it but he was in bad health then.

ROSEN: I'd like to hear about your film directing.

SHEPARD: I haven't done the second one yet. It was all set to go in October but now we're delayed. I've just done one.

ROSEN: There are certain things you can do on film you can't do on stage or in a novel. There are several images in *Far North* – the loon, the shot of an eagle flying with a horse, the shot of the horse's profile turning into Katie's profile – certain images that are filmic, certain visual techniques that can't be achieved on-stage or in a novel.

SHEPARD: One thing that's great about film, I think, if you actually are lucky enough to get to make one, is the thing of parallel time, which is very difficult on-stage. I tried it in *A Lie of the Mind* to a certain extent, but it's very cumbersome. It works, but with film it's immediate. You can follow three or four stories in parallel time. It's like music – you just move into time. Or you can go to the past or the future or wherever you want. Whereas on-stage, it's much more awkward to do that kind of instantaneous time shift.

ROSEN: On-stage, flashbacks have to emerge from language.

SHEPARD: Or from some sort of standard shadow of the character in the background. Backlighting, whatever.

ROSEN: You know all the tricks, right?

SHEPARD: Well, I've been doing it for 25 years.

ROSEN: When you structure a play in an unusual way, then, you have made a conscious choice. It's not that you aren't familiar with conventional techniques. Are you aiming for particular effects?

SHEPARD: Not effects so much, it's territory, emotional territory. I am interested in effects only to the extent that they serve some purpose of emotional terrain. Developing a new style of theatre is not something I'm interested in.

ROSEN: You've used that term 'emotional territory' in the past to suggest the destination of your plays. Which of your plays do you think go there? To emotional territory.

SHEPARD: Oh, they all do.

ROSEN: All of them?

SHEPARD: Yes, but some of them do it better than the others. When you begin, your great hope is that it moves into something that is true. Sometimes that happens, sometimes it doesn't happen. Like with *Fool for Love*, it began to move into a certain kind of territory. I don't think it eventually succeeded. It became too formal toward the end. But it attempted to move into a certain kind of emotional terrain that was true to itself. It depicted itself. That's what I'm looking for – something that is its own feature.

ROSEN: It's not imitating something else.

SHEPARD: Right. Or it's not trying to represent something else. It becomes its own animal.

ROSEN: Reality is just the jumping-off point.

SHEPARD: Well, we could talk about reality forever.

ROSEN: But you are making an important distinction between art and biography.

SHEPARD: It's all real. I don't mean to be difficult, but I don't see where these distinctions lie, really, between so-called realism and super-realism and naturalism and surrealism and absurdism and – you know what I mean?

ROSEN: Pigeonholing.

SHEPARD: All of these things that have so conveniently been delineated over the years don't really seem to make any sense. And in fact, in some ways, they do nothing but curtail something from happening, which is the reason, I think, a big reason why *States of Shock* wasn't received by the critics. They couldn't find a place to put it . . . Some of them called it absurdism or . . . they couldn't fit it into anything. It was so radically different from *A Lie of the Mind*, and I guess their expectations were in that vein.

ROSEN: I think you have a really nice definition of realism in *Fool for Love*. The old man turns to this picture of Barbara Mandrell on the wall and says, 'I'm married to her in my mind. That's realism.' Or is realism just a 'lie of the mind'?

SHEPARD: No, what I'm saying is I think those definitions are fruitless, they don't get anywhere, they don't make anything new possible. All they do, really, is put a fence around something. And why is a play like *A Lie of the Mind* more realistic than a play like *States of Shock*? It doesn't make any sense. *A Lie of the Mind* isn't realistic. You've got two parallel situations going on. One guy's running around the stage in his underwear with an American flag. And somebody else is rubbing somebody's feet. Why is that considered realism? Or why should it be considered absurd? It's just . . . it is what it is.

ROSEN: Which is?

SHEPARD: I don't know. I don't have a name for it. Why should I put a name on it?

ROSEN: You called *A Lie of the Mind* a love ballad.

SHEPARD: OK, yeah.

ROSEN: And it felt like a very old story.

SHEPARD: I guess when you start something, you always kind of have a half-baked notion about what you hope it to be. But it may not go in that direction at all. It may go somewhere completely different, which isn't to say that you failed, it's just that it turns and becomes something . . . But I think one of the thrills about writing is to remain open to all its possibilities, and not to try to put a bridle on it and squeeze it down into what your notion of it is. Not to say that you lose control, but I think you have to remain open.

ROSEN: Did *Lie of the Mind* start out one way and end up another?

SHEPARD: I wrote about 11, 12 drafts of that thing. It changed, it shifted directions a lot of times. But then I discovered something in rewriting that was interesting. I would trace back to the moment where I thought it started to go wrong and then I would throw everything away up to that – past that point and start again at that moment. Sometimes it would go back 25, 30 pages. And I'd just take that and throw it away and start over.

ROSEN: *A Lie of the Mind* opened really well, with the two levels and that phone call from nowhere. I think Jake was calling his brother from nowhere. He didn't know where, somewhere on a highway, from one nowhere to another. But you never used that level of the stage again.

SHEPARD: No, we did. See, originally the play was much longer. I cut a lot out of it in production. We had a lot of scenes come out. There was one scene where he's walking up there on the highway and a couple other scenes that we cut out.

ROSEN: Of your stage plays, the only one you've adapted for film is *Fool for Love. A Lie of the Mind* would be a good candidate for film.

SHEPARD: Yes, because of that parallel time thing. Actually, Milos Forman wanted to make it into a movie. But I said no.

ROSEN: Much has been made about that eagle and tomcat story in the monologue that ends *Curse of the Starving Class*.

SHEPARD: I didn't intend it as a metaphor. It was just an image, which actually happened. I remember that happening, not exactly as it was written, but I remember that was the case. When you castrated ram lambs, there would always be a hawk or something around. And then I think later I came across a story similar to that in an old Western magazine, about an eagle. But I think it was with calf testes. I just kind of adapted it. But I didn't mean it as a metaphor. It can be taken that way, if you want. It's not about masculinity or anything like that. Unless you want it to be.

ROSEN: I'd like to ask you about all your imagery of food.

SHEPARD: [*Laughs*]

ROSEN: I can't think of a single play of yours where characters haven't been having breakfast, or boiling artichokes, or burning toast, or spilling cream of broccoli soup all over the bed, or . . .

SHEPARD: Well, it was an interesting thing, because I don't think I really discovered the meaning of it, if you want to put it that way, until I worked with Joe [Chaikin] on *Tongues*. In *Tongues* we have a little monologue about hunger, where he gets into: do you want to eat, why do you want to eat now? You know, I have a hunger. And it builds into this momentum. When we got into that, Joe started to talk about it in a way that suddenly revealed what it really was to me, I think. Because I don't think I'd really understood it before. But his sense of it was that a person's profound emptiness, the profound sense of

220

emptiness in a person's life is answered by eating in many ways. Somehow, when you eat, food fills some kind of void that's not only physical but emotional. And I think that there's something to that. People who have the hunger for anything – the hunger for drugs, the hunger for sex – this hunger is a direct response to a profound sense of emptiness and aloneness, maybe, or disconnectedness. And I think that there's some truth to that.

ROSEN: With *States of Shock* I thought you finally decided, 'I'm going to give you a food fight to end all food fights.'

SHEPARD: Yes. There were a couple of things in production which I thought were great, but then after the first night Wynn Handman hit the roof because we started getting all the cleaning bills from the front row. 'We can't have these cleaning bills.'

ROSEN: I saw it a few times and every time it was different, depending on how long it took for the banana split to melt.

SHEPARD: But John [Malkovich] would really aim it to that front row. I love slapstick comedy. I just think that if theatre loses the ability to enjoy slapstick because the audience has become too cool, then we have really cut ourselves off, we've shot ourselves in the foot.

ROSEN: There's lots of slapstick in *True West*. When Malkovich played Lee, he seemed just crazy. It was as if he was going to destroy the stage.

SHEPARD: Yes, with the golf club.

ROSEN: And then there was slapstick when the toast was hurled everywhere. Do you aim for that kind of anarchy in production?

SHEPARD: It's a controlled anarchy. It's not 'everybody go crazy and have fun'. It's really controlled. Like, for instance, when Malkovich hit his partner, Gary Sinise [who played Austin in the Steppenwolf production of *True West*], Sinise had glasses on, and Malkovich tapped his glasses with the golf club. That's controlled, that's absolute control. The character is freaking out, and the actor has the ability to be able to draw that stroke with the golf club so that he can tap his glasses like that and not hurt somebody. That's what we're looking for.

ROSEN: This is a point that was often made by Lee Strasberg at the Actors Studio.

SHEPARD: I think Strasberg ruined more actors than he helped. He set American acting back about 100 years.

ROSEN: Why do you think that?

SHEPARD: Well, because now you have this whole generation of young actors who think James Dean was where it was at. James Dean was brilliant at what he did. But he was kind of a phenomenon. He wasn't somebody you'd want to imitate. That wasn't the penultimate American actor. There is this whole kind of self-indulgent, neurotic belief that somehow the purpose for doing a play for these actors is to work out their private problems. They don't have the sense of serving the script. It's serving their own . . . unravelling their emotional problems. Which is a disaster.

ROSEN: I want to ask you about myth.

SHEPARD: You've never seen that word in my plays. It comes up after the fact.

ROSEN: In an interview you once said a myth is a lie of the mind.

SHEPARD: Yes, but our language has been so laundered that we don't . . . We can say the same word to each other and not know what we mean.

ROSEN: That's why I ask what you mean.

SHEPARD: There's myth in the sense of a lie. There's myth in the sense of fantasy. There's myth in all those senses. But the traditional meaning of myth, the ancient meaning of myth, is that it served a purpose in our life. The purpose had to do with being able to trace ourselves back through time and follow our emotional self. Myth served as a story in which people could connect themselves in time to the past. And thereby connect themselves to the present and the future. Because they were hooked up with the lineage of myth. It was so powerful and so strong that it acted as a thread in culture. And that's been destroyed. Myth in its truest form has been demolished. It doesn't exist anymore. All we have is fantasies about it. Or ideas that don't speak to our inner self at all, they just speak to some lame notions about the past. But they don't connect with anything. We've lost touch with the essence of myth.

ROSEN: Many of your characters try to connect with that essence, don't they?

SHEPARD: Fruitlessly, yes.

ROSEN: In *Buried Child*, Vince has that speech about the face reflected in the windshield. And in *Far North*, Katie has a very similar speech, tracing her lineage.

SHEPARD: Well, those instances are more in terms of just immediate hereditary things, having to do with family. But see, myth not only connects you and me to our personal families, it connects us to the family of generations and generations of races of people, tribes, the mythology of the ancient people. The same with the American Indians – they were connected to their ancestors, people they never knew but are connected to through myth, through prayer, through ritual, through dance, music, all of those forms that lead people into a river of myth. And there was a connecting river, not a fragmented river.

ROSEN: And that's gone.

SHEPARD: It's gone, yes.

ROSEN: Does Wesley attempt to create a ritual that will lead into a river of myth in *Curse of the Starving Class*? He fails.

SHEPARD: Yes, but all contemporary efforts will fail. They have to be connected to ancient stuff. They can't be just contemporary or else it will come apart. It will become a fashion show, like rap music.

ROSEN: Do you think you might write a 'musical'?

SHEPARD: What is a musical? *Guys and Gals*?

ROSEN: *Tooth of Crime* is a musical.

SHEPARD: Yes, well so is *States of Shock*. *Lie of the Mind* is a musical. It's got a lot of music in it. You don't have to have actors standing around singing to each other for it to be a musical. I think the traditional American musical is pretty hard to pull off these days. I mean, how are you going to do *that*? I haven't found a good . . . You need a good story to write a musical.

ROSEN: What was the process involved in writing the music for *States of Shock*?

SHEPARD: I worked with a composer I've worked with for a long, long time, J. A. Deane. He did some of the music for *Far North* and we worked a lot in San Francisco with the improvisational group. They did *Angel City* and all kinds of stuff. So I kind of composed it with him. He's just an incredible guy to work with. And I've worked with one of those drummers who's backstage, Joe [Joseph Sabella].

ROSEN: In terms of musical structure, do your plays end the way music ends?

SHEPARD: I hate endings. You have to end it somehow. I like beginnings. Middles are tough, but endings are just a pain in the ass. It's very hard to end stuff.

ROSEN: *Lie of the Mind* ended perfectly.

SHEPARD: Yeah, I found a good ending for that. I liked the ending of *True West*.

ROSEN: Yes, but *True West* doesn't end.

SHEPARD: No, but that's why I like it.

ROSEN: *A Lie of the Mind* ends with a silhouette, one of those images that Peter Brook talks about in *The Empty Space*.

SHEPARD: Yes, I finally discovered an ending for that. Endings are so hard. Because the temptation always is a sense that you're supposed to wrap it up somehow. You're supposed to culminate it in something fruitful. And it always feels so phony when you try to wrap it all up.

ROSEN: That's why it seems more like music, because music is not supposed to wrap it up, it's supposed to keep going in your mind.

SHEPARD: Yes, I think that's the right kind of ending. That it leaves you on the next note. See, what interested me is the seven-note scale. That the first and the seventh are the same note, just an octave higher, so things are cycled. So you go through something you are really returning to – the place you began. But then you get into scales from other countries, like China or Japan, and they go on . . . What are they, 13-note scales or 21 sometimes?

ROSEN: Do you ever think about *Far North* or *A Lie of the Mind* as feminist pieces?

SHEPARD: What does that mean? What is a feminist piece? Following the feminist cause or something?

ROSEN: That they perceive the world from the point of view of women as opposed to superimposing a male view on history.

SHEPARD: To a certain extent, yes. But what became curious for me was . . . There was that certain period of time, and now I think it's actually over, or it's changed into something else, but there was a period of time when there was a kind of awareness happening about the female side of things. Not necessarily women but just the female force in nature becoming interesting to people. And it became more and more interesting to me because of how that female thing relates to being a man. You know, in yourself, that the female part of one's self as a man is, for the most part, battered and beaten up and kicked to shit just like some women in relationships. That men themselves batter their own female part to their own detriment. And it became interesting from that angle – as a man, what is it like to embrace the female part of yourself that you historically damaged for one reason or another? So from that point of view, it was interesting to me. But not from the cultural feminist point of view because I don't really understand that. I would never try to be a spokesman for it.

ROSEN: Starting with Emma in *Curse of the Starving Class*, you create some really vibrant women characters. And in *A Lie of the Mind* and in *Far North*, you explore the female side of character, even in the men.

SHEPARD: I felt that too. That was one of the big changes for me in those few pieces, that the women suddenly took on a different light than they had before. Because before it felt so sort of overwhelmed by the confusion about masculinity, about the confusion about how these men identify themselves. That sort of overwhelmed the female. There wasn't even any room to consider the female, because the men were so fucked up. You spent the whole play trying to figure out what these men were about, who had no idea themselves. But then, when the women characters began to emerge, then something began to make more sense for the men, too.

ROSEN: To explore the 'female side of things', did you ever think of doing *True West* with women? Two sisters?

SHEPARD: No. People get funny ideas about writers, like, for instance, Beckett stopped a production of *Endgame* that was a black production. He didn't stop it because he's a racist, he stopped it because he wrote it with a certain inclination. And to cast it black, regardless of how good the actors are, is going to completely throw something else into it. He's just protecting his play. I wouldn't want to see *True West* done by women because it's a scam on the play, it's not the play. I don't have anything against women. I'm just telling you it would distort the play.

ROSEN: Your plays have a lot of broken pacts. In *Fool for Love*, May has to break the pact in order to escape. *A Lie of the Mind* has a pact that can't be broken. The premise of *Paris, Texas* is a broken pact. And in *Far North*, there's a pact between the daughter and the father, which is really a one-way pact. I ask you, as you once asked Bob Dylan, do you believe in a pact?

SHEPARD: I think we don't really know anymore what a pact is. That's another thing that's been lost, along with myths. If you make a pact, you're suddenly cut off from the whole territory of so-called independence. Which is the reason a lot of people don't want to get married, or when they do get married, they make a contract. They don't make a pact, they make a contract, so that one can't sue the other. Well, a contract isn't a pact. A pact is something that has to do with something *felt*. In order to have a pact, you have to know that both of you feel the same thing. It's very difficult because hardly anybody knows it.

ROSEN: In your plays there are a lot of presumed pacts.

SHEPARD: Broken, yes. But there are even pacts of friendship. They don't have to be between men and women necessarily. It has to do with honour, an exchange of honour in the real sense. You don't betray each other in any way. Not just sexually, but any way.

ROSEN: Who breaks the pact in *States of Shock*?

SHEPARD: Well, I'm not sure there ever was an actual pact made between the two of them, but the betrayal is definitely on the side of the father. There's no such thing as a one-sided pact, so you would both have to know about it or it ain't a pact.

ROSEN: In some of your plays there are one-sided pacts. In *Far North* the father demands that Katie keep her end of a pact she never agreed to.

SHEPARD: Kind of a deal, yes.

ROSEN: Yes. In *Paris, Texas* there's a one-sided pact the wife rejected. Characters presume they have a pact when they don't.

SHEPARD: 'Everything is Broken' – Dylan. It's a great tune.

ROSEN: How does your work with Chaikin feed your other work?

SHEPARD: It's a long story. For years I hung around with Joe in the Open Theatre, but for a long time I never actually worked with him. I just listened and sat in on sessions and was greatly influenced by what he had to say, particularly about the relationship between the audience and the stage. These were notions that I hadn't really considered strongly before, because I was so wrapped up in my writing that, for some reason, I was pushed off into the world of writing a play and kind of disregarding the aspect of the audience. Which is a grave mistake, I think. What are we doing to an audience? What's an audience doing to us? What do we want to have done and how are we being influenced back and forth? So I think that was the first big idea that galvanized me to him as a theatre person. Then much later, I got lucky enough to work with him, and to write and direct – and the music and all the rest of it. Then we just kind of moved into a kind of agreement about how to work.

228

ROSEN: Does it affect the way you create characters? Or think about character?

SHEPARD: To some extent, yes. But it also affected the way I thought about play, the plays, the whole . . . I mean, one of the great things he said to me when we'd just started to do *Tongues*, the first time we'd worked directly together, was, he says, 'You know, it doesn't have to be a play'.

ROSEN: What would you call it?

SHEPARD: A bunch of monologues. It can be a presentation. It can be something not pretending to be a play. It's just something between an audience and a performer. And we don't even have to call it a performance piece. You don't have to call it anything.

ROSEN: In *Angel City* and in other plays, you sometimes leave characters, as you've put it, 'marooned with language', isolated with long reveries of transformation.

SHEPARD: Yes, that whole severe break with so-called naturalism happened back there. And I think it was a healthy thing. Why should we be anchored to these notions of Eugene O'Neill and all this burden of having your character be believable from the outside in terms of the artist saying, well, he really is in a living room serving tea to his mother. And he's really talking the way he would be talking in real life. What the hell is that? Where is that going to take us? Why doesn't he pour the tea on her head and start screaming and carrying on, climbing walls, and then come back and sit down and . . . You know what I mean?

ROSEN: Why not just jump through the wall?

SHEPARD: Yes, or whatever. And I think that a lot of those breaks back then had to do with incredible frustration, the straitjacket of that kind of theatre that we had been told was great theatre.

ROSEN: Dead theatre.

SHEPARD: Dead theatre, yes. Living room theatre.

ROSEN: Is character larger than personality?

SHEPARD: Well see, I don't think character really has anything to do with personality. I think character and personality are two entirely different animals. Really. When you get right down to it. See, I think character is something that can't be helped, that can't be . . . It's like destiny. And maybe it includes personality, but personality is something so frivolous compared to character, they're not even in the same ballpark. Personality is putting on a different hat.

ROSEN: But character is permanent?

SHEPARD: Character is an essential tendency. It can be covered up, it can be messed with, it can be screwed around with, but it can't be ultimately changed. It's like the structure of our bones, the blood that runs through our veins.

ROSEN: Is character the same for a whole family?

SHEPARD: There is a character, characteristics, if you want to call them that, that run through families that are undeniable. So many people get screwed up because they try to deny them, try to say, 'I'm not like my father, I'm not like my mother, I'm not going to be this way, I'm not going to be that way.' When, in fact, there's nothing you can do about it [*laughs*].

ROSEN: So many of your plays revolve around the hopelessness of getting out of that bind. Unless a character embraces that family character, or accepts it, he is doomed.

SHEPARD: Yes, I think so. I think that there is no escape, that the wholehearted acceptance of it leads to another possibility. But the possibility of somehow miraculously making myself into a different person is a hoax, a futile game. And it leads to insanity, actually [*laughs*].

ROSEN: In the plays?

SHEPARD: No, in people. People go insane trying to deny what they really are.

ROSEN: I want to know about angels.

SHEPARD: What do you want to know about angels?

ROSEN: Sometimes you write about angels, and you often allude to them. You wrote an angel's monologue for Chaikin.

SHEPARD: Well, you know there is a hierarchy of angels. It's been around a long, long time. And there are all kinds of angels. Just like there are all kinds of demons.

ROSEN: It's not a facetious question.

SHEPARD: No, I'm not answering flippantly, it's just that I'm not an authority on the subject, but I do know that there's considerable historical evidence that there are these creatures, or this world exists, the world of angels and demons.

ROSEN: Where would this world be in your plays? How would it affect the plays?

SHEPARD: Well, just that it's a part of the world of the character's notions about good and evil, his notions about fate and chance and this, that, and the other. Or his lack of that. Certain characters might be surrounded by certain things. I don't mean to sound esoteric [*laughs*] but . . . influences. It's just influences, we're influenced.

ROSEN: The characters are influenced?

SHEPARD: Um hum. Just like we are.

ROSEN: By angels and demons. Which are real forces.

SHEPARD: Well, I think so, yes. I think forces exist that –

ROSEN: In many of your plays, such as *A Lie of the Mind*, characters fight with these internalized angels and demons. And now you've written a character in *The War in Heaven* who is an angel.

SHEPARD: Yes. To me, it [the angel] is a great character for Joe [Chaikin], because, particularly nowadays, it's very

231

difficult to write a hero or to write a good person or a person pure of heart or a person with spiritual integrity or whatever you want to call it. It's very difficult to write that and not have it be the corniest thing on earth. So the only way to take it was to this absolute extreme – the world of angels. And I thought it would be very risky to try the premise of an angel crashing to earth. So that's where . . . I thought if any actor could play it, it would be Joe, because he has that amazing innocence about him.

ROSEN: Do you think about heroes the way you did when you wrote all those plays about the hero corrupted by his society and facing danger?

SHEPARD: Did I write those? [*Laughs*]

ROSEN: In *Geography of a Horse Dreamer* the hero's got to do what he's got to do because he gets kidnapped and forced to serve. And in *Angel City* –

SHEPARD: Yeah. The exploited artist.

ROSEN: Do you still have that feeling about the exploited artist as hero?

SHEPARD: Not to the extent that I want to defend it anymore. I've grown out of that phase of being outraged that the artist isn't treated with real respect anymore. It doesn't matter to me now. It did then.

ROSEN: Many plays recall *Angel City*, plays about the artist devoured by movies.

SHEPARD: Yes, but they've been singing that song forever. What was the great . . . *Day of the Locust*? It was such a brilliant book. There's no reason . . . I mean, that book says the whole thing about Hollywood and dealing with Hollywood and dealing with the machinery of it. And the thing of it is, Hollywood is impervious to criticism. You cannot puncture the skin of that mechanism. Even more so today. It's like steel armour. You can't even get next to it, because it's so completely locked up, guarded by the mechanism.

ROSEN: I thought you got around that with *Paris, Texas* by working with Wim Wenders, a German film-maker who sees America the way you do. You don't see America the way an American does. You step away from it and look at it from a distance.

SHEPARD: [*Laughs*] Right. It's true Europeans, particularly Germans, have a very critical eye – not a critical eye but an eye that *embraces* a certain thing about America that I don't think Americans have. For the most part, I think Americans have lost compassion for their own country.

ROSEN: I'd like to know about this movie you're working on. What is the title?

SHEPARD: *Silent Tongue.*

ROSEN: Which of course I would recognize as one of your titles.

SHEPARD: Yeah, I'm running out of titles.

ROSEN: Is it true that you used to make up titles first and plays later?

SHEPARD: I did that a couple of times. *Unseen Hand.* I just liked the title so much I wrote a play to fit the title.

ROSEN: And *Tooth of Crime?* Is that from Mallarmé?

SHEPARD: Yeah. Actually, I may have had that title before the play, I'm not sure. *The Unseen Hand* – I know for sure I had the title first.

ROSEN: What is *Silent Tongue* about?

SHEPARD: It's about a woman who had her tongue cut out for lying. It takes place in 1876, and there's a medicine show. And a half-breed woman who has her tongue cut out. I don't want to say too much about it. Suffice it to say it's a period piece.

ROSEN: A great deal has been written about medicine shows as popular entertainment.

SHEPARD: I've researched a lot of it. It's a pretty amazing era. It lasted up into the '50s, which is incredible, before it disappeared. The mid-1800s to the 1950s.

ROSEN: Touring America.

SHEPARD: Wagons and all that stuff. It says something about Americans. There's a cure somewhere and the cure resides in some kind of magic potion, a miracle. The gullibility of it is incredible.

ROSEN: Yes, the magic solution. What did you think of Jack Gelber calling you 'the playwright as shaman'?

SHEPARD: It's very flattering, but the problem I find with that kind of stuff is that in a way it's embarrassing, because having come across some of this stuff for real, you realize how far you personally are, say, from real shamanism or real magic or real wisdom, that kind of stuff.

ROSEN: In many of your plays, characters try to come up with 'potions'. In *Fool for Love*, Eddie's coming up with something that's going to fix everything.

SHEPARD: Yeah, it fails.

ROSEN: But in *Silent Tongue* are you dealing with characters who are real shamans? Concocting real potions?

SHEPARD: Oh, no, those guys were all bogus. None of those medicine show guys were for real. They sold snake oil and actually the mixture was 70 per cent alcohol. So people got drunk and felt great, and the next day woke up and discovered they'd been duped and the medicine show was out of town. But no, none of those guys were shamans in any sense of the word. They were just charlatans. Those were sideshows.

ROSEN: But your title character – is she genuine, but involved with this fake world?

SHEPARD: She was and then got out of it.

ROSEN: And can she really cure people?

SHEPARD: No. It's not about . . . She's not a holy person.

ROSEN: What brought about *States of Shock*? Where did that come from?

SHEPARD: When that war started [in Iraq] – I was in Kentucky when the war opened. I was in a bar that I go to a lot down there because it's a horsemen's bar. Normally that bar is just a din of conversation and people having a great time and talking about horses and this, that, and the other. And I walked in the bar and it was stone silence. The TV was on, and these planes were coming in, and suddenly . . . It just seemed like doomsday to me. I could not believe the systematic kind of insensitivity of it. That there was this punitive attitude – we're going to just knock these people off the face of the earth. And then it's devastating. Not only that, but they've convinced the American public that this was a good deed, that this was in fact a heroic fucking war, and welcome the heroes back. What fucking heroes, man? I mean, they bombed the shit out of these people. They knocked the stew out of them over there with bombing and bombing and bombing. The notion of this being a heroic event is just outrageous. I couldn't believe it. I still can't believe it. I can't believe that, having come out of the '60s and the incredible reaction to Vietnam, that voice has all but disappeared. Vanished. There's no voice anymore. This is supposed to be what America's about? This fucking military . . . I had just spent eight weeks on the Pine Ridge Indian Reservation in South Dakota, the most devastated culture in America – 80 per cent alcoholism and the poverty rate is just . . . You can't even believe the poverty [Shepard was there on location filming *Thunderheart*]. And watching these F-104s and F-15s, these fighter jets flying across every day to Ellsworth air base. I don't know. You really start to wonder.

ROSEN: So that's how the play started?

SHEPARD: *States of Shock*, yes. I just got so outraged by the whole hoax of it, and the way everything is choked down and censored in the media. Frightening situation.

ROSEN: But *States of Shock* doesn't only respond to the Gulf War.

SHEPARD: No. I wanted to create a character of such outrageous, repulsive, military, fascist demonism that the audience would recognize it, and say, 'Oh, this is the essence of this thing'. I thought Malkovich came pretty close to it. Just creating this monster fascist.

ROSEN: What was the purpose of all that stage business about balancing?

SHEPARD: Just a way to get the waitress across the stage.

ROSEN: He [the Colonel played by Malkovich] also had a lot of bits about rhythm and timing and . . .

SHEPARD: Oh yes, manipulating is a better word. Manipulating things. He knew how to manipulate – manipulate the public, manipulate machinery, whatever.

ROSEN: But the play didn't do that. Do you think the play succeeded in getting audiences galvanized against the war?

SHEPARD: No, not at all. I don't know what happened. It only succeeded in pissing off the critics, it seems like. [*Laughs*] That was part of its purpose. I don't know.

ROSEN: Do you think you'll ever offer another playwrights' workshop like the ones you led in Mill Valley?

SHEPARD: Yes, actually, I do want to do something like that again. I'm not sure when or where, you know, but I wouldn't mind working with writers.

ROSEN: Why have you created this wall around yourself and made yourself so inaccessible?

SHEPARD: Well, you have to protect a certain territory. Otherwise, it becomes exploited and taken away from you.

ROSEN: But I don't mean the private self, I mean the public self – the artist, the writer, the director.

SHEPARD: Same thing, same thing. I mean, particularly with your work, you have to protect the air around it. Otherwise, it gets co-opted and taken over. It's not a paranoid statement. Writers are isolated individuals, for good reason.

ROSEN: How do your plays take shape?

SHEPARD: Every single one of them comes about in a different way. I don't systematically sit down every morning and write three hours and then have a sandwich and then write for another two hours. I never have been able to work like that. If I have a piece of work that begins to have momentum and force, then I'll pay attention to it and I'll work very systematically. But I don't just sit down and arbitrarily punch keys on the typewriter, hoping for the best. I think that's a lost cause, for me anyway. I've never had any luck with that.

ROSEN: So you wait for the work to announce itself?

SHEPARD: To a certain extent, yes. And then it happens differently each time. Sometimes it turns in a different way or another idea comes out and you begin something else and abandon that one and go off to this one. So right now I'm working on a book, two books.

ROSEN: Fiction?

SHEPARD: Yes. I've got one up to 200 pages and the other more than 30 pages.

ROSEN: Somebody said he started out being a novelist, but then he noticed that when you type a play, it takes a lot of space on the page for the name of the character.

SHEPARD: Who was *that* person? [*Laughs*]

ROSEN: Right, *you* said that.

SHEPARD: You fill up the pages faster. Yeah, it's true, dialogue flies [*laughs*].

237

ROSEN: But now you're writing novels.

SHEPARD: Well, I wouldn't call them novels. They're books, you know, just books. I don't know if they're novels.

ROSEN: You mean like *Motel Chronicles*?

SHEPARD: No. One of them is an actual long story. It's about 150 pages. Might be a novel. And the other one is a kind of chronicle, but it's mixed with fiction and fact. I don't know what you would call them.

ROSEN: Where do you stand on the question of an artist's privacy in regard to notebooks and first drafts being made available?

SHEPARD: It depends on what people are interested in. Are they interested in the life of the artist or the artist's work?

ROSEN: Sometimes one is interested in the artist's process.

SHEPARD: I doubt that very seriously. I think most people are just interested in gossip. The process has nothing to do with it. In fact, I don't think anybody has ever been able to objectively explain process. How can you explain process? Did you ever read those interviews – *Paris Review* did a whole great series of interviews – the one with Céline in it? The Céline one just knocks me out. The end of it is they're sitting on some park bench somewhere. The interviewer says something to him about, 'Well, how are you going to go on from here?' Céline turns to him and says, 'I just want to be left alone.' [*Laughs uproariously*] I just want to be left alone.

ROSEN: Are there playwrights working today whom you admire?

SHEPARD: I don't know any playwrights.

ROSEN: You don't pay attention to anybody else's work?

SHEPARD: I don't know playwright one. I don't hang out with playwrights. I can't say I dislike them, but for the most part theatre doesn't interest me. I like writing plays because they have so much movement, there's so much

238

possibility of movement, and language moves. But I'm not a theatre buff. Most theatre bores the hell out of me. But I do like the possibilities. I think of all the forms that we've got now, probably theatre has more possibilities than anything else. Really. Of real experimentation and real surprise and real emotional contact with an audience. More than movies. Movies have just become a kind of hallucination. An excuse to go hallucinate, like drugs. Movies are a dream world. Eat popcorn and dream. But theatre still has that very exciting possibility because you can put all the elements in there. You've got music and actors and so many possibilities. And language: language can do so many things.

ROSEN: Are movies anti-language?

SHEPARD: Yes. They don't want to know about language. Nobody listens anymore. Listening is not part of the programme.

ROSEN: When you direct a film, what is your attitude toward language?

SHEPARD: Oh, well, I intend . . . I mean, I wrote *Silent Tongue* as a screenplay. It's intended to be filmed. It's not an adaptation of anything. So a good screenplay is intentionally a visual event. That's what the medium is about. So you do tend to shy away from dialogue. Whereas in plays, entirely composed of dialogue, that's the meat and potatoes of it.

ROSEN: Language is one of the strongest elements of your plays. When you write a movie, you're really working without a net.

SHEPARD: Yes, although I think there's a lot of exciting possibilities with film. I'm not saying it's without possibilities. One great thing about theatre, too, is the nuts and bolts aspect of it. You're just working at a very physical level. Like when we were doing *States of Shock*, we were

239

trying to figure out a good whipping sound for the drummers in the back. And everybody was checking out everybody's belts. People would go, 'Try this one.' Whap! 'That's pretty good. Let's try that one over there.' And that's what it's about, you know – okay, let's try everybody's belt. The light technician, 'Do you have a good belt?' Till we get the right sound. That kind of thing. You never in a million years see that in a movie. You go to the prop person who's got 20 different varieties of belts hanging there. But you wouldn't be going around asking the caterer to take his belt off.

ROSEN: You never go to the theatre at all?

SHEPARD: Oh no. But I've been to a lot of rodeo lately [*laughs*].

ROSEN: Do you romanticize the rodeo?

SHEPARD: Romanticize it? Well, I suppose, to a certain extent. But on the other side, you can't romanticize it if you *do* it.

ROSEN: The rodeo is not a representation of anything. It's real.

SHEPARD: Yes. If you rope an 800-pound steer and dally off your saddle on him and pull all that steer, and the rope comes across your leg, it's real.

ROSEN: Should theatre be real, and dangerous, in the same way?

SHEPARD: Well, to a certain extent. You don't want to hurt anybody. I don't think that's what Artaud meant by 'the theatre of cruelty'. But on the emotional level, there can be a comparable experience without hurting anyone.

ROSEN: On the emotional level, are you aiming toward Artaud's idea of theatre exteriorizing latent cruelty? Your plays do put audiences in touch with things they don't think about when they think about themselves as civilized.

240

SHEPARD: Yes, hopefully, although it sounds highfalutin' when you couch it with Artaud, because Artaud has become so misused over the years. He's become an excuse for a whole kind of theatre that he probably wouldn't endorse if he was alive today. He'd laugh at it. Or maybe he wouldn't; I don't know because I never met the man.

ROSEN: Are you aware of all the playwrights who have been influenced by you?

SHEPARD: No. Well, I mean, I heard tell of it. But see, I don't follow theatre so I don't know.

ROSEN: You've had a tremendous impact on the way people shape plays, and the kind of language and energy that they think is possible on-stage.

SHEPARD: It's an interesting thing, though, that question of energy. Because I think there is a certain capacity, and if you try to push past that capacity you shoot yourself in the foot. I think there's only a certain *amount* of energy that can be contained on-stage. I think it's finite. I don't think that it just goes on forever. A lot of the time, the mistake I see is that there is an effusiveness that doesn't have a focus. So it becomes just chaotic. It needs to have a leash on it to a certain extent so that it can do something. Otherwise, it's just like a force with no handle.

ROSEN: In *Fool for Love*, when Ed Harris was lassoing bedposts, he was very focused, very contained.

SHEPARD: Yes, but full of energy. Right to the brim. Malkovich is the same way.

ROSEN: Why do you act? Is it just a way to raise money?

SHEPARD: Actually, it's become more interesting over the years, I must say. At first, I was really disappointed in film acting. Not only by its possibilities, but by mine. I felt very limited. I felt very intimidated, and unable to take many risks. Now I feel like more and more I can . . . I'm actually beginning to find a way to make an expression of character and to follow something that wasn't possible when I started out. I don't know how that's happened, but it's evolved over the years of doing it, I guess, just from practice. It's become more interesting. But still, the difficult part of film acting is not the acting, but the hanging around and the waiting and all the time that's burned up.

ROSEN: Becoming an actor made you famous in a way that you could not have anticipated. Could becoming a movie star have been a bad move on your part as an artist?

SHEPARD: Yeah, it may have been, yeah. But life has a lot of surprises.

ROSEN: Ironically, Eddie in *Fool for Love* is really the best role you've ever had.

SHEPARD: I suppose. Yes.

ROSEN: If you were playing him now, would you do it differently?

SHEPARD: I don't know. I was so confused during that time about what exactly I was doing. See, originally, Jessie [Jessica Lange] and I were supposed to do it, with Robert Altman. And then she decided, because she was pregnant at the time, that it would probably be better not to. And I just said, well, I'd go ahead with it even though I was sort of halfhearted since she wasn't going to do it. I would never want to redo it. But on the other hand, it wasn't bad. It was just kind of ill thought-out. Like, for instance, Altman wanting all the flashbacks to be random and disconnected and deliberately confusing.

ROSEN: Do you get some kind of pleasure out of acting?

SHEPARD: Well, I'm not saying pleasure, but it's starting to become more interesting, the whole process of being able to contact the character and to manipulate your concentration and your attention and move into areas that are more risky and that have real feeling and stuff like that. I couldn't do that when I first started. All I could do was sit and hang onto the saddle horn and go.

ROSEN: Do you think you might ever act on-stage again?

SHEPARD: No, I doubt it. Unless it was a very, very particular situation and it lasted a very short time. I did a play with Patti Smith, *Cowboy Mouth*. I think we did it one night. A one-night stand.

ROSEN: Are you still fond of any of your early plays?

SHEPARD: Yes, I like *Action*. And I like *Rock Garden*, all right. The funny thing about *Rock Garden* is, if you look at that play, it's surprising even to me because when I look at it, I see the germ right in that little play of a whole lot of different things. The germ is in that play of many, many to come, much more so than *Cowboys*, for instance, or a lot of those other plays. *Rock Garden* was sort of the beginning of something that reverberated from there, which I didn't realize at the time.

ROSEN: And why are you fond of *Action*?

SHEPARD: Because it was such a complete breakaway from anything I'd done before. It's completely in another domain. The play itself surprised me, the way it moved and the idiosyncrasy of it and the way it shifted. I thought it was a satisfying combination of slapstick and something more serious. I don't know what you call it, realism or something like that.

ROSEN: *Action* has that haunting speech about the moths.

SHEPARD: The moths and the breaking of the chair and the clothes on the clothesline and things like that. And I think it's an interesting play. And, in fact, *States of Shock* is probably an outcome of that play, in form, in structure, in its quirkiness, its instant changes. Things like that.

ROSEN: And do you have any fondness for *Tooth of Crime*?

SHEPARD: To some extent. But I think it's dated now. A lot of that early stuff I couldn't really say was dated. But *Tooth of Crime* seems too topical. The combat thing is interesting, the clash of forces, but then the whole thing about pop culture kind of turns me off. There's this pretence of being a commentary on pop culture.

ROSEN: There's a scene in *Tooth of Crime* where Hoss is talking to his father, and it connects . . . I suppose everything connects.

SHEPARD: Yes, whether you've connected it or not is another story, but I think it all *is* connected by itself.

ROSEN: What are you reading lately?

SHEPARD: Oh, I read *The Thoroughbred Times* [*laughs*]. I was reading a lot of short fiction and some history, about the Plains country, the grassland country.

ROSEN: What are you doing next?

SHEPARD: I'm working on these two books. It's a huge amount of work because one of them is totally handwritten and I've got to retype the whole thing. And the other one . . . They both basically have got to be reworked with the machines.

ROSEN: So you revise it as you type?

SHEPARD: Yes, as I go. And then also, when I start typing, there's new writing that goes into that, that isn't necessarily in the handwritten version.

ROSEN: Is it a very lonely process?

SHEPARD: Oh, I don't feel it as being that. I've heard writers complain about that, but I don't think they're writers. That's what writing is, an act of isolation. You either accept it or you don't. I don't think there's any complaining about it.

ROSEN: I've read that you've wished you would never have to write another play.

SHEPARD: That was a little period I was going through.

ROSEN: But not anymore? You no longer feel it's some kind of curse: you have to write and you would like to be free of it?

SHEPARD: No, not necessarily. Because see, the thing that's interesting about writing is if it really is something that you get in your blood, it keeps opening and opening and opening. It doesn't shut down. I think to a certain extent the play thing has narrowed. But then there's other kinds of writing that have opened up as a result of that narrowing down. And you get involved in that and then maybe, who knows, the playwriting all comes back up again. You can't really predict that stuff.

ROSEN: You can't turn your back on a gift like that.

SHEPARD: It's not only a gift, it's a kind of way of life. I feel lucky that I have something like that where experience can be shuffled back into another form, as opposed to not having a form or structure to put an expression into. I suppose you do that with anything, but with writing . . . It's really lucky to be a writer, I think.

Appendix I
Chronological List of First Productions of Stage Plays and Screenplays, First Publications of Prose

Stage Plays

Cowboys
First production: Theatre Genesis, New York, 16 Oct 1964. *Cowboys # 2* (revised version). First production: Mark Taper Forum, Los Angeles, Nov 1967, dir. Edward Parone. Later productions: The Old Reliable, New York, 12 Aug 1967; Pindar of Wakefield, London, July 1972, dir. Kenneth Chubb; New York, 1973.
Publication: (*Cowboys #2*): in *'Mad Dog Blues' and Other Plays; in 'Angel City', 'Curse of the Starving Class' and Other Plays* (Applause, 1981); and in *Collision Course*, ed. Edward Parone (New York: Random House, 1968).

The Rock Garden
First production: Theatre Genesis, St Mark's Church in the Bowery, New York, 10 Oct 1964. Excerpt produced in *Oh! Calcutta!* New York, 1969; London, 1970.
Publication: in *'Mad Dog Blues' and Other Plays*: and in *'Angel City', 'Curse of the Starving Class' and Other Plays*. Excerpt in *Oh! Calcutta!* (New York: Grove 1969). Film produced by Tigon, 1972.

Up to Thursday
First Production: Village South Theatre, 23 Nov 1964 and Theatre 65, Playwrights Theatre, 10 Feb 1965.
Unpublished: Typescript at the Mugar Memorial Library.

Dog
First Production: La Mama Experimental Theatre Club, New York, 10 Feb 1965.
Unpublished.

Rocking Chair
First Production: La Mama Experimental Theatre Club, New York, 10 Feb 1965.
Unpublished.

Appendix I

Chicago

First production: Theatre Genesis, St Mark's Church in the Bowery, New York, 16 Apr 1965, dir. Ralph Cook. Later productions: La Mama Experimental Theatre Club, 13 Mar 1966; Martinique Theatre, New York, 12 Apr 1966; Mercury Theatre, London, Sept 1967 (during the La Mama season); King's Head Theatre, London, 15 Aug 1972. Revived by Signature Theatre Company at the Public Theatre, New York, as part of its season devoted to plays by Shepard, 1996, dir. Joseph Chaikin.

Publication: in *Five Plays*, repr. as '*Chicago*' *and Other Plays*, with notes by Ralph Cook, and in *Eight Plays from off-off Broadway*, ed. Nick Orzel and Michael Smith (New York: Bobbs-Merrill, 1966).

4-H Club

First production: Theatre 65, Cherry Lane Theatre, New York, Sept 1965.

Publication: in '*The Unseen Hand*' *and Other Plays* (New York: Applause, 1981).

Icarus's Mother

First production: Café Cino, New York, 16 Nov 1965, dir. Michael Smith.

First London production: Open Space Theatre, Spring 1971, dir. David Benedictus.

Publication: in *Five Plays*, repr. as '*Chicago*' *and Other Plays* with notes by Michael Smith.

Fourteen Hundred Thousand

First production: Firehouse Theatre, Minneapolis, 1966, dir. Sydney Schubert Walter; recorded by National Educational Television for NET Playhouse, 1969.

Publication: in *Five Plays*, repr. as '*Chicago*' *and Other Plays*, with notes by Sydney Schubert Walker.

Red Cross

First production: Judson Poets Theatre, New York, 20 Jan 1966, dir. Jacques Levy. Later productions. Provincetown Playhouse, New York, 28 Apr 1968; Glasgow, 1969: London, 1970: King's Head Theatre, London, 15 Aug 1972.

Publication: In *Five Plays*, repr. as '*Chicago*' *and Other Plays*, with notes by Jacques Levy; in *The New Underground Theatre*, ed. Robert J. Schroeder (New York: Bantam, 1968); and in *Off-Broadway Plays 2*, ed. Charles Marowitz (Harmondsworth: Penguin, 1972).

La Turista

First production: American Place Theatre, New York, 4 Mar 1967, dir. Jacques Levy. First London production: Theatre Upstairs at the Royal Court Theatre, 19 Mar 1969.

247

Publication: *La Turista* (New York and Indianapolis: Bobbs-Merrill, 1968; and London: Faber, 1969); in *Four Two-Act Plays* (New York: Applause, 1980); and in *Seven Plays* (New York: Bantam, 1981).

Melodrama Play
First production: La Mama Experimental Theatre Club, New York, 18 May 1967, dir. Tom O'Horgan. First London production: Mercury Theatre, 11 Sept 1967 (during the La Mama season).
Publication: in *Five Plays*, repr. as '*Chicago*' *and Other Plays*, with notes by Shepard; and in '*Fool for Love*' *and Other Plays* (New York: Bantam, 1984).

Forensic and the Navigators
First production: Theatre Genesis, St Mark's Church in the Bowery, New York, 29 Dec 1967, dir. Ralph Cook. Later production: Astor Place Theatre, New York, 1 Apr 1970.
Publication: in '*The Unseen Hand*' *and Other Plays*; and in *The Best of Off-Off Broadway*, ed. Michael Smith (New York: Dutton, 1969).

The Holy Ghostly
First production: New Troupe branch of La Mama on tour, 1969, dir. Tom O'Horgan; New York, 1970. First London production: King's Head Theatre, 3 July 1973, dir. Kenneth Chubb.
Publication: in '*The Unseen Hand*' *and Other Plays*.

The Unseen Hand
First production: La Mama Experimental Theatre Club, New York, 26 Dec 1969, dir. Jeff Bleckner. Later productions: Astor Place Theatre, New York, 1 Apr 1970; Theatre Upstairs at the Royal Court, London, 12 Mar 1973, dir. Jim Sharman; revived 6 Jan 1982, redirected by Jim Sharman (transferred to Provincetown Playhouse).
Publication: in '*The Unseen Hand*' *and Other Plays*; in *The Off-Off Broadway Book*, ed. Albert Poland and Bruce Mailman (New York and Indianapolis: Bobbs-Merrill, 1972); in *Plays and Players*, May 1973, with a new introduction by Sam Shepard and 'It'll Get You in the End' by Jim Sharman; and in '*Action*' *and* '*The Unseen Hand*', with Shepard's introduction (London: Faber, 1975).

Operation Sidewinder
First production: Repertory Theatre of Lincoln Centre, New York, 12 Mar 1970, dir. Michael A. Schultz.
Publication: *Operation Sidewinder* (New York and Indianapolis: Bobbs-Merrill, 1970); in *Four Two-Act Plays* (earlier version); in *Esquire*, May 1969; and in *The Great American Life Show: Nine Plays from the Avant-Garde Theatre*, ed. John Lahr and Jonathan Price (New York: Bantam, 1974).

Appendix I

Shaved Splits
First production: La Mama Experimental Theatre Club, New York, 20 July 1970, dir. Bill Hart.
Publication: in '*The Unseen Hand*' *and Other Plays*.

Mad Dog Blues
First production: Theatre Genesis at St Mark's Church in the Bowery, New York, 4 Mar 1971, dir. Robert Glaudiini.
Publication: in '*Mad Dog Blues*' *and Other Plays*: and in '*Angel City*', '*Curse of the Starving Class*' *and Other Plays*.

Cowboy Mouth, co-authored with Patti Smith
First production: Traverse Theatre, Edinburgh, 12 Apr 1971, dir. Gordon Stewart. American premiere in a special performance at the American Place Theatre, New York, 29 Apr 1971, as an afterpiece to Shepard's *Back Bog Beast Bait*, dir. Robert Glaudini, with the following cast: Slim played by Sam Shepard, Cavale played by Patti Smith, Lobster Man played by Robert Glaudini. First London production: King's Head Theatre, 11 July 1972, dir. Kenneth Chubb.
Publication: in '*Mad Dog Blues*' *and Other Plays*; in '*Angel City*', '*Curse of the Starving Class*' *and Other Plays*; and in '*Fool for Love*' *and Other Plays*.

Back Bog Beast Bait
First production: American Place Theatre, 29 Apr 1971, dir. Tony Barsha. Later production: in *Shepard Sets*, La Mama Experimental Theatre Club, New York, Nov 1984, dir. George Ferencz, music by Max Roach.
Publication: in '*The Unseen Hand*' *and Other Plays*.

The Tooth of Crime
First production: Open Space Theatre, London, 17 July 1972, dir. Walter Donohue and Charles Marowitz. Later productions: Royal Court Theatre, 5 June 1974, dir. Jim Sharman; McCarter Theatre, Princeton, NJ, 2 Nov 1972, dir. Lou Criss. Environmental version of the play presented (without playwright's sanction) by the Performance Group at the Performing Garage, New York, dir. Richard Schechner, 8 Mar 1973; this production was filmed. *Tooth of Crime, new version subtitled Second Dance,* was revived as part of the Signature Theatre season devoted to plays by Sam Shepard, Lucille Lortel Theatre, 1 Nov 1996, dir. Bill Hart.
Publication: in '*The Tooth of Crime*' *and* '*Geography of a Horse Dreamer*' (New York: Grove, 1974): in *Four Two-Act Plays*; and in *Seven Plays* (New York: Bantam, 1981).

Nightwalk, a 'collective work' of the Open Theatre, to which Shepard, along with Jean-Claude van Itallie and Megan Terry, was a 'contributing writer'
First production: Open Theatre, New York, 1972. First London production: Round House, June 1973 (during Open Theatre season).

Publication: in *Three Works by the Open Theatre*, ed. Karen Malpede (New York: Drama Book Specialists, 1974).

Blue Bitch
First production: BBC television, Open House, Spring 1973; New York, 1973. Unpublished.

Geography of a Horse Dreamer
First production: Theatre Upstairs at the Royal Court Theatre, London, 21 Feb 1974, dir. Sam Shepard. First US production: Yale Repertory Theatre, New Haven, CT, 8 Mar 1974, dir. David Schweizer
Publication: in *'The Tooth of Crime' and 'Geography of a Horse Dreamer'*; in *Four Two-Act Plays*; and in *'Fool for Love' and Other Plays*.

Man Fly, a play with music in two acts, adapted from Christopher Marlowe's *Dr. Faustus*, 1974 (?)
Unproduced.
Unpublished: typescript at the Bancroft Library, University of California at Berkeley.

Little Ocean
First production: Hampstead Theatre Club, London, 25 Mar 1974, dir. Stephen Rae.
Unpublished: typescript at the Mugar Memorial Library, Boston University.

Action
First production: Theatre Upstairs at the Royal Court Theatre, London, Sep 1974 dir. Nancy Meckler. Later productions: American Place Theatre, New York, 1975, dir. Nancy Meckler; Magic Theatre, San Francisco, 1975, dir. Sam Shepard.
Publication: in *'Action' and 'The Unseen Hand'*; in *'Angel City'*, *'Curse of the Starving Class' and Other Plays*; and in *'Fool for Love' and Other Plays*.

Killer's Head
First production: American Place Theatre, New York, 1975, dir. Nancy Meckler. Revived by the Signature Theatre Company at the Public Theatre, New York, 1996.
Publication: in *'Angel City'*, *'Curse of the Starving Class' and Other Plays*.

Angel City
First production: Magic Theatre, San Francisco, 2 July 1976, dir. Sam Shepard. Later productions: McCarter Theatre, Princeton, NJ, March 1977, dir. Michael Kahn; in *Shepard Sets*, La Mama Experimental Theatre, New York, Nov 1984, dir. George Ferencz, music by Max Roach.
Publication: in *'Angel City'*, *'Curse of the Starving Class' and Other Plays*; and in *'Fool for Love' and Other Plays*.

Appendix I

Suicide in B Flat
First production: Yale Repertory Theatre, New Haven, CT, 15 Oct 1976, dir. Walt Jones in association with Denise A. Gordon. Later production: in *Shepard Sets*, La Mama Experimental Theatre, New York, Nov 1984, dir. George Ferencz, music by Max Roach.
Publication: in '*Buried Child*', '*Seduced*', and '*Suicide in B Flat*' (New York: Applause, 1984); and in '*Fool for Love*' and Other Plays.

Seduced
First production: American Place Theatre, New York, 19 Jan 1976, dir. Jack Gelber.
Publication: in '*Buried Child*', '*Seduced*', and '*Suicide in B Flat*': and in '*Fool for Love*' and Other Plays.

Inacoma
First production: Magic Theatre, San Francisco, 18 Mar 1977, dir. Sam Shepard.
Unpublished: typescript at the Bancroft Library, University of California at Berkeley. For a detailed critical analysis of this work, see William Kleb, 'Sam Shepard's *Inacoma* at the Magic Theatre', *Theatre*, Fall 1977, 59–64.

The Sad Lament of Pecos Bill on the Eve of Killing his Wife
First production: Magic Theatre, San Francisco, 1976. Later production: La Mama 1983.
Publication: in '*Fool for Love*' and '*The Sad Lament of Pecos Bill on the Eve of Killing his Wife*' (San Francisco, CA: City Lights, 1983).

Curse of the Starving Class
First production: Royal Court Theatre Upstairs, London, 21 Apr 1977; New York Shakespeare Festival at the Public Theatre, 2 Mar 1978, dir. Robert Woodruff. Later production: Magic Theatre, San Francisco, 1981–82, dir. John Lion. Film version, 1994, dir. Bruce Beresford.
Publication: in *Seven Plays*: and in '*Angel City*', '*Curse of the Starving Class*' and Other Plays.

Re-arrangements, with others
First production: Joseph Chaikin's Winter Project, 1979.
Unpublished.

Buried Child
First production: Magic Theatre, San Francisco, 27 June 1978, dir. Robert Woodruff. New York premiere: Theatre for the New City, 1978, dir. Robert Woodruff. Revival by the Steppenwolf Theatre Company, Chicago, 4 Oct 1995, and Broadway, Apr 1996, dir. Gary Sinise.
Publication: in *Seven Plays*: and in '*Buried Child*', '*Seduced,*' and '*Suicide in B Flat*'.

Tongues, a piece for voice and percussion, co-authored with Joseph Chaikin
First performed by the authors, along with *Savage/Love*, a companion piece on
which they also collaborated, at the Magic Theatre, San Francisco, in 1978.
New York premiere: New York Shakespeare Festival at the Public Theatre.
Publication: in *Seven Plays*, with notes by Shepard.

Savage/Love, co-authored with Joseph Chaikin
First performed by the authors, along with *Tongues*, a companion piece on
which they also collaborated, at the Magic Theatre in 1978, New York
premiere: New York Shakespeare Festival at the Public Theatre. Videotape
of the New York production, dir. Shirley Clarke, available at the New York
Public Library Theatre Collection at Lincoln Center.
Publication: in *Seven Plays*, with notes by Joseph Chaikin.

Drum War, a jazz 'concert'
First production: Overtone Theatre, 1979.
Unpublished.

True West
First production: Magic Theatre, San Francisco, 10 July 1980, dir. Robert
Woodruff. New York premiere: New York Shakespeare Festival at the
Public Theatre, 23 Dec 1980, dir. Robert Woodruff. Later productions:
Steppenwolf Theatre Company, Chicago, then New York Cherry Lane
Theatre, dir. Gary Sinise, 1983. The Chicago production was videotaped
for PBS as part of their American Playhouse Presentation series, 1984. First
London production: National Theatre, dir. John Schlesinger, 1981.
Broadway revival, 9 Mar 2000, dir. Matthew Warchus.
Publication: in *Seven Plays*.

Jacaranda, a dance, written for Daniel Nagrin
Performed by Daniel Negrin, 1979.
Unpublished: manuscript at the Bancroft Library, University of California at
Berkeley.

Superstitions, a theatre piece based on the journal entries published in *Motel
Chronicles* (1982), written under the pseudonym, Walker Hayes.
First production: Overtone Theatre, San Francisco, 1981. Revived by the
Overtone Theatre, La Mama E.T.C., and New Writers at the Westside at La
Mama E.T.C., New York, September 1983. According to the Playbill for
the La Mama production, '*Superstitions* was first performed by the
Overtone Theatre in 1981 at the Intersection Theatre in San Francisco.
Shepard wrote *Superstitions* as a collection of prose and poetry for his book
Motel Chronicles. The Overtone Theatre with Shepard adapted these pieces
into a play with music, mistaken sounds and silences. A day and a night on
the desert.'
Unpublished.

Fool for Love
First production: Magic Theatre, San Francisco, 8 Feb 1983, dir. Sam Shepard.
New York premiere: Circle Repertory Theatre, May 1983, dir. Sam Shepard
and with the complete cast from the original Magic Theatre production. First
London production: Cottesloe at the National Theatre, Oct 1984, dir. Peter
Gill. Revival by the Roundabout Theatre company at the American Airliner
Theatre (Broadway premiere), Winter 2005. Film version 1985, screenplay
by Shepard, who also plays Eddie on screen, dir. Robert Altman.
Publication: in '*Fool for Love*' and '*The Sad Lament of Percos Bill on the Eve
of Killing his Wife*'; and in '*Fool for Love*' and Other Plays.

A Lie of the Mind
First production: Promenade Theatre, New York, 5 Dec 1985, dir. Sam Shepard.
Revival at the Donmar Warehouse, London, July 2001, dir. Wilson Milam.
Publication: '*A Lie of the Mind*' and '*The War in Heaven*' (New York: New
American Library, 1987).

The War in Heaven, a radio play co-written with Joseph Chaikin
Performed by Joseph Chaikin in New York on the WBAI radio station, 8 Jan
1985, and at American Place Theatre.
Publication: '*A Lie of the Mind*' and '*The War in Heaven*'

True Dylan
Unproduced.
Publication: *Esquire*, July 1987.

States of Shock
First production: American Place Theatre, New York, 30 Apr 1991, director Bill
Hart.
Publication: *States of Shock: A Vaudeville Nightmare*, in '*States of Shock*', '*Far
North*', and '*Silent Tongue*': A Play and Two Screenplays (New York:
Random House, 1992).

Simpatico
First production: New York Shakespeare Festival at the Public Theatre, New
York, 14 Nov 1994, director Sam Shepard. Film version, 2000, dir. Matthew
Warchus.
Publication: *Simpatico* (New York: Random House, 1996).

When the World Was Green (A Chef's Fable), co-written with Joseph Chaikin
First production: Seven Stages Company, Atlanta, 1996 Olympic Arts Festival,
dir. Joseph Chaikin. Produced in New York by the Signature Theatre
Company at the Public Theatre, 22 Oct 1996, dir. Joseph Chaikin.
Publication: in '*The Late Henry Moss*', '*Eyes for Consuela*', and '*When the
World Was Green*' (New York: Random House, 2002).

Eyes for Consuela Adapted from the story, 'The Blue Bouquet', by Octavio Paz
First production: Manhattan Theatre Club, 10 Feb 1998, dir. Terry Kinney.
Publication: in *'The Late Henry Moss'*, ' *Eyes for Consuela'*, and *'When the World Was Green'*.

The Late Henry Moss
First production: Magic Theatre, San Francisco, 7 November 2000, dir. Sam Shepard. Signature Theatre Company, New York, 23 Sept 2001, dir. Joseph Chaikin. The rehearsal process of the Magic Theatre production is the subject of the documentary, *This so-called Disaster: Sam Shepard Directs 'The Late Henry Moss'*, 2004, dir. Michael Almereyda.
Publication: in *'The Late Henry Moss'*, *'Eyes for Consuela,'* and *'When the World Was Green'*.

The God of Hell, work-in-progress, 2004.

Screenplays

Me and My Brother, with Robert Frank, 1967, dir. Robert Frank.
Zabriskie Point, with Michelangelo Antonioni, Fred Gardner, Tonnino Guerra and Claire Peploe, 1968, dir. Michelangelo Antonioni. Produced by MGM–United Artists, 1970. Published by Simon and Schuster, 1972.
Ringaleerio, with Murray Mednick, 1971. Unproduced: in Mugar Library Archive, Boston University.
Maxagasm, for the Rolling Stones, early 1970s. Unproduced: in Mugar Library Archive, Boston University.
The Bodyguard, modern version of Middleton and Rowley's *The Changeling*, 1975. Unproduced.
Fractured. Unproduced: in Mugar Library Archive, Boston University.
Seventh Son. Unproduced: in Mugar Library Archive, Boston University.
Oh! Calcutta! Screenplay by Shepard with others. Produced by Tigon, 1972.
Renaldo and Clara, with Bob Dylan, 1978.
Paris, Texas, adaptation of story by L. M. Kit Carson, 1984, dir. Wim Wenders. Produced by 20th Century Fox. Awarded Palme d'Or, Cannes, 1984. Nominated for Academy Award for Best Screenplay, 1984. Published by Road Movies, Berlin, 1984, distributed by Ecco Press, New York.
Fool for Love, 1985, dir. Robert Altman. Produced by Cannon Group.
Far North, 1988, screenplay and dir. Sam Shepard. Produced by Cannon Group. Published in *'States of Shock'*, *'Far North'* and *'Silent Tongue'*: A Play and Two Screenplays (New York: Vintage, 1993).
Silent Tongue, 1993, screenplay and dir. Sam Shepard. Produced by Belbo Films. Published in *'States of Shock'*, *'Far North'* and *'Silent Tongue'*: A Play and Two Screenplays (New York: Vintage, 1993).

Curse of the Starving Class, with Bruce Beresford, dir. Bruce Beresford, 1994. Produced by Breakheart Films.

See You In My Dreams, stories from *Cruising Paradise* and *Motel Chronicles*, teleplay by H. Haden Yelin, dir. Graeme Clifford, adapted for TV, 2000.

Don't Come Knocking, dir. Wim Wenders, a Reverse Angle production, filming in 2004.

Prose

'Autobiography', *News of the American Place Theatre*, III (Apr 1971), 1–2.

Hawk Moon, a collection of short stories, poems and monologues (New York: Performing Arts Journal Publications, 1973; repr. 1981).

'News Blues', *Time Out*, 31 May–6 Jun 1974, 17.

'Less than Half a Minute', *Time Out*, 12–18 July 1974, 16–17.

'Time', American Place Theatre Newsletter, 1975; repr. in *Theatre*, IX (Spring 1978), 9; repr. in *American Dreams: The Imagination of Sam Shepard*, ed. Bonnie Marranca (New York: Performing Arts Journal Publications, 1981), pp. 210–11.

Rolling Thunder Logbook (New York: Viking, 1977).

'American Experimental Theatre: Then and Now', *Performing Arts Journal*, II (Fall 1977); repr. in *American Dreams: The Imagination of Sam Shepard*, ed. Bonnie Marranca (New York: Performing Arts Journal Publications, 1981), pp. 212–13.

'Language, Visualization, and the Inner Library', *Drama Review*, XXI (Dec 1977), 49–58; repr. in *American Dreams: The Imagination of Sam Shepard*, ed. Bonnie Marranca (New York: Performing Arts Journal Publications, 1981), pp. 214–19.

'The Fastest Man in the World: A Kid's Fable', in *Wonders: Writings and Drawings for the Child in Us All*, ed. Jonathan Cott and Mary Gimbel (New York: Summit Books/Rolling Stone Press, 1980), pp. 532–6.

Motel Chronicles (San Francisco: City Lights, 1982).

Joseph Chaikin & Sam Shepard: Letters and Texts, 1972–1984, ed. Barry V. Daniels (New York: New American Library, 1989).

'Brownsville Girl', song co-written with Bob Dylan, appears on Bob Dylan's album, *Knocked Out Loaded*, 1986.

Excerpts from *Slave of the Camera*, in *Plays in One Act*, ed. Daniel Halpern (Hopewell, NJ: Ecco Press, 1991), pp. 421–9.

'True Dylan', an interview in the form of a play, *Esquire*, July 1987, 57–68.

Cruising Paradise: Tales (New York: Knopf, 1996).

'My First Year in New York; 1963', *The New York Times*, 17 Sep 2000.

Great Dream of Heaven: Stories (New York: Knopf, 2002).

[*ALSO OF INTEREST* (an anthology by Shepard's son) JESSE SHEPARD, *JUBILEE KING: STORIES* (New York: Bloomsbury, 2003).]

Appendix II
Playwriting Awards

1966 Obie Award, Distinguished Playwriting, for *Chicago*, *Icarus's Mother*, and *Red Cross* at Café La Mama in New York and on tour abroad

1967 Obie Award, Distinguished Playwriting, for *La Turista* at the American Place Theatre

1968 Obie Award, Distinguished Playwriting, for *Melodrama Play* at La Mama and for *Forensic and the Navigators* at Theatre Genesis

1968 Rockefeller Foundation Grant

1968 Guggenheim Foundation Grant

1968 Office for Advanced Drama Research Grant

1968 Yale University Fellowship

1971 Guggenheim Foundation Grant

1972 Obie Award, Distinguished Playwriting, for *The Tooth of Crime* at the McCarter Theatre, Princeton, NJ, and at the Open Space, London

1974 Obie Award, Distinguished Playwriting, for *Action* at the Theatre Upstairs in London, at The American Place Theatre, New York, and Magic Theatre, San Francisco

1974, renewed 1975–76 Rockefeller Foundation Grant as 'Playwright in Residence' at the Magic Theatre, San Francisco

1975 National Institute of Arts and Letters Award in Literature

1976 Brandeis University Creative Arts Medal

1977 Obie Award, Best New Play, for *Curse of the Starving Class* at the Royal Court Theatre in London and at the Public Theatre in New York

1978 Obie Award, Distinguished Playwriting, for *Buried Child* at the Magic Theatre, San Francisco

1979 Pulitzer Prize for Drama, for *Buried Child*

1980 Obie Award, Sustained Achievement in Playwriting

1983 Obie Award, Best New Play, for *Fool for Love* at the Magic Theatre in San Francisco and at the Circle Repertory Theatre in New York
(Also, 1984 Obie Award, Direction, *Fool for Love*)

1984 Golden Palm Award from the Cannes Film Festival for *Paris, Texas*
(Also, 1984 Academy of Motion Picture Arts and Sciences Award nomination. for Best Supporting Actor in *The Right Stuff*)

1986 Drama Desk Award, Outstanding New Play, for *A Lie of the Mind*

1986 New York Drama Critics Circle Award, Best New Play, for *A Lie of the Mind*

1986 Elected to the American Academy and Institute of Arts and Letters

1992 Gold Medal for Drama from the American Academy of Arts and Letters

1994 Inducted into the Theatre Hall of Fame

1996 Antoinette Perry (Tony) Award nomination, Best New Play, for revival of *Buried Child*

(Also, 1999 American Academy of Television Arts and Sciences Emmy Award nomination for Best Lead Actor in a Miniseries or Movie for *Dash and Lily*)

2000 Antoinette Perry (Tony) Award nomination, Best Play, for revival of *True West*

Appendix III
Acting Career

Stage

Student productions at Mount San Antonio College in Walnut, California, for two semesters, early 1960s.

Plays with the Bishop's Company Repertory Players, Burbank, California, 1963.

Cowboy Mouth, American Place Theatre, New York, 1971.

Tongues and *Savage/Love*, Magic Theatre, San Francisco, 1978.

Salter, in *A Number*, by Caryl Churchill, NY Theatre Workshop, New York, Nov 2004.

Film

Brand X, dir. Win Chamberlin, 1970.

Renaldo and Clara, dir. Bob Dylan, 1977.

Days of Heaven, dir. Terence Malick, 1978.

Resurrection, dir. Daniel Petrie, 1980.

Raggedy Man, dir. Jack Fisk, 1981.

Frances, dir. Graeme Clifford, 1982.

The Right Stuff, dir. Philip Kaufman, 1983; nomination for Academy Award as best supporting actor.

Country, dir. Richard Pearce, 1984.

Fool for Love, dir. Robert Altman, 1985.

Crimes of the Heart, dir. Bruce Beresford, 1986.

Baby Boom, dir. Charles Shyer, 1987.

September, dir. Woody Allen, 1987 – unreleased version. (The film was reshot and substantially recast, with Sam Waterston replacing Shepard – who had himself replaced Christopher Walken – in the final, theatrically released version of *September*. John Lahr writes in his New Yorker profile of Woody Allen, reprinted in *Show and Tell* [Berkeley: University of California Press, 2002], 'On *September*, Sam Shepard was granted permission to improvise a speech, and according to [actress, Diane] Wiest, ended up talking about leaving Montana to go East to medical school. As Wiest and Allen were walking back to the dressing room, Allen turned to her. "Montana? Montana?" he said. "The word 'Montana' is gonna be in my movie?" It wasn't.')

Steel Magnolias, dir. Herbert Ross, 1989.

Bright Angel, adapted from Richard Ford's short story collection, *Rock Springs*, 1990.

Appendix III

Homo Faber, a.k.a. *Voyager,* dir. Volker Schlondorff, 1991.
Defenseless, dir. Martin Campbell, 1991.
Thunderheart, dir. Michael Apted, 1992.
The Pelican Brief, dir. Alan J. Pakula, 1993.
Safe Passage, dir. Robert Alan Ackerman, 1994.
Larry McMurty's Streets of Laredo, 1995.
The Good Old Boys, with Tommy Lee Jones, 1995.
Lily Dale, screenplay by Horton Foote, 1996.
The Only Thrill, dir. Peter Masterson, 1997.
Curtain Call, dir. Peter Yates, 1999.
Snow Falling on Cedars, dir. Scott Hicks, 1999.
Purgatory, with Randy Quaid, 1999.
Dash and Lily, dir. Kathy Bates, 1999; Emmy Award nomination for lead actor
    in a miniseries or movie.
All the Pretty Horses, dir. Billy Bob Thornton, 2000.
Hamlet, with Ethan Hawke, dir. Michael Almereyda, 2000.
One Kill, 2000.
Shot in the Heart, 2001.
Kurosawa, dir. Adam Low (Shepard is narrator), 2001.
After the Harvest, 2001.
Swordfish, dir. Dominic Sena, 2001.
Black Hawk Down, dir, Ridley Scott, 2001.
The Pledge, dir. Sean Penn, 2001.
Leo, 2002
Blind Horizon, 2003.
The Notebook, dir. Nick Cassavetes, 2004.
Stealth, dir. Rob Cohen, 2004.
Don't Come Knocking, dir. Wim Wenders, 2004.

Appendix IV
Selected Bibliography

Chronological List of Principal Editions of Stage Plays, Screenplays and Prose

(See Appendix I for additional publication information.)

Five Plays (New York and Indianapolis: Bobbs-Merrill, 1967; and London: Faber, 1969), repr. as '*Chicago' and Other Plays* (New York: Applause, 1981). Includes *Chicago, Icarus' Mother, Fourteen Hundred Thousand, Red Cross* and *Melodrama Play.*

La Turista (Indianapolis: Bobbs-Merrill, 1968).

Operation Sidewinder (New York and Indianapolis: Bobbs-Merrill, 1970).

'*The Unseen Hand' and Other Plays* (New York and Indianapolis: Bobbs-Merrill, 1971), repr. as '*The Unseen Hand' and Other Plays* (New York: Applause, 1981). Includes *The Unseen Hand, Forensic and the Navigators, The Holy Ghostly, Back Bog Beast Bait, Shaved Splits* and *4-H Club.*

'*Mad Dog Blues' and Other Plays* (New York: Winter House, 1972). Includes *Mad Dog Blues, Cowboy Mouth, Rock Garden* and *Cowboys # 2.*

Hawk Moon: A Book of Short Stories, Poems and Monologues (Los Angeles, CA: Black Sparrow, 1972).

'*The Tooth of Crime' and 'Geography of a Horse Dreamer'* (New York: Grove, 1974).

'*Action' and 'The Unseen Hand'* (London: Faber, 1975).

'*Angel City', 'Curse of the Starving Class' and Other Plays* (New York: Urizen, 1976; repr. New York: Applause, 1981). 'Sam Shepard: The Playwright as Shaman' by Jack Gelber, *Angel City, Curse of the Starving Class, Killer's Head, Action, The Mad Dog Blues, Cowboy Mouth, The Rock Garden, Cowboys # 2,* and Patti Smith, 'Sam Shepard: 9 Random Years [7+2]'.

Rolling Thunder Logbook (New York: Viking, 1977).

'*Buried Child', 'Seduced' and 'Suicide in B-Flat'*, introduction by Jack Richardson (New York: Urizen, 1979; repr. New York: Applause, 1984).

Four Two-Act Plays, introduction by Elizabeth Hardwick (New York: Applause, 1980). Includes *La Turista, The Tooth of Crime, Geography of a Horse Dreamer* and *Operation Sidewinder.*

'The Fastest Man in the World: A Kid's Fable', in *Wonders: Writings and Drawings for the Child in Us All*, ed. Jonathan Cott and Mary Gimbel (New York: Summit Books/Rolling Stone Press, 1980), pp. 532–6.

True West (Garden City, New York: Doubleday, 1981; London: Faber, 1981).

Seven Plays, intro. Richard Gilman (New York: Bantam, 1981). Includes *True West, Buried Child, Curse of the Starving Class, The Tooth of Crime, La Turista, Tongues* and *Savage/Love.*

'Time' (1978), 'American Experimental Theatre: Then and Now' (1977) and 'Language, Visualization and the Inner Library' (1977), in *American Dreams: The Imagination of Sam Shepard*, ed. Bonnie Marranca (New York: Performing Arts Journal Publications, 1981), pp. 210–20.

Motel Chronicles (San Franciso, CA: City Lights, 1982).

'*Fool for Love*' *and* '*The Sad Lament of Pecos Bill on the Eve of Killing his Wife*' (San Francisco, CA: City Lights, 1983).

'*Fool for Love*' *and Other Plays*, introduction by Ross Wetzsteon (New York: Bantam, 1984). Includes *Fool for Love, Angel City, Geography of a Horse Dreamer, Action, Cowboy Mouth, Melodrama Play, Seduced* and *Suicide in B-Flat.*

'Brownsville Girl', song co-written with Bob Dylan, appears on Bob Dylan's album, *Knocked Out Loaded*, 1986.

'True Dylan', an interview in the form of a play, *Esquire*, July 1987, 57–68.

'*A Lie of the Mind*' *and* '*The War in Heaven*' (New York: New American Library, 1987).

Joseph Chaikin & Sam Shepard: Letters and Texts, 1972–1984, ed. Barry Daniels (New York: New American Library, 1989).

Excerpts from *Slave of the Camera*, in *Plays in One Act*, ed. Daniel Halpern (Hopewell, NJ: Ecco Press, 1991) pp. 421–9.

'*States of Shock*', '*Far North*' *and* '*Silent Tongue*': *A Play and Two Screenplays* (New York: Vintage, 1993).

Simpatico (New York: Random House Vintage, 1996).

Cruising Paradise: Tales (New York: Knopf, 1996).

'*The Late Henry Moss*', '*Eyes for Consuela*' *and* '*When the World Was Green*' (New York: Random House Vintage, 2002).

Great Dream of Heaven: Stories (New York: Knopf, 2002).

Archives

Magic Theatre Archives at the Bancroft Library, University of California, Berkeley, California.

Shepard Archive at the Mugar Memorial Library, Boston University, Boston, Massachusetts.

Southwestern Writers Collection, Southwest Texas State University, San Marcos, Texas.

Toby Cole Collection in the Shields Library at the University of California, Davis, California.

Yale Repertory Theatre Archives at the Yale School of Drama Library.

Selected Interviews

(and selected articles including interviews)

Boyd, Blanche McCrary, 'The Natural', *American Film* (Oct 1984) 23–6, 91–2.

Sam Shepard: A 'Poetic Rodeo'

Coe, Robert, 'Saga of Sam Shepard', *New York Times Magazine*, 23 Nov 1980, pp. 56–8, 118–24.

Cott, Jonathan, 'The Many Faces of Sam Shepard', *New York Daily News*, 25 Jan 1987, City Lights section, p. 3.

Dark, Johnny, 'Sam Shepard on Myths and Heroes', *San Francisco* (Sep 1983) 66–72.

Editors of *Theatre Quarterly* and Kenneth Chubb, 'Metaphors, Mad Dogs and Old Time Cowboys: Interview with Sam Shepard', *Theatre Quarterly*, IV (Aug–Oct 1974) 3–16. Repr. in *American Dreams: The Imagination of Sam Shepard*, ed. Bonnie Marranca (New York: Performing Arts Journal Publications, 1981) pp. 187–209.

Fay, Stephen, 'Renaissance Man Rides Out of the West', *London Sunday Times Magazine*, 26 Aug 1984, pp. 16–19.

Goldberg, Robert, 'Sam Shepard: American Original', *Playboy* (Mar 1984) 90ff.

— —, 'Sam Shepard: Off-Broadway's Street Cowboy', *Rolling Stone College Papers* (Winter 1980) 42–5.

Gussow, Mel, 'From Plays to Fiction: Thanks, Dad', New York Times, 15 Oct 2002, p. E1, E8.

— —, 'Sam Shepard: Writer on the Way Up', *New York Times*, 12 Nov 1969, p. 42.

Hamill, Pete, 'The New American Hero', *New York* (5 Dec 1983) 74–102.

Kakutani, Michiko, 'Myths, Dreams, Realities – Sam Shepard's America', *New York Times*, 29 Jan 1984, B1, B26–28. Repr. in Kakutani, Michiko, *The Poet at the Piano* (New York: Times Books, 1988), pp. 178–85.

Kroll, Jack, 'Who's That Tall, Dark Stranger', *Newsweek*, 11 Nov 1985, pp. 68–74.

Lippman, Amy, 'Rhythm and Truths: An Interview with Sam Shepard', *American Theatre*, I (Apr 1984) 9–13, 40–1.

Marks, Peter, 'Sam Shepard is Happy to be on Broadway but It's Just a Visit', *New York Times*, 28 May 1996, C11, C15.

Oppenheim, Irene, and Fascio, Victor, 'The Most Promising Playwright in America Today is Sam Shepard', *Village Voice* (27 Oct 1975) 81–2.

Rosen, Carol, ' "Emotional Territory": An Interview with Sam Shepard', *Modern Drama*, XXXVI (Mar 1993) 1–11.

— —, ' "Silent Tongues": Sam Shepard's Explorations of Emotional Territory', *Village Voice* (4 Aug 1992) 32–41. Reprinted in this book.

Roudane, Matthew, 'Shepard on Shepard: An Interview', in *The Cambridge Companion to Sam Shepard* (Cambridge: Cambridge University Press, 2002) ch 3.

Schiff, Stephen, 'Showcase: Shepard on Broadway', *New Yorker*, 22 Apr 1996, 84–6.

Sessums, Kevin, 'Geography of a Horse Dreamer', *Interview* (Sep 1988) 70–8.

Shewey, Don, 'Rock-and-Roll Jesus with a Cowboy Mouth (Revisited)', *American Theatre* XXI (Apr 2004) 20–5, 82–4.

Simpson, Mona, McCulloch, Jeanne, and Howe, Benjamin, 'Sam Shepard: The Art of Theatre XII', *Paris Review*, 142 (Spring 1997) 204–23; reprinted in *Playwrights at Work*, ed. George Plimpton (New York: Modern Library, 2000) pp. 329–45.

Taylor, Belinda, 'Sam Shepard's Gift to the Magic Theatre', *Theatre Bay Area Magazine* (21 Feb 2002) 1.

VerMeulen, Michael, 'Sam Shepard: Yes, Yes, Yes', *Esquire* (Feb 1980) 79–86.

Wetzsteon, Ross, 'Unknown Territory', *Village Voice* (10 Dec 1985) 55–6.

Wren, Scott Christopher, 'Camp Shepard: Exploring the Geography of Character', *West Coast Plays: 7* (Berkeley, CA.: California Theatre Council, Fall 1980) pp. 73–103.

— —, 'Duck Hunting in Marin: On the Second Shepard Workshop', *West Coast Plays: 11/12*, ed. Rick Foster (Berkeley, CA: California Theatre Council, 1982) pp. 210–19.

Note: See also 'Sam Shepard: Stalking Himself', a production of Teale/Oren Jacoby Productions, Thirteen/WNET and BBC. Premiered as part of the Great Performances series on PBS 8 July 1998. Video also includes performances of excerpts from eight of his plays (including *Chicago, Fourteen Hundred Thousand, The Tooth of Crime, Action, Killer's Head, Curse of the Starving Class* and *Buried Child*).

See also, *This so-called Disaster: Sam Shepard Directs 'The Late Henry Moss'*, dir. Michael Almereyda) 2004.

Suggested Secondary Reading

Books

Auerbach, Doris, *Sam Shepard, Arthur Kopit, and the Off Broadway Theatre* (Boston, MA: Twayne, 1982).

Bottoms, Stephen J., *The Theatre of Sam Shepard* (Cambridge: Cambridge University Press, 1998).

Callens, Johan (ed.), *Sam Shepard: Between the Margin and the Centre, Contemporary Theatre Review*, VIII, # 3–# 4 (Amsterdam, The Netherlands: Harwood Academic Publishers, 1996).

Cohn, Ruby, *New American Dramatists: 1960–1980* (London: Macmillan; New York: Grove Press, 1982).

De Rose, David J., *Sam Shepard* (New York: Twayne, 1992).

Dugdale, John, *File on Shepard* (London: Methuen, 1989).

Hart, Lynda, *Sam Shepard's Metaphorical Stages* (Westport, CT: Greenwood Press, 1987).

Howard, Patricia (ed.), *Sam Shepard and Contemporary American Drama*: Special Edition of *Modern Drama*, XXXVI (Toronto: *Modern Drama*, Mar 1993), 1–177.

Sam Shepard: A 'Poetic Rodeo'

King, Kimball (ed.), *Sam Shepard: A Casebook* (New York: Garland, 1989).

Marranca, Bonnie (ed.), *American Dreams: The Imagination of Sam Shepard* (New York: Performing Arts Journal Publications, 1981).

McGhee, Jim, *True Lies: The Architecture of the Fantastic in the Plays of Sam Shepard* (New York: Peter Lang, 1993).

Mottram, Ron, *Inner Landscapes: The Theatre of Sam Shepard* (Columbia, MO: University of Missouri Press, 1984).

Oumano, Ellen, *Sam Shepard: The Life and Work of an American Dreamer* (New York: St. Martin's Press, 1986).

Roudane, Matthew (ed.), *The Cambridge Companion to Sam Shepard* (Cambridge: Cambridge University Press, 2002).

Shewey, Don, *Sam Shepard: The Life, the Loves, Behind the Legend of a True American Original* (New York: Dell, 1985).

Wilcox, Leonard (ed.), *Rereading Shepard: Contemporary Critical Essays on the Plays of Sam Shepard* (New York: St. Martin's Press, 1993).

Articles

Bigsby, C.W. et al., 'Theatre Checklist No. 3, Sam Shepard', *Theatrefacts*, Aug 1974.

Blau, Herbert, 'The American Dream in American Gothic: The Plays of Sam Shepard and Adrienne Kennedy', *Modern Drama*, XXVII (Dec 1984) 520–39.

Blumenthal, Eileen, 'Chaikin and Shepard Speak in Tongues', *Village Voice* (26 Nov 1979).

— —, *Joseph Chaikin* (Cambridge: Cambridge University Press, 1984) pp. 171–84.

— —, 'The Voyage Back', *American Theatre*, VIII (June 1991) 12–17, 53.

Carroll, Dennis, 'The Filmic Cut and "Switchback" in the Plays of Sam Shepard', *Modern Drama*, XXVIII (Mar 1985) 125–38.

Chubb, Kenneth, 'Fruitful Difficulties of Directing Shepard', *Theatre Quarterly*, IV (Aug–Sept 1974) 17–23.

Cohn, Ruby, 'Sam Shepard', *Contemporary Dramatists* (New York: Scarecrow Press, 1983) pp. 171–86.

De Rose, David, 'Slouching towards Broadway: Shepard's *A Lie of the Mind*', *Theatre*, XVII (Spring 1986) 69–74.

Eder, Richard, 'Sam Shepard's Obsession is America', *New York Times*, 4 Mar 1979, II, 1, 27.

Falk, Florence, 'The Role of Performance in Sam Shepard's Plays', *Theatre Journal*, XXIII (May 1981) 182–98.

Freedman, Samuel G., 'Sam Shepard's Mythic Vision of the Family', *New York Times*, 1 Dec 1985, Sec. 2, p.1, 20.

Gelber, Jack, 'Sam Shepard: The Playwright as Shaman', intro. to Sam Shepard, '*Angel City*', '*Curse of the Starving Class*' and Other Plays (New York: Applause, 1981) pp. 1–4; repr. in *American Dreams: The Imagination of Sam Shepard*, ed. Bonnie Marranca (New York: Performing Arts Journal Publications) pp. 45–8.

Appendix IV

Gilman, Richard, Introduction to *Sam Shepard, Seven Plays* (New York: Bantam, 1981) pp. ix–xxv.

Grant, Gary, 'Writing as a Process of Performing the Self: Sam Shepard's Notebooks', *Modern Drama*, XXXIV (1991) 549–65.

Hayes, Michael, 'Sam Shepard', in *American Drama*, ed. Clive Bloom (New York: St. Martin's Press, 1995) 131–41.

Hardwick, Elizabeth, Introduction to *La Turista* (New York: Bobbs-Merrill, 1968); repr. as Introduction to *Four Two-Act Plays* (New York: Applause, 1980) pp. 11–16; also repr. in *American Dreams: The Imagination of Sam Shepard*, ed. Bonnie Marranca (New York: Performing Arts Journal Publications, 1981) pp. 67–71.

Hughes, Catherine, 'Sam Shepard', in *American Playwrights, 1945–1975* (London: Pitman, 1976) pp. 72–80.

Kauffmann, Stanley, '*True West/Tooth of Crime*', in *Theatre Criticisms* (New York: Performing Arts Journal Publications, 1983) pp. 165–8.

Kleb, William, 'Sam Shepard's *Inacoma* at the Magic Theatre', *Theatre*, IX (Fall 1977) 59–64.

Lahr, John, 'Jules Feiffer and Sam Shepard: Spectacles of Disintegration', in *Astonish Me: Adventures in Contemporary Theatre* (New York: Viking, 1973) pp. 102–9.

— —, 'Sam Shepard', in *Automatic Vaudeville: Essays on Star Turns* (New York: Limelight, 1985).

Lion, John, ' "Rock and Roll Jesus with a Cowboy Mouth" ', *American Theatre*, I (Apr 1984) 4–8.

Mazzocco, Robert, 'Heading for the Last Round-Up', *New York Review of Books*, XXXII, 9 May 1985, 21–7.

Reuben, Paul P., 'Chapter 8: American Drama – Sam Shepard', *PAL: Perspectives in American Literature – A Research and Reference Guide* (URL: http://www.csustan.edu/english/reuben/pal/chap8/shepard.html).

Savran, David, 'Sam Shepard's Conceptual Prison: *Action* and the Unseen Hand', *Theatre Journal*, XXXVI (Mar 1984) 57–73.

Schechner, Richard, 'Sam Shepard', *Contemporary Dramatists*, ed. J. Vinson (New York: Scarecrow Press, 1973) pp. 696–9.

— —, 'The Writer and the Performance Group: Rehearsing *The Tooth of Crime*', *Performance*, I (Mar–Apr 1973) 60–5.

Wetzsteon, Ross, 'The Genius of Sam Shepard', *New York* (24 Nov 1980) 20–5.

Notes

Introduction

1. See Elizabeth Hardwick, Introduction to *La Turista*, in Sam Shepard, *Four Two-Act Plays* (New York: Applause, 1980) p.14; and Sam Shepard, quoted in Ruby Cohn, 'Sam Shepard', *Contemporary Dramatists* (New York: Scarecrow Press, 1983) p. 722.

2. Sam Shepard, 'Visualization, Language and the Inner Library', *Drama Review*, XXI (Dec 1977) 53.

3. Sam Shepard, 'Autobiography', *News of the American Place Theatre*, III (Apr 1971).

4. Quoted in Robert Goldberg, 'Sam Shepard: Off-Broadway's Street Cowboy', *Rolling Stone College Papers* (Winter 1980) 44.

5. Quoted in Jack Kroll, 'Who's That Tall, Dark Stranger?', *Newsweek*, 11 Nov 1985, p. 74.

6. Sam Shepard, quoted in Amy Lippman, 'Rhythm and Truths: An Interview with Sam Shepard', *American Theatre*, 1 (Apr 1984) 11; and John Simon,'Theater: Woolly Shepard, Unstately Holmes', *New York* (16 Dec 1985) 99.

7. Paraphrased in Scott Christopher Wren, 'Camp Shepard: Exploring the Geography of Character', in *West Coast Plays: 7*, ed. Rick Foster (Berkeley, CA: California Theatre Council, Fall 1980) pp. 92–3.

8. Sam Shepard, '1/6/80, Homestead Valley, Ca.', quoted in *Playbill* for *Superstitions* and *The Sad Lament of Pecos Bill on the Eve of Killing His Wife*, La Mama, E.T.C., New York, Sept 8–Oct, 2 1983.

1. 'Ain't the Highway Fine'

1. Sam Shepard, *Motel Chronicles* (San Francisco: City Lights Books, 1982) p. 49.

2. Ibid, p. 32.

3. Ibid, pp. 30, 18.

4. Quoted in Goldberg, 'Sam Shepard: Off-Broadway's Street Cowboy', *Rolling Stone College Papers* (Winter 1980) 43; 'Sam Shepard: American Original', *Playboy* (Mar 1984) 192; and Stephen Fay, 'Renaissance Man Rides out of The West', *Sunday Times Magazine*, 26 Aug 1984, p. 16.

5. Shepard, *Motel Chronicles*, p. 56.

6. Quoted in Pete Hamill, 'The New American Hero', *New York* (5 Dec 1983) 80, 84.

7. 'The Holy Modal Rounders Talk about the Holy Modal Rounders', *Playbill* for the Repertory Theatre of Lincoln Center/Vivian Beaumont Theatre production of Shepard's *Operation Sidewinder* (New York: Saturday Review,

1970) p. 26. See also Michael VerMeulen, 'Sam Shepard: Yes, Yes, Yes', *Esquire* (Feb 1980) 80.

8. Sam Shepard, 'California', in *Rolling Thunder Logbook* (New York: Viking, 1977) p. 4.

9. Quoted in Hamill, 'The New American Hero', *New York* (5 Dec 1983) 84, 86.

10. Quoted ibid., p. 84.

11. Quoted in Editors and Kenneth Chubb, 'Metaphors, Mad Dogs and Old Time Cowboys: Interview with Sam Shepard', *Theatre Quarterly*, IV (Aug–Oct 1974) 4.

12. Quoted in Goldberg, 'Sam Shepard, American Original', *Playboy* (Mar 1984) 192 .

13. Quoted in Hamill, 'The New American Hero', *New York* (5 Dec 1983) 86 .

2. 'Just Like Rock and Roll'

1. This and following quotes from Editors and Chubb, 'Metaphors, Mad Dogs and Old Time Cowboys', *Theatre Quarterly*, IV (1974), 5, 8 and 6.

2. Quoted ibid. p. 9.

3. Shepard, 'Visualization, Language and the Inner Library', *Drama Review*, XXI (Dec 1977) 53.

4. Ibid., pp. 53, 58, 53–4.

5. Ruby Cohn, *New American Dramatists, 1960–1980* (London: Macmillan; New York: Grove, 1982) p. 173.

6. Shepard, 'Visualization, Language and the Inner Library', *Drama Review*, XXI, 55.

7. Ibid., pp. 53–4.

8. Ibid., p. 58.

3. 'In this Desert'

1. Irene Oppenheim and Victor Fascio, 'The Most Promising Playwright in America Today is Sam Shepard', *Village Voice* (27 Oct 1975) 81.

2. Ibid.

3. Ibid.

4. Quoted in Goldberg, 'Sam Shepard: Off-Broadway's Street Cowboy', *Rolling Stone College Papers* (Winter 1980) 45; and Editors and Chubb, 'Metaphors, Mad Dogs and Old Time Cowboys', *Theatre Quarterly*, IV (Aug–Oct 1974), 13.

5. Ibid.

6. Mel Gussow, 'Sam Shepard: Writer on the Way Up', *New York Times*, 12 Nov 1969, p. 42.

7. Quoted in Goldberg, 'Sam Shepard: Off-Broadway's Street Cowboy', *Rolling Stone College Papers* (Winter 1980) 43–4.

4. 'Where Does a Hero Live?'

1. Quoted in Goldberg, 'Sam Shepard: Off-Broadway's Street Cowboy', *Rolling Stone College Papers* (Winter 1980) 44.

2. Quoted in Editors and Chubb, 'Metaphors, Mad Dogs and Old Time Cowboys', *Theatre Quarterly*, IV (Aug–Oct 1974), 11–12.

3. Ibid., p. 14.

4. Ibid., p.11.

5. Quoted in Richard Schechner, 'The Writer and the Performance Group: Rehearsing *The Tooth of Crime*', *Performance*, I (Mar–Apr 1973) 63; repr. in Schechner, *Environmental Theatre* (New York: Hawthorne, 1973) p. 235.

6. Quoted in Schechner, 'The Writer and the Performance Group', *Performance*, I, 62.

7. Kenneth Chubb, 'Fruitful Difficulties of Directing Shepard', *Theatre Quarterly*, IV (Aug–Oct 1974) 21–2.

8. Charles Marowitz, 'Sam Shepard: Sophisticate Abroad', *Village Voice* (7 Sep 1972) 59.

9. Chubb, 'Fruitful Difficulties of Directing Shepard', *Theatre Quarterly*, IV, 21.

10. Quoted in Editors and Chubb, 'Metaphors, Mad Dogs and Old Time Cowboys', *Theatre Quarterly*, IV, 12.

11. Quoted ibid., p. 13.

12. Chubb, 'Fruitful Difficulties of Directing Shepard', *Theatre Quarterly*, IV, 22.

13. Quoted in Schechner, *Environmental Theatre*, p. 239.

14. Chubb, 'Fruitful Difficulties of Directing Shepard', *Theatre Quarterly*, IV, 24.

15. Quoted in Editors and Chubb, 'Metaphors, Mad Dogs and Old Time Cowboys', ibid., p. 14.

16. Quoted ibid., p. 15.

17. Shepard, *Rolling Thunder Logbook* (New York: Viking, 1977) p. 43.

18. Sam Shepard, *Hawk Moon* (New York: Performing Arts Journal Publications, 1981) p. 91.

19. Sam Shepard, 'The House and the Fish', in *Three Works by the Open Theatre*, ed. Karen Malpede (New York: Drama Book Specialists, 1974) p. 142, and *Nightwalk*, ibid., p. *.

20. Shepard, 'Visualization, Language and the Inner Library', *Drama Review* XXI, 53–4. Subsequent page references in the text, cited as Shepard.

Notes

5. 'One Special Rhythm'

1. Antonin Artaud, *The Theatre and its Double*, trans. Mary Caroline Richards (New York: Grove Press, 1958) p. 133.

2. Sam Shepard, 'Time', *Theater*, IX (Spring 1978) 9.

3. Quoted in Gussow, 'Sam Shepard: Writer on the Way Up', *New York Times*, 12 Nov 1969, p. 42.

4. Shepard 'Autobiography', *News of the American Place Theatre*, III (Apr 1971) 1–2.

5. Shepard, *Motel Chronicles* (San Francisco, CA: City Lights Books, 1982) pp. 40–1.

6. Kroll, 'Who's That Tall, Dark Stranger?' *Newsweek*, 11 Nov 1985, pp. 72–4.

7. Quoted in Richard Schechner, 'Sam Shepard', in *Contemporary Dramatists*, ed. James Vinson (New York: Scarecrow Press, 1973) p. 697.

8. F. Scott Fitzgerald, *The Love of the Last Tycoon: A Western*, ed. Matthew J. Bruccoli (Cambridge: Macmillan, 1993) p. 32.

9. Shepard, 'Visualization, Language and the Inner Library', *Drama Review*, XXI, 54; and 'Autobiography', *News of the American Place Theatre*, III (Apr 1971) 1–2.

10. Shepard, 'Visualization, Language and the Inner Library', *Drama Review*, XXI, 53.

11. Jack Kroll, 'High-Pressure Jazz', *Newsweek*, 8 Nov 1976, p. 109.

12. John Pareles, 'Music to Match the Beat in Early Shepard', *New York Times*, 18 Nov 1984, II, 4, 20.

13. Ibid.

14. Jennifer Dunning, 'A Nagrin Dance to a Shepard Libretto', *New York Times*, 31 May 1979, p. C13. See also Kay Larson, '2-Part Invention', *Village Voice* (18 June 1979) 99.

15. Quoted in William Kleb, 'Sam Shepard's *Inacoma* at the Magic Theatre', *Theater*, IX (Fall 1977) 59–64. The script of *Inacoma* is in the Sam Shepard Archive at the Bancroft Library, University of California at Berkeley.

16. Quoted in Lippman, 'Rhythm and Truths', *American Theatre*, I (Apr 1984), 13.

17. Sam Shepard Archive, Bancroft Library, University of California at Berkeley, quoted with permission of the author.

6. 'Dynamite in the Blood'

1. Shepard, 'Visualization, Language and the Inner Library', *Drama Review*, XXI (1977), 55.

2. Quoted in Robert Coe, 'Saga of Sam Shepard', *New York Times Magazine*, 23 Nov 1980, p. 122.

3. Quoted in Robert Coe, 'Interview with Robert Woodruff', in *American Dreams: The Imagination of Sam Shepard*, ed. Bonnie Marranca (New York: Performing Arts Journal Publications, 1981) p. 156.

4. Quoted in Lippman, 'Rhythm and Truths', *American Theatre*, I, 9.

5. Quoted in Wren, 'Camp Shepard: Exploring the Geography of Character', in *West Coast Plays: 7*, pp. 76, 80, 95.

6. Quoted in Lippman, 'Rhythm and Truths', *American Theatre*, I, 9–10.

7. Quoted in VerMeulen, 'Sam Shepard: Yes, Yes, Yes', *Esquire* (Feb 1980) 85.

8. Walter Kerr, 'Sam Shepard – What's the Message?' *New York Times*, 10 Dec 1978, II, 3.

9. Quoted in Carol Rosen, 'Sharp Corners: Gary Sinise's Long Ride with Sam Shepard', *Village Voice* (1 May 1996) pp. 76, 78.

10. Ibid. Subsequent references to this interview will appear in the text.

11. Benedict Nightingale, 'Even Minimal Shepard is Food for Thought', *New York Times*, 25 Sept 1983, II, 26.

12. John Lahr, 'Sam Shepard', in *Automatic Vaudeville* (New York: Limelight, 1985) p. 47.

13. Quoted in Stephen Fay, 'Renaissance Man Rides out of the West', *London Sunday Times Magazine*, 26 Aug 1984, p. 19.

14. See Nightingale, 'Even Minimal Shepard is Food for Thought', *New York Times*, 25 Sep 1983, II, 5, 26. This comparison to *Phèdre* is alluded to in Irving Wardle, 'Theatre: Violence between Dream and Reality', *The Times*, 6 Oct 1984. In Wardle's view, however, 'It is in [these] closing passages that you feel most strongly the absence of a governing myth. If this were *Phèdre* or *Hippolytus* the inexorable rules would be implicit in the story and there would be no need for explanations. As it is, Shepard is driven back into the wearisome American device of prolonged memory speeches – three of them – which still fail to account for the rhythm of fatality that has accumulated up to that point.'

15. See Cohn, 'The Word is my Shepard', in *New American Dramatists, 1960–1980*, pp. 171–86.

16. John Lion, 'Rock 'n Roll Jesus with a Cowboy Mouth', *American Theatre*, I (Apr 1984) 6.

7. 'Destination': Emotional Territory

1. Quoted in Ross Wetzsteon, 'Unknown Territory', *Village Voice* (10 Dec 1985) 56.

2. Quoted in Fay, 'Renaissance Man Rides out of the West', *London Sunday Times Magazine*, 26 Aug 1984, p. 19.

3. Quoted in Wetzsteon, 'Unknown Territory', *Village Voice* (10 Dec 1985) 56.

4. Quoted in 'Camp Shepard: Exploring the Geography of Character', in *West Coast Plays: 7*, p. 81.

Notes

5. Hélène Cixous, 'The Laugh of the Medusa', trans. Keith Cohen and Paula Cohen, *Signs*, I. 4 (Summer 1976) 880.

6. Jeanie Forte, 'Women's Performance Art: Feminism and Postmodernism', in *Performing Feminisms: Feminist Critical Theory and Theatre*, ed. Sue-Ellen Case (Baltimore, MD: Johns Hopkins University Press, 1990) p. 258. Shepard is hilariously objectified in Meghan Daum's novel, *The Quality of Life Report* (New York, Viking, 2003).

7. Joseph Chaikin, *The Presence of the Actor* (New York: Atheneum, 1972) pp. 25–6; also Shepard, quoted in Wren. 'Camp Shepard: Exploring the Geography of Character', *West Coast Plays 7*, p. 81.

8. Morgan, Robin, *The Word of a Woman* (New York: Norton, 1992) pp. 275–7.

8. 'Ghosts and Sacrifices'

1. Ed Harris, quoted in Carol Rosen, 'Playing Anxiety: Ed Harris on his Reunion with Sam Shepard in *Simpatico*', *TheatreWeek*, VIII, 28 Nov 1994, 13–17. Subsequent page references to this interview appear in the text, cited as Harris.

2. James Houghton, quoted in Carol Rosen, 'Signature Presents Shepard', *TheatreWeek*, X (9 Sept 1996) 16–20.

3. Chaikin, *The Presence of the Actor*, p. 132.

4. *Joseph Chaikin and Sam Shepard: Letters and Texts, 1972–1984*, ed. Barry Daniels (New York: New American Library, 1989), pp. 121–2.

5. Chaikin, *The Presence of the Actor*, p. 22.

6. Sam Shepard, quoted in Belinda Taylor, 'Sam Shepard's Gift to the Magic Theatre', *Callboard: Theatre Bay Area Magazine* (21 Feb 2002) 1.

7. Ibid.

Epilogue: In America

1. William Butler Yeats, *Essays* (New York: Macmillan, 1924) pp. 302–3.

2. Chaikin, *The Presence of the Actor*, pp. 25–6.

3. Ibid.

4. Shepard, quoted in Michiko Kakutani, *The Poet at the Piano* (New York: Random House, 1988) pp. 178–85.

5. Wim Wenders, 'The Inspiration', *New York Times Magazine*, 12 Nov 2000, p. 97.

6. Shepard, quoted in Ruby Cohn, 'Sam Shepard', *Contemporary Dramatists*, p. 722.

7. Shepard, quoted in Mel Gussow, 'From Plays to Fiction: Thanks, Dad', *New York Times*, 15 Oct 2002, pp. E1, E8.

8. Finally, it is worth noting that although Shepard's name is nowhere to be found in the end-credits of *Masked and Anonymous* (2003), written by and starring Bob Dylan as 'Jack Fate', this desultory film may also be of interest to readers of this book.

Index

Index

Index

279

Index

281